FORMATIVE WORKS for THE FLAMENCO/ CLASSICAL GUITARTRADITION

VOLUMES 1 and 2

BY COREY WHITEHEAD
AND RICARDO MARLOW

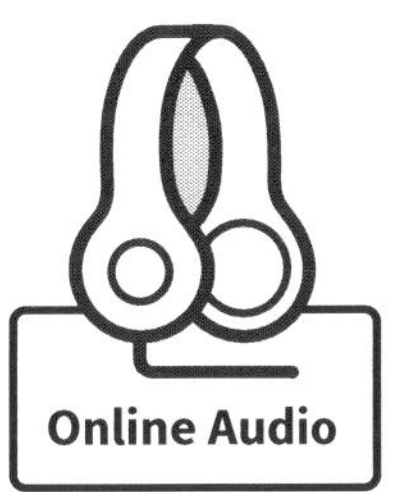

To access the online audio recording go to:
WWW.MELBAY.COM/31022MEB

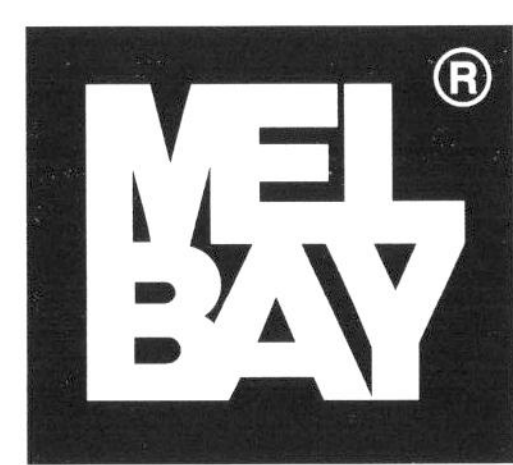

WWW.MELBAY.COM

Preface

This book is the repertoire supplement for the introductory guitar method, *The Flamenco/ Classical Guitar Tradition, Vol. I* (21029). This book also expands the repertoire and bridges the gap between beginning and intermediate level study.

Part I

This group of 60 etudes begins with two etudes that explore the diatonic and chromatic scales on each string from the open string to the 12th fret and back. These first two etudes are also intended for reference when reading the subsequent etudes, should one need to find a duplicate note location on the guitar quickly. One should use *apoyando* or "rest stroke" as much as possible with right-hand fingers *a-m-i* on the treble strings to emphasize the melodic voice, and to produce a sound that projects above the accompaniment or bass voices. Indications for rest stroke were omitted in this edition to leave that choice up to the personal taste of the performer and/or teacher. The 27 classical guitar etudes were selected for their musical and technical qualities to prepare the classical or flamenco guitarist to read standard musical notation throughout the entire fretboard in keys with up to no flats or sharps to those with one flat and up to four sharps.

Part II

For the classical guitarist, this section is helpful in learning about the palos or musical forms found in flamenco: *Soleares, Siguiriyas, Tangos*, and *Fandangos*. Also shown are common related sub-forms: *Bulerías, Alegrías, Tarantas, Verdiales, Soleá por bulerías,* and *Soleá por medio.*

Each of these forms are used as vehicles for teaching the fundamental techniques of flamenco guitar: *alzapúa, picado, rasgueado, trémolo, arpegio,* and golpe. Learning these techniques within the authentic musical language of flamenco palos aids in discernment when interpreting classical guitar works and transcriptions of the great Spanish masters. Learning a palo means learning not only metric and rhythmic patterns, but also chord progressions, chord voicings, melodies, and cadential formulas.

The division between classical and flamenco-style guitar is mainly in the application of rasgueados and chord voicings. As a flamenco teacher, rasgueados and chord voicings are the base of one's knowledge and need to be learned first. We are trying to bridge the two worlds, and rasgueado along with the *alzapúa* and flamenco trémolo are the primary differences between the worlds of classical and flamenco guitar, as is playing with only *pulgar*. Additionally, the use of pulgar (right-hand thumb) as an anchor and also in alternation with the right-hand index finger (*i*) is another important distinction in flamenco guitar technique. Each flamenco example (except the two *trémolos* and some *arpegios*) contains some strumming to contextualize the palo, and assumes the student already knows some correct patterns from previous study.

Every falseta example is only one to three (1-3) pages and graded according to level with the title giving the palo name, and technique and subtitle describing what is being studied. In the table of contents: *A=arpegios, P=pulgar (thumb),* which includes *alzapúa (*to "raise-up or come-forth" with the thumb) and other thumb work, Pic=picado (finger alternation for scales/melodies),

R=rasgueados (strumming), T=trémolo (single-note repetition). Everything in this set of studies is at Level 1 and is material typically used by/with beginning guitarists in Spain. The siguiriya rasgueado *a-m-i* is not shown until R4, however, as all beginners can do those "scary-looking" strums after getting the R1 and R2 down; but again, this is because *"compas"* (rhythm patterns) and *rasgueados* are the basis of flamenco guitar pedagogy. The lower-level examples can be learned concurrently with the idea that as one advances, you can go back and "upgrade" the *rasgueados* that appear in the non-R examples. For example, Pic.2 focuses on *picado,* but the strumming responses benefit a student who has already studied R8 abanicos, the fan-motion strum.

These examples function both as repetitive technical exercises and may also be connected like "Legos" to the song form so that a "composition" is created by linking the variations or *falsetas* together. One can also listen to anthologies of *cante flamenco (flamenco song)* and learn the accompaniment (chords and rhythms) by ear, using the strum and arpeggio patterns from this book to accompany a singer. Often this requires the use of a *cejilla or "capo"* to change the lowest sounding note to a higher pitch. All of these *falsetas* work when using a *cejilla to change the pitch or "position."* When a guitarist accompanies a singer for the first time, they would find the ideal position, and then use their knowledge of accompanying for example tangos; then between verses interject the tangos falsetas learned from this book until the singer gives the guitarist a cue to reenter, or *vice-versa.*

Practice Tips

The tempo markings you see are goals or upper-threshold speeds; it is recommended to use various tempi (tempos) to achieve mastery. For example, the Pic.6 "fandango" features a very fast picado, but working it much slower for example, at 100 bpm is acceptable. Also, when linking the A2 Soleá por medio arpegios, R3 Soleá por bulería rasgueado, Pic.3 Soleá por bulería picado, P7 Alzapúa, and T3 trémolo, the tempo ranges are 100-135, so a middle ground should be found. For example, A1 arpegios graduate internally and to construct a Soleá "composition" one could take any of the five patterns or two mixed variations and separate them between P2 or P4 variations and R1 strumming patterns at a tempo that works for all of the techniques used in a composition.

The only complete "piece" in this book is the "Alegrías silencio en Mi menor" used to introduce Pic.1, and T1. The A5 arpegios are based on the same song form and work fine along with it. The R8 "verdiales" is an accompaniment for a complete letra, for a lyrical verse. The Pic.6 "fandango" is a complete *copla,* or melody for a popular song with enough material to construct several solo compositions.

The material in this book ranges from Level 1 to intermediate, and provides everything needed technique-wise to take a serious flamenco student to a professional level. Some very short examples are extremely challenging, Pic. 5, for example. All musical content in this book is either original or derived from traditional flamenco material.

Corey Whitehead

Contents

Title	Page	Audio

Classical Studies
Part 1/Unit 1

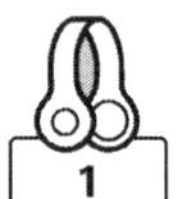

Modal Scales on Each String

Corey E. Whitehead

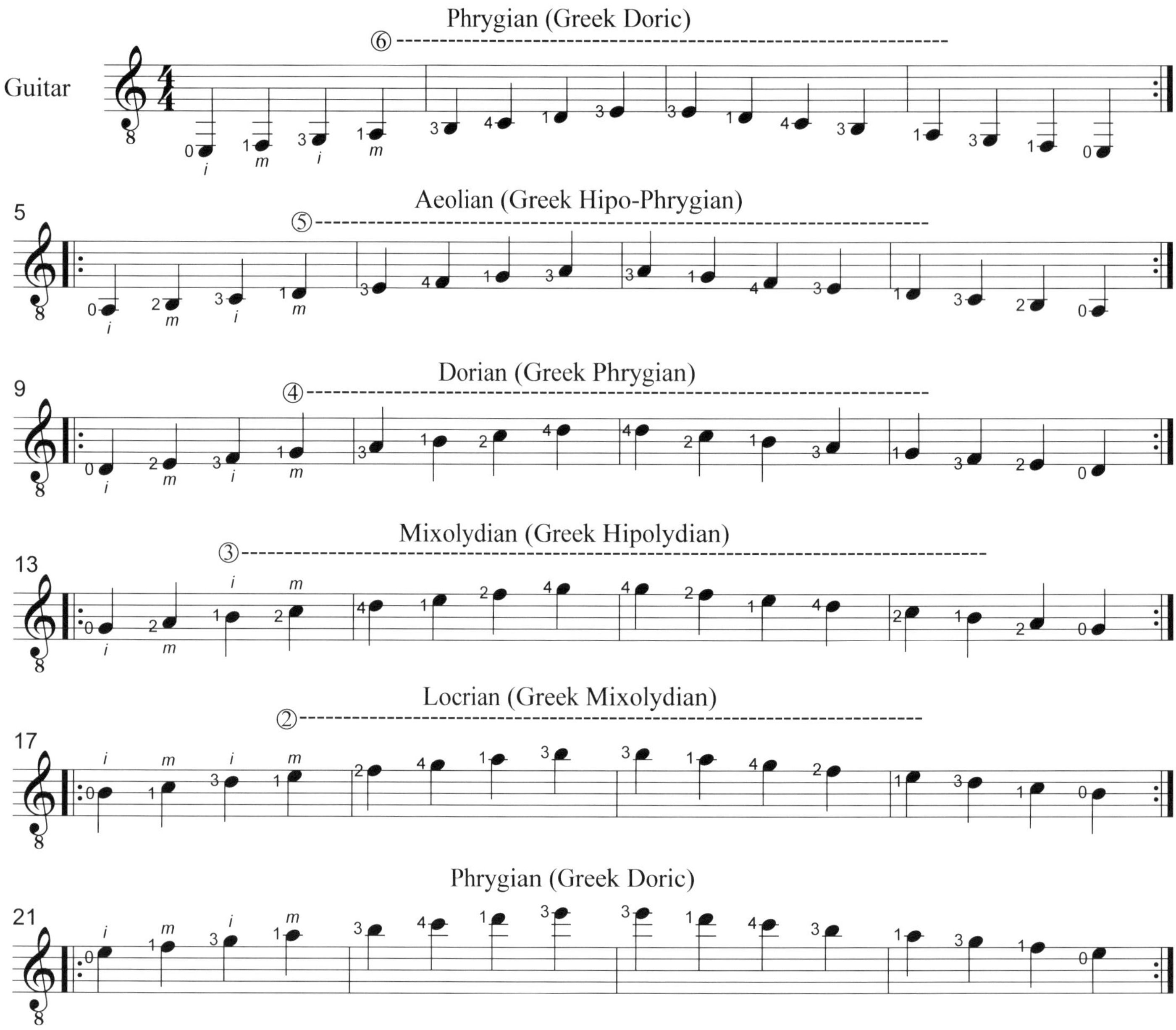

Phrygian (Greek Doric)

⑥

Guitar

Aeolian (Greek Hipo-Phrygian)

⑤

Dorian (Greek Phrygian)

④

Mixolydian (Greek Hipolydian)

③

Locrian (Greek Mixolydian)

②

Phrygian (Greek Doric)

Performance Notes: Both the modern Roman-ecclesiastical and ancient Greek names of the modes are given for each scale. Note that Greek musical scales are perceived only in descending order, whereas Roman modes ascend and descend.

1) Alternate the index and middle fingers of the right hand using rest-stroke (apoyando).

2) Vary this study by playing each note twice, thrice, or four times in eighth-notes, triplet eighth-notes, or sixteenth-notes.

3) Anchor the thumb of the right hand on one of the bass strings, such as the 4th string when playing picado on the first, etc.

4) Apply other right-hand formulas such as (i-a), (a-i), (a-m), (m-a), or (a-m-i-m) or (i-m-a-m).

5) Anchor the thumb of the right hand on one of the bass strings, such as the 4th string when playing picado on the first, etc.. When playing the 5th or 6th string, anchor the thumb of the right hand on the golpeador or soundboard.

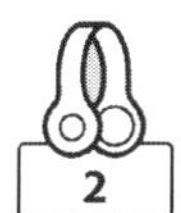

The Chromatic Scale on Each String

Corey E. Whitehead

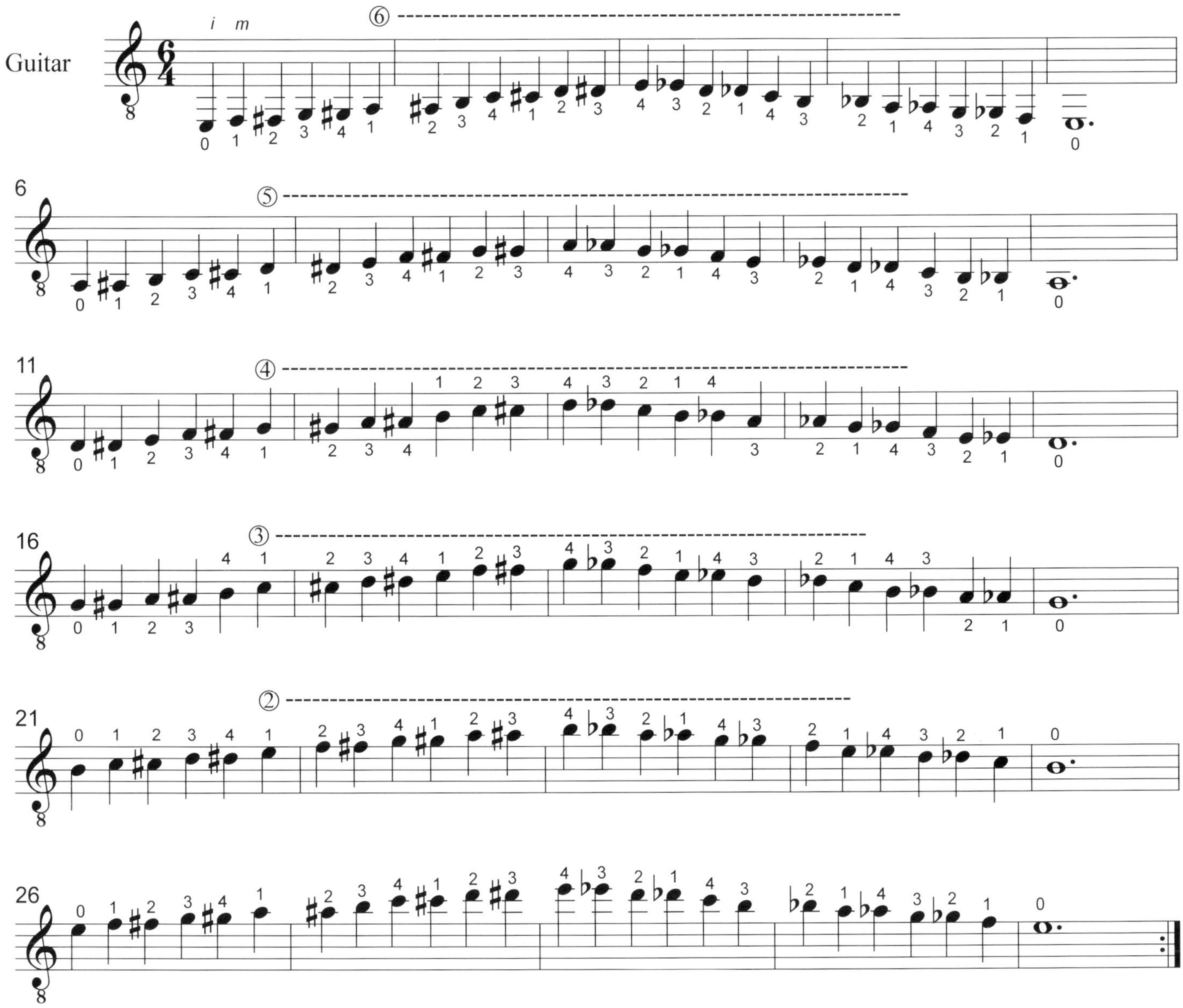

Guitar

Performance Notes

1) Alternate the index and middle fingers of the right hand using rest-stroke (apoyando).

2) Vary this study by playing each note twice, thrice, or four times in eighth-notes, triplet eighth-notes, or sixteenth-notes.

3) Anchor the thumb of the right hand on one of the bass strings, such as the 4th string when playing picado on the first, etc. When playing the 5th or 6th string, anchor the thumb of the right hand on the golpeador or soundboard.

4) Apply other right-hand formulas such as (i-a), (a-i), (a-m), (m-a), or (a-m-i-m) or (i-m-a-m).

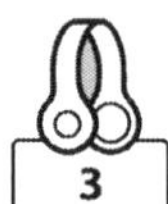

Exercise on the Major Scale, No. 14

Fernando Sor and Napoleon Coste
Edited by Corey Whitehead

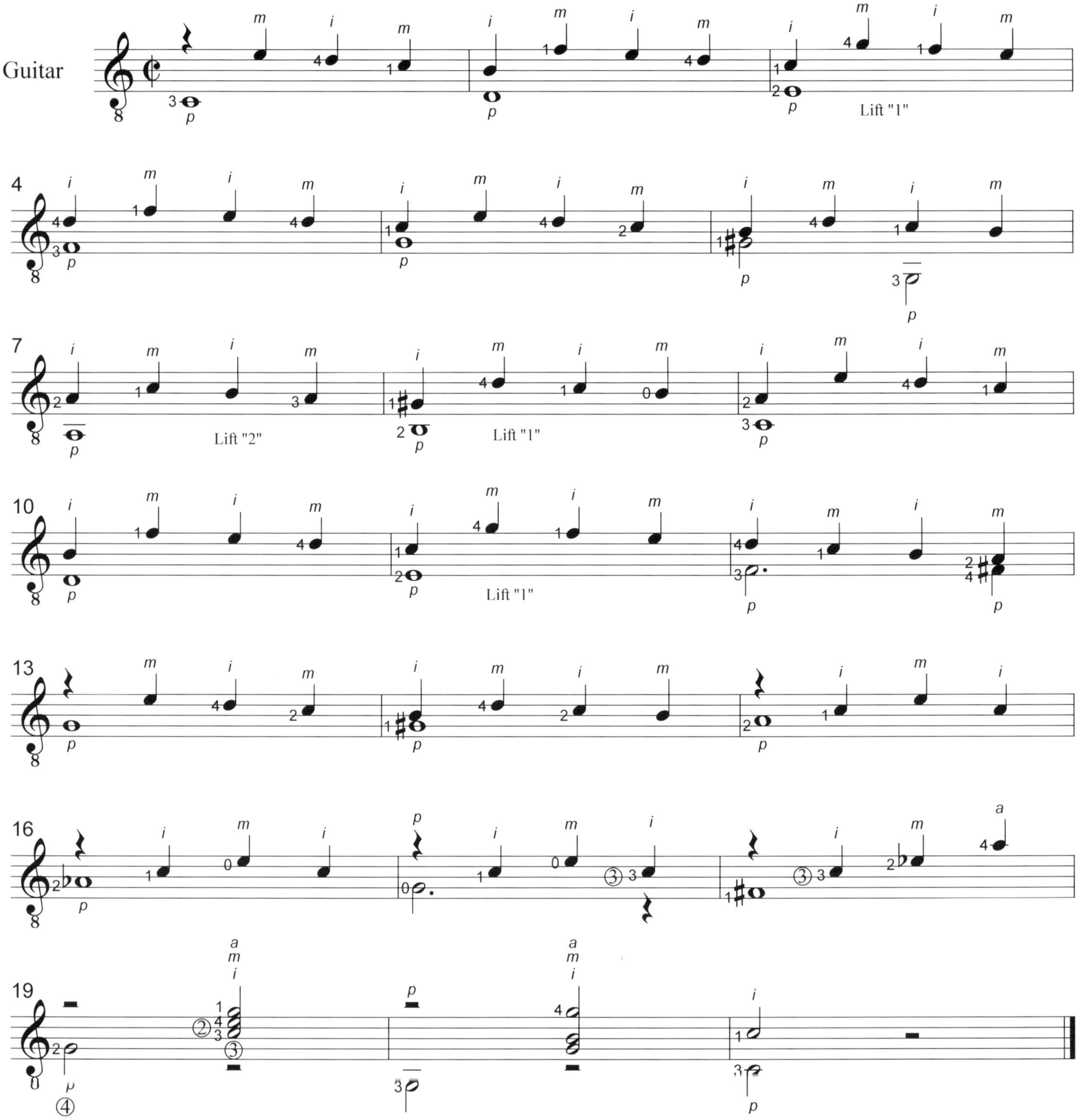

Performance Notes

1) The bass notes should ring for the full measure.
2) Allow notes with stems up to ring together (finger pedal) within a measure when desired.
3) The 2nd finger (L.H) is used on beat four at times to facilitate crossing the barline with legato.
4) Lift the 1st finger (L.H.) on beat two in mm. 3, 7, 8, and 11.
5) In measure 17, on beat four, play the "C" on the 3rd string to facilitate the next chord change.

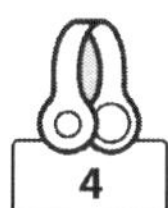

Exercise on the Major Scale. No. 16

Fernando Sor and Napoleon Coste
Edited by Corey Whitehead

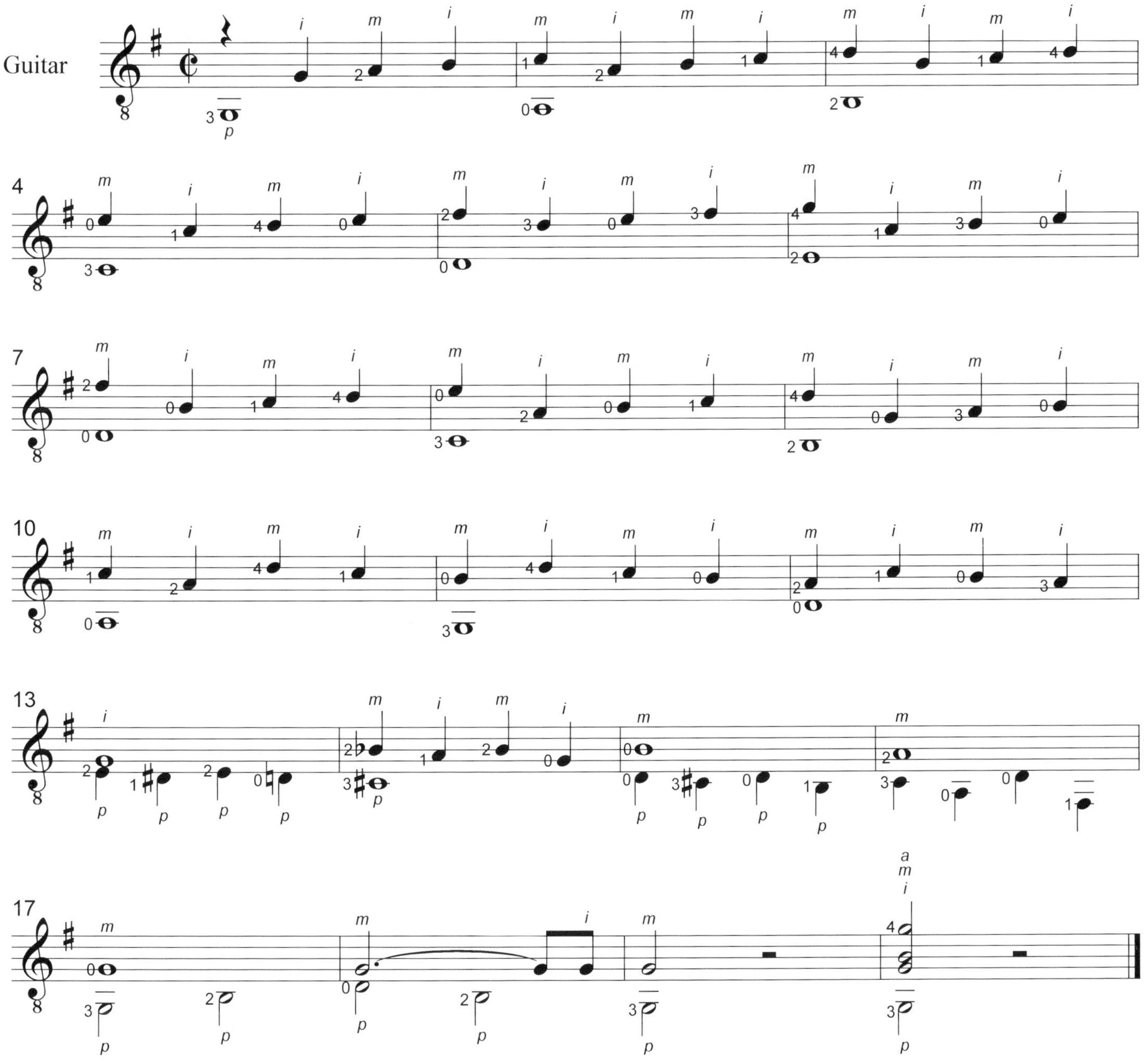

Guitar

Performance Notes

1) The bass notes should ring for the full measure.
2) Allow the notes with stems up to ring together (finger pedal) as desired.
3) In 2/2 or "cut" time, the beat is represented by the half-note. Beat one is strong, and beat two is weaker.
4) Use rest strokes (apoyando) on the melodic notes (stems up) as desired.
5) The use of the "a" finger is optional, and typically avoided in this style period.

Exercise on the Major Scale, No. 19

Fernando Sor and Napoleon Coste
Edited by Corey Whitehead

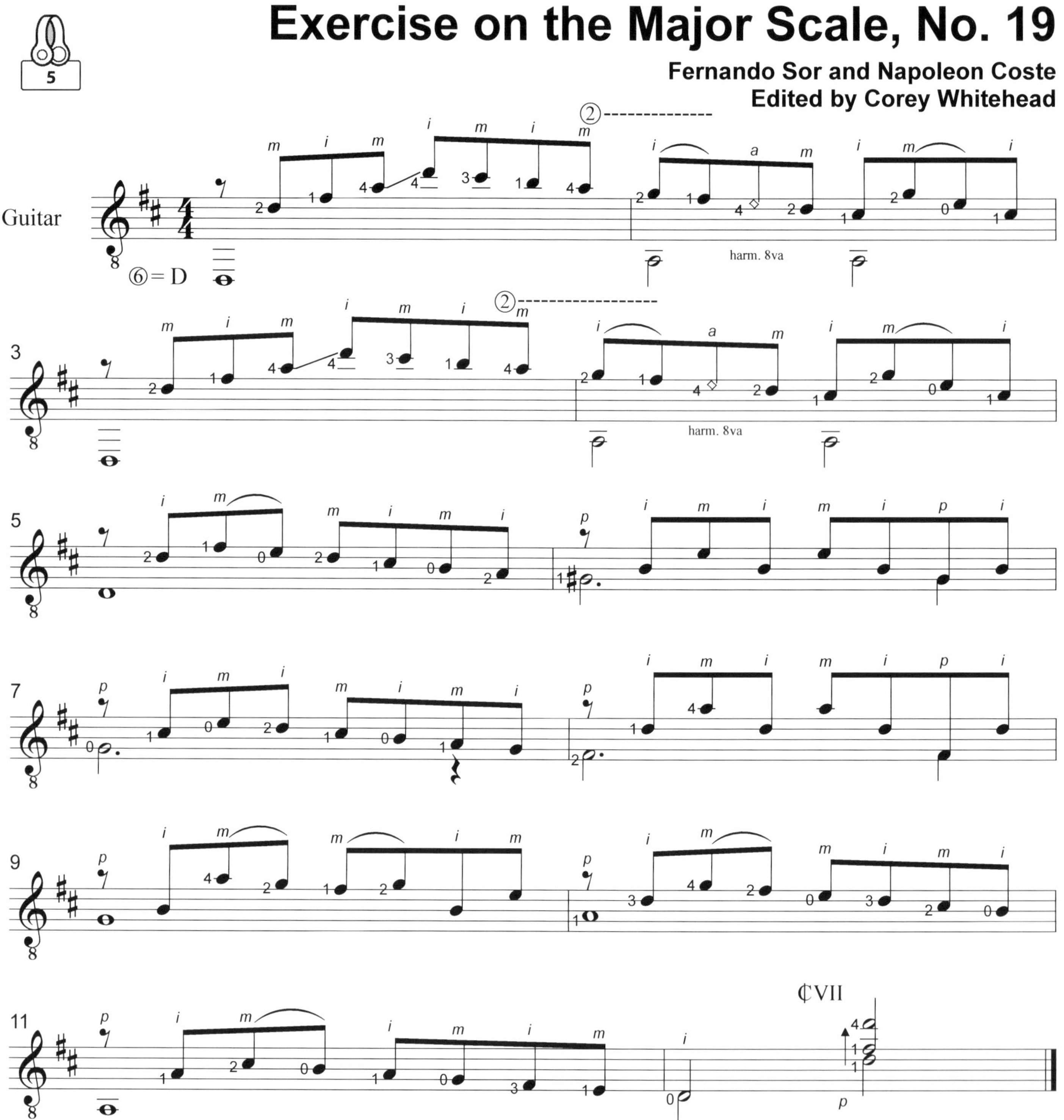

Performance Notes

1) The sixth string is tuned a whole-step (whole tone) lower to D, matching the 4th string, 8va lower.
2) The harmonic at m. 2, beat two is played on the 12th fret, first string by touching above the fret w/o pressure.
3) The "a" finger is used when needed to facilitate the movement of "i" and "m."
4) Use rest strokes (apoyando) as desired.
5) Mind the duration of the first note of the slurs: do not shorten or "compress" the first note's duration.
6) Allow the notes within a measure to ring together as desired.

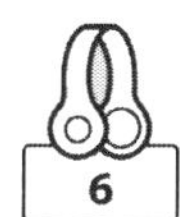

Exercise on the Major Scale, No. 21

Fernando Sor and Napoleon Coste
Edited by Corey Whitehead

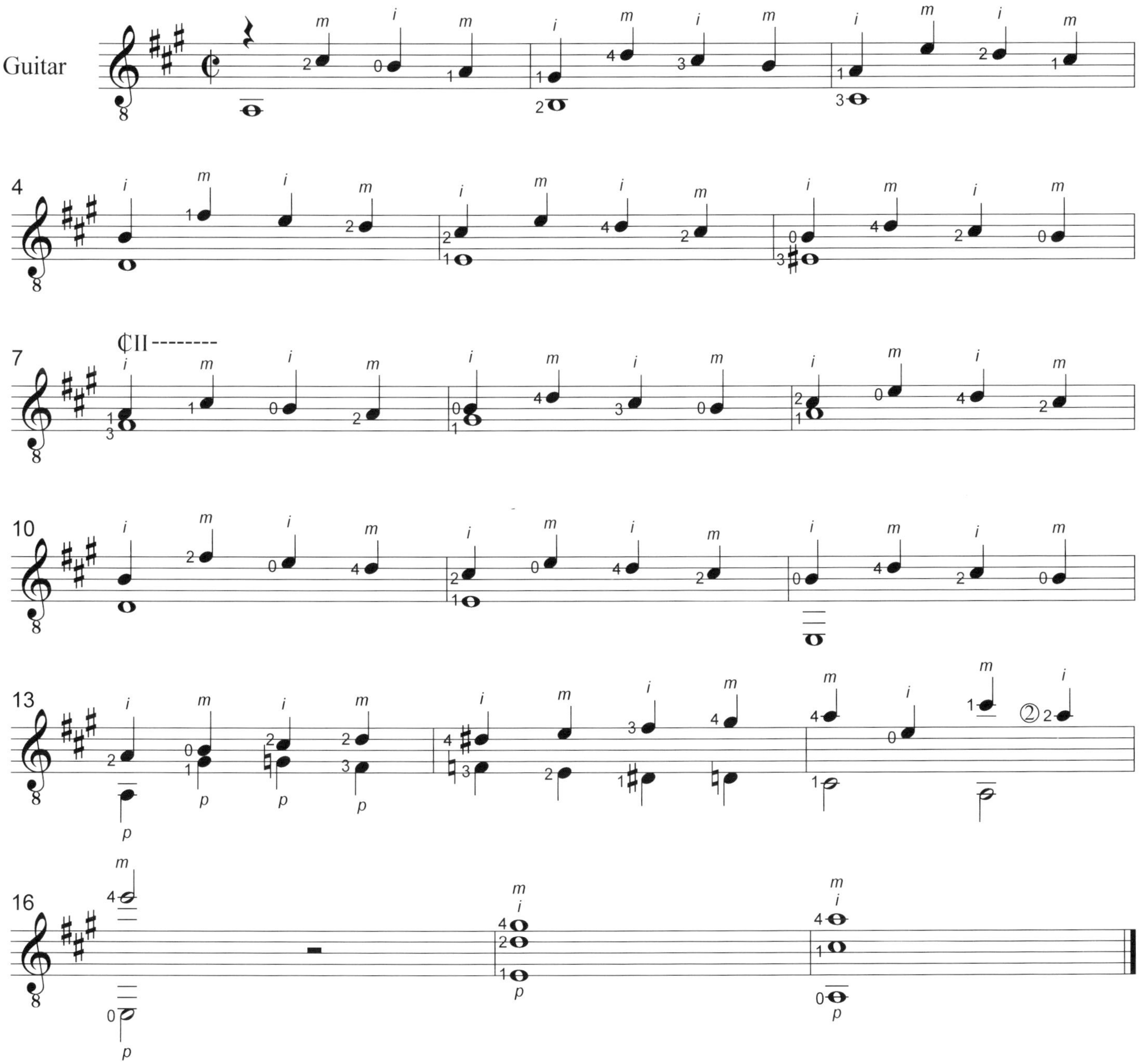

Guitar

Performance Notes

1) The bass notes should ring for the full measure in mm. 1-12.
2) Allow the notes with stems up to ring together (finger pedal) as desired.
3) In 2/2 or "cut" time, the beat is represented by the half-note. Beat one is strong, and beat two is weaker.
4) Use rest strokes (apoyando) on the melodic notes (stems up) as desired.
5) The use of the "a" finger is optional, but is typically avoided in this style period.
6) The last "A" note of measure 15 is played on the second string at the 10th fret.

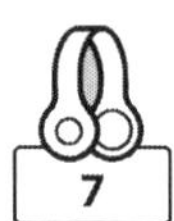

Della tenuto de tuono, No.1 "Maestoso"

Mauro Giuliani
Edited by Corey Whitehead

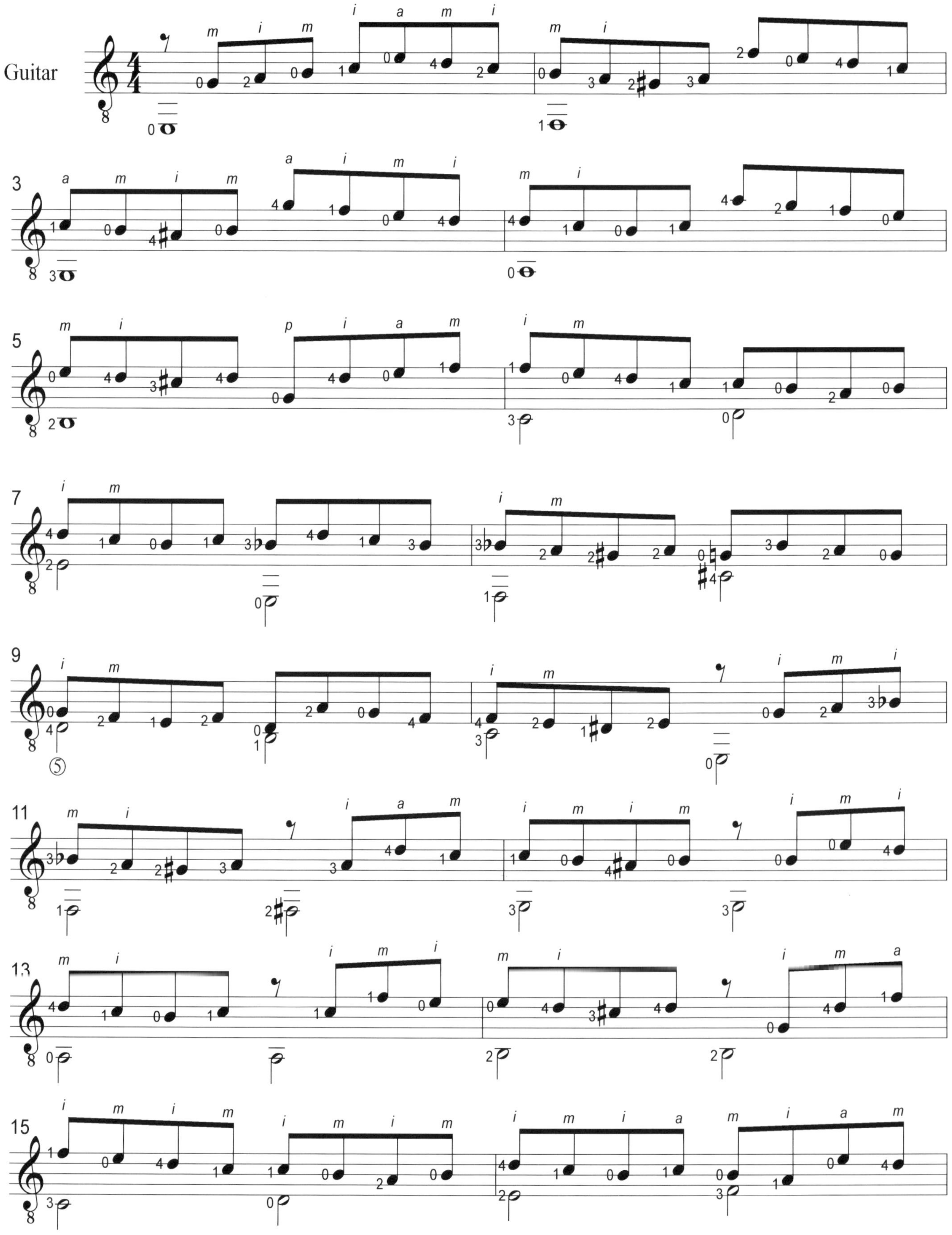

Guitar

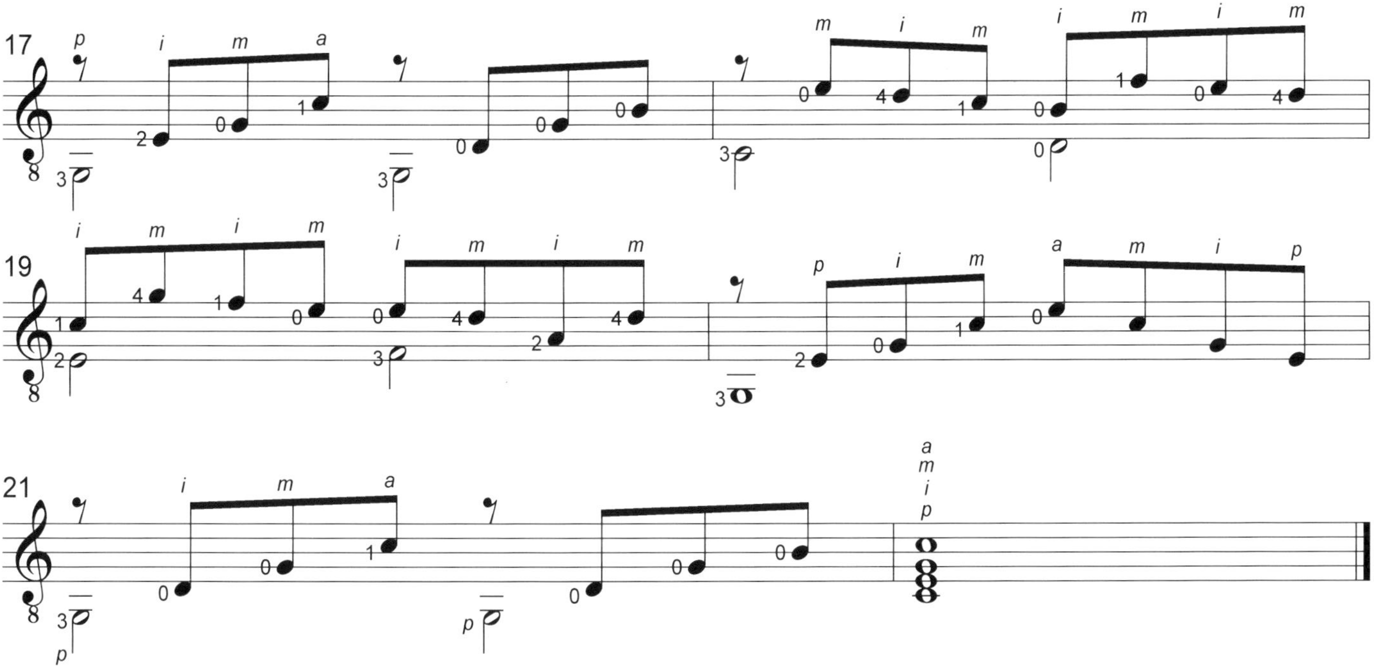

Perfomance Notes

1) Use apoyando when possible or tirando strokes imitating the sound of "apoyando." Experiment by pushing inward in the direction of the soundboard with the right-hand finger, and allow the same finger to avoid contact with the adjacent string by use of the medial-phalangeal joint (middle joint) of the finger.

2) Emphasize the upper voice (stems up).

3) Allow bass notes to ring for their full value.

4) Allow voices within the measure to blend when they sound good together (finger pedal).

5) Strive for a legato connection in the melodic voice (stems up).

6) Improvise your own dynamics as no dynamics are indicated by the composer.

7) Dissonances should be emphasized and then resolved to consonances which are relatively softer.

8) Often, the dissonances appear as "accidentals," i.e., sharps or flats not included in the key signature.

9) The key signature and last melodic note indicate C Major with no sharps or flats, but the piece uses many accidentals to "tonicize" other notes.

10) "Tonicization" of a note other than the root of the scale (C) requires a temporary key change.

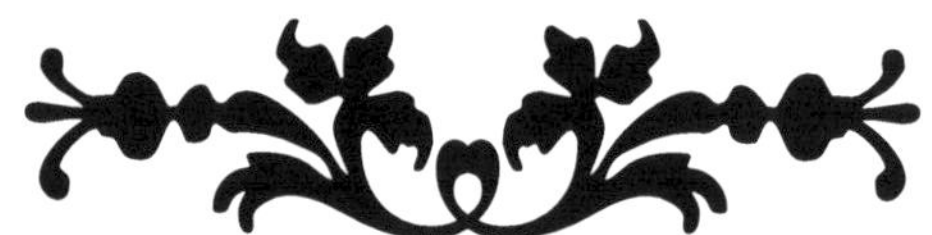

Classical Studies Part 1/Unit 2

Exercise in Thirds, No. 1

Fernando Sor and Napoleon Coste
Edited by Corey Whitehead

Lower voice may be played with "*p*" (R.H. thumb)

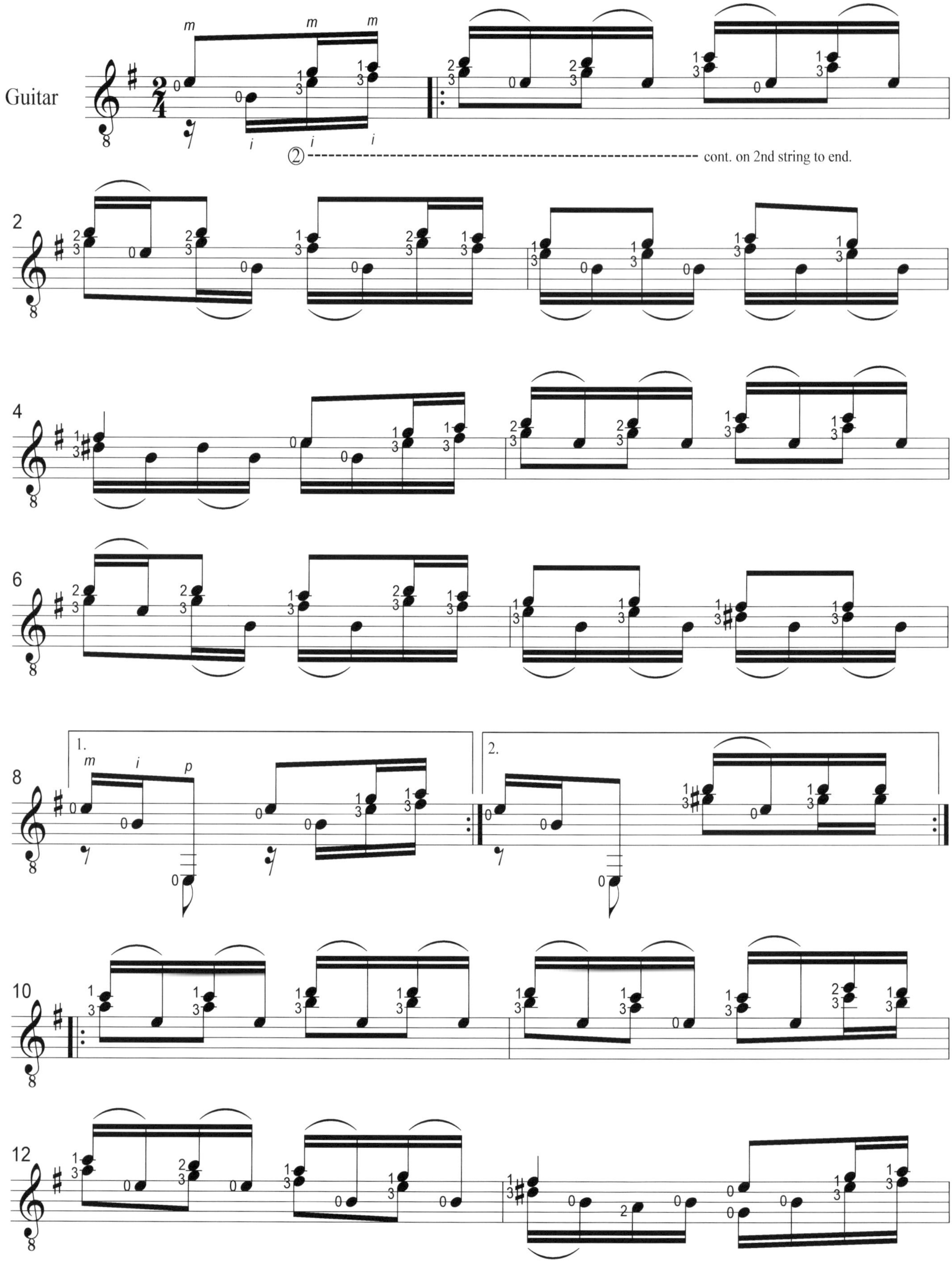

Guitar

cont. on 2nd string to end.

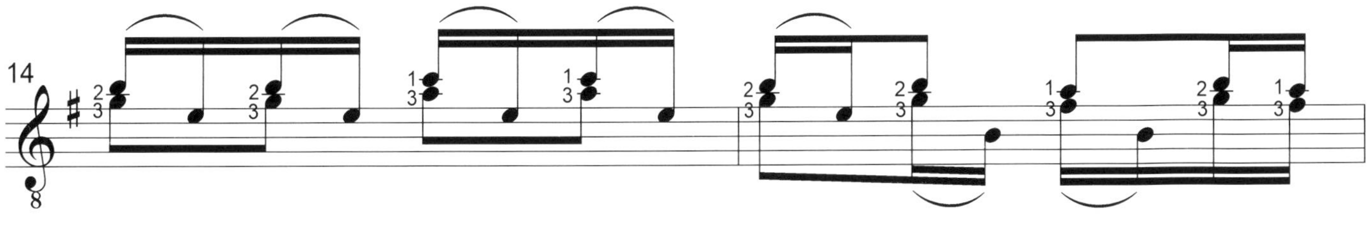

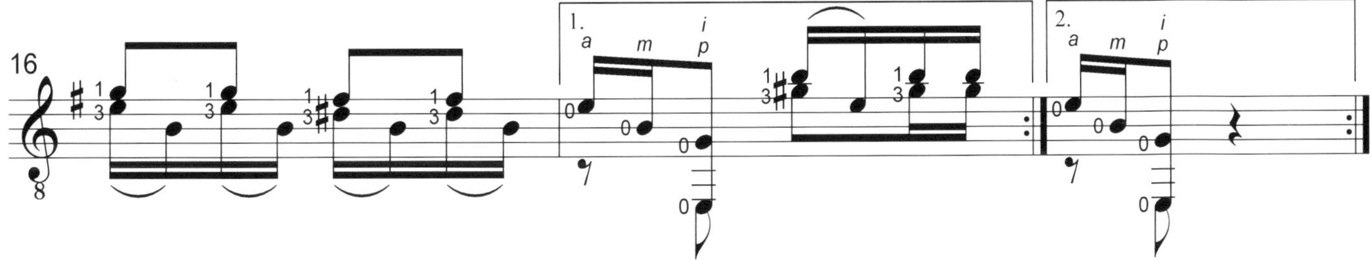

Performance Notes:

1) The lower notes of the "dyads" (two notes sounding together) should be played on the 2nd string.

2) Allow the melodic notes with stems up to ring for their full eighth-note duration.

3) In 2/4 time, the beat is represented by the quarter-note. Beat one is strong, and beat two is weaker.

4) Use free strokes (tirando) on the melodic notes (stems up).

5) Use the "a" finger only when necessary.

6) Slurred notes (the second note of a slur) are ***melodic*** *when on the 1st string.*

7) Slurred notes are ***harmonic accompaniment*** *when on the 2nd string.*

8) Keep L.H. "guide fingers" in contact with the string when the same finger is used more than once on the same string.

9) Minimize movement in both hands.

10) Watch L.H. movement and eliminate any "bouncing."

11) Right-hand finger movement should come from the middle joint (medio-phalangeal).

12) Anchor the right-hand thumb "p" on the 4th string in mm. 1-16.

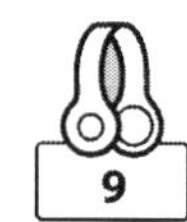

Exercise in Thirds, No. 2

Fernando Sor and Napoleon Coste
Edited by Corey Whitehead

Performance Notes

1) Play accompaniment softly and lightly.

2) Make the melody sing, imitating "apoyando" with "tirando" strokes.

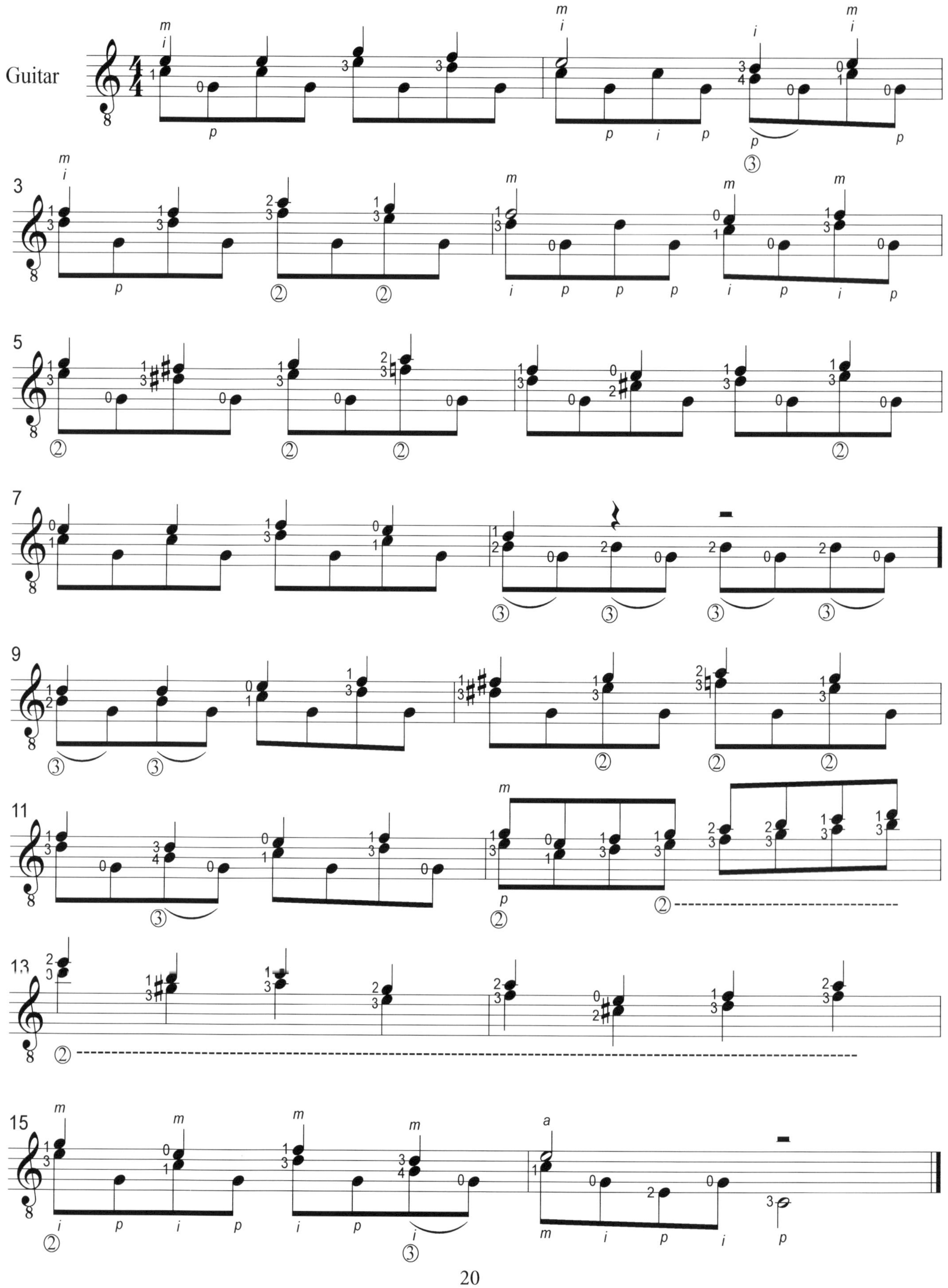

Guitar

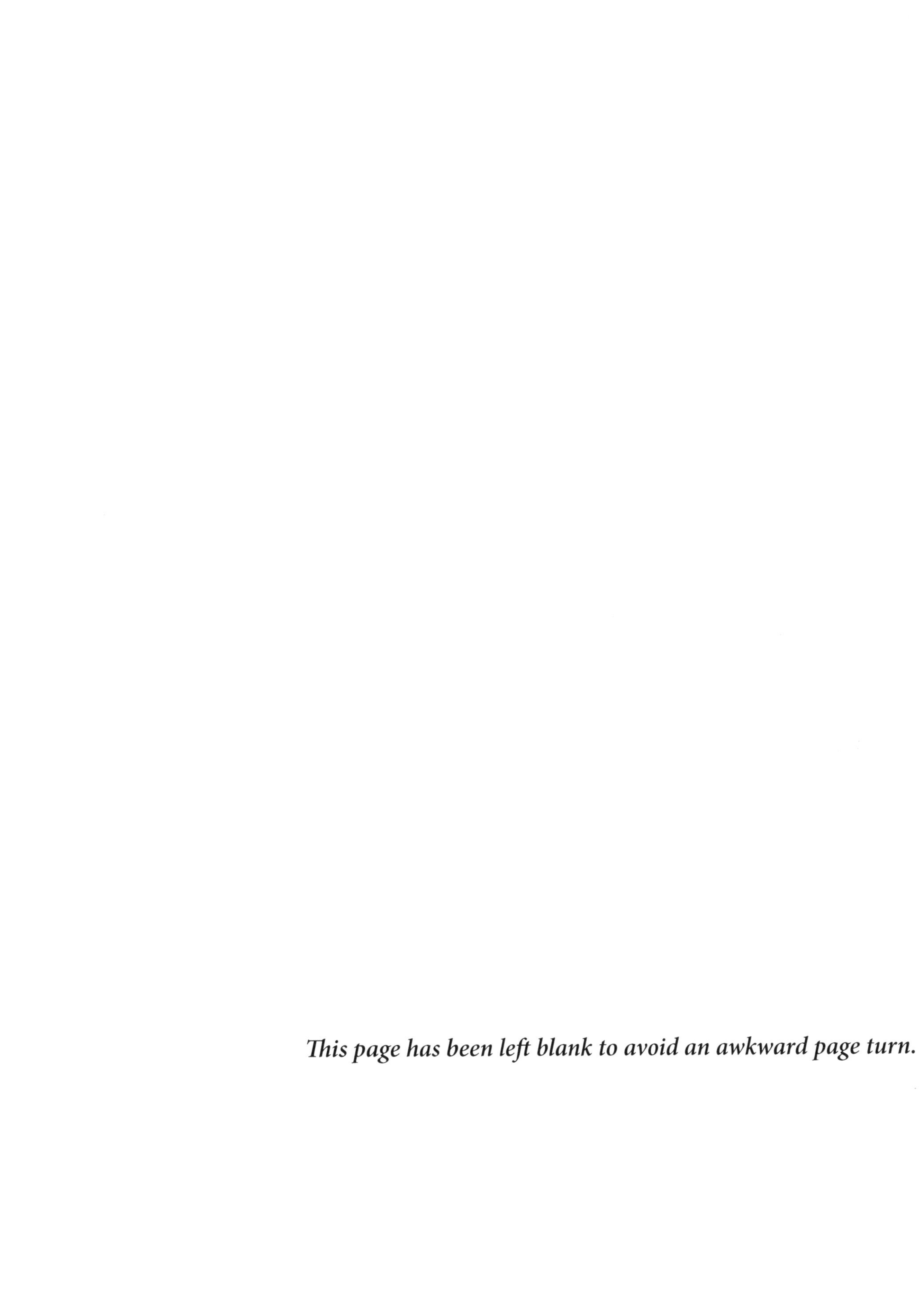

This page has been left blank to avoid an awkward page turn.

Exercise in Thirds, No. 3

Fernando Sor and Napoleon Coste
Edited by Corey Whitehead

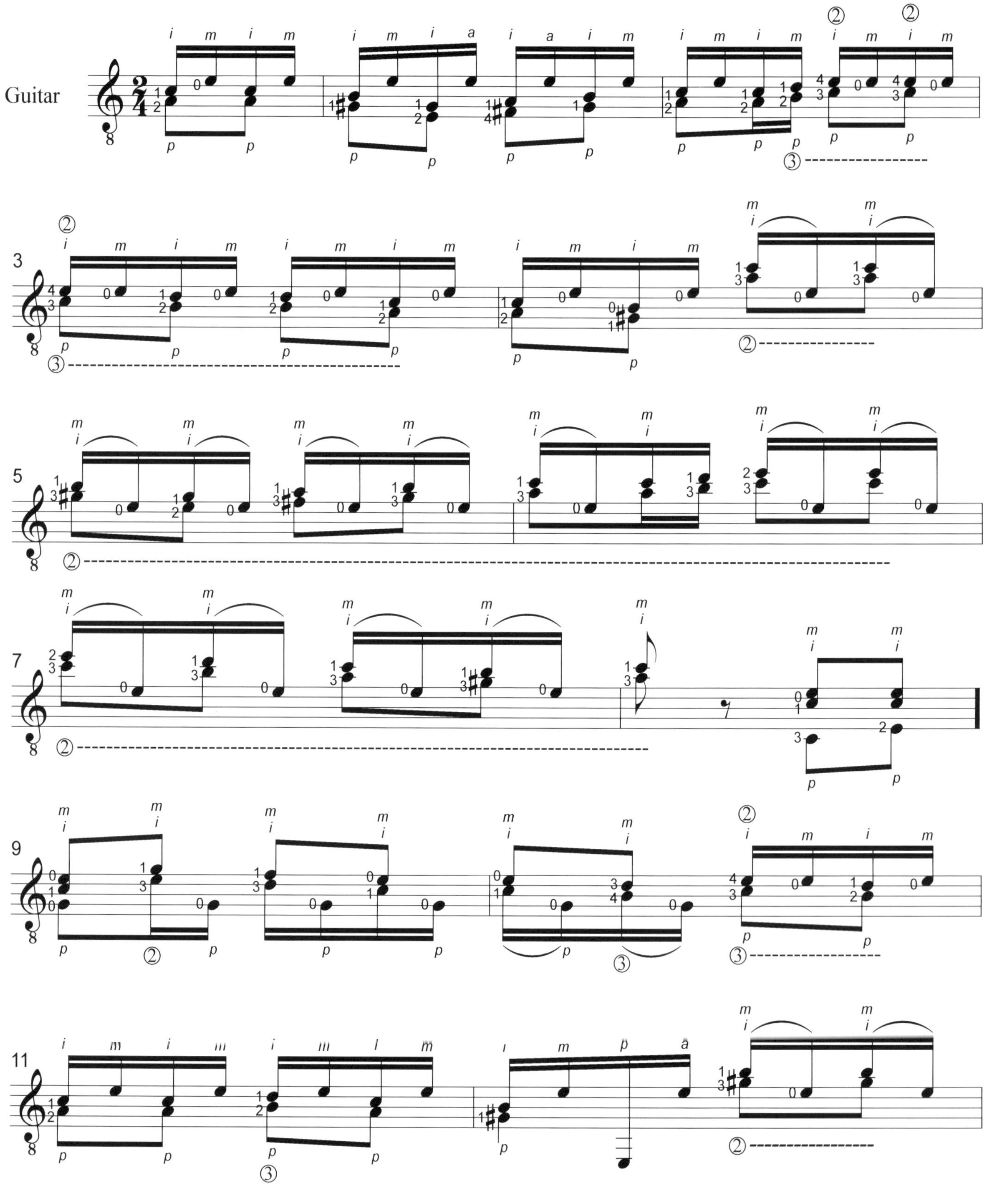

Guitar

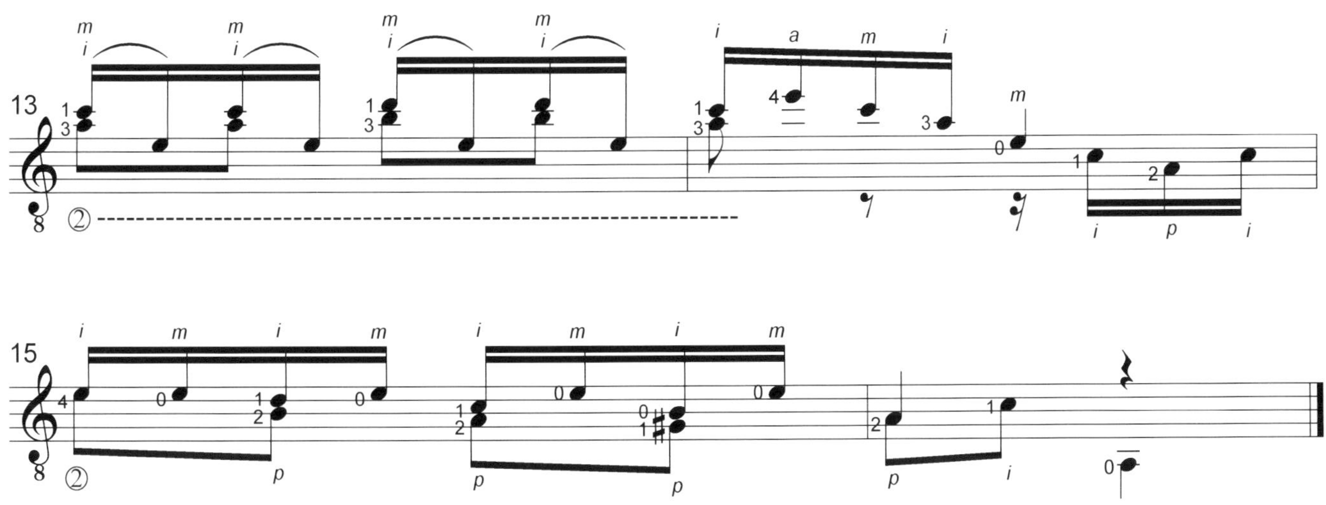

Performance Notes

1) Use "tirando" or free-strokes with the right hand and "pull-off" (descending slur technique) with the left hand.

2) Play the melodic or bass voice (stems down) louder by pressing inward toward the soundboard with "p-i."

3) When a L.H. finger is repeated on the same string, keep this "guide-finger" in contact with the string when shifting.

4) In 2/4 meter, the quarter-note duration represents the beat. Beat one is strong, and beat two is weaker.

*5) Place the emphasis on the first beat of each measure for "rhythmic" phrasing. (See James Thurmond)**

6) In general, play lightly after the downbeat of each measure.

7) Balance of volume should favor the melodic voice, which in this case is in the (stems down) lower voice.

* Thurmond, James. *"Note Grouping: A Method for Achieving Expression and Style in Musical Performance."* Catholic University Press, Merideth Music Publications, 1952.

Exercise in Thirds, No. 4

Fernando Sor and Napoleon Coste
Edited by Corey Whitehead

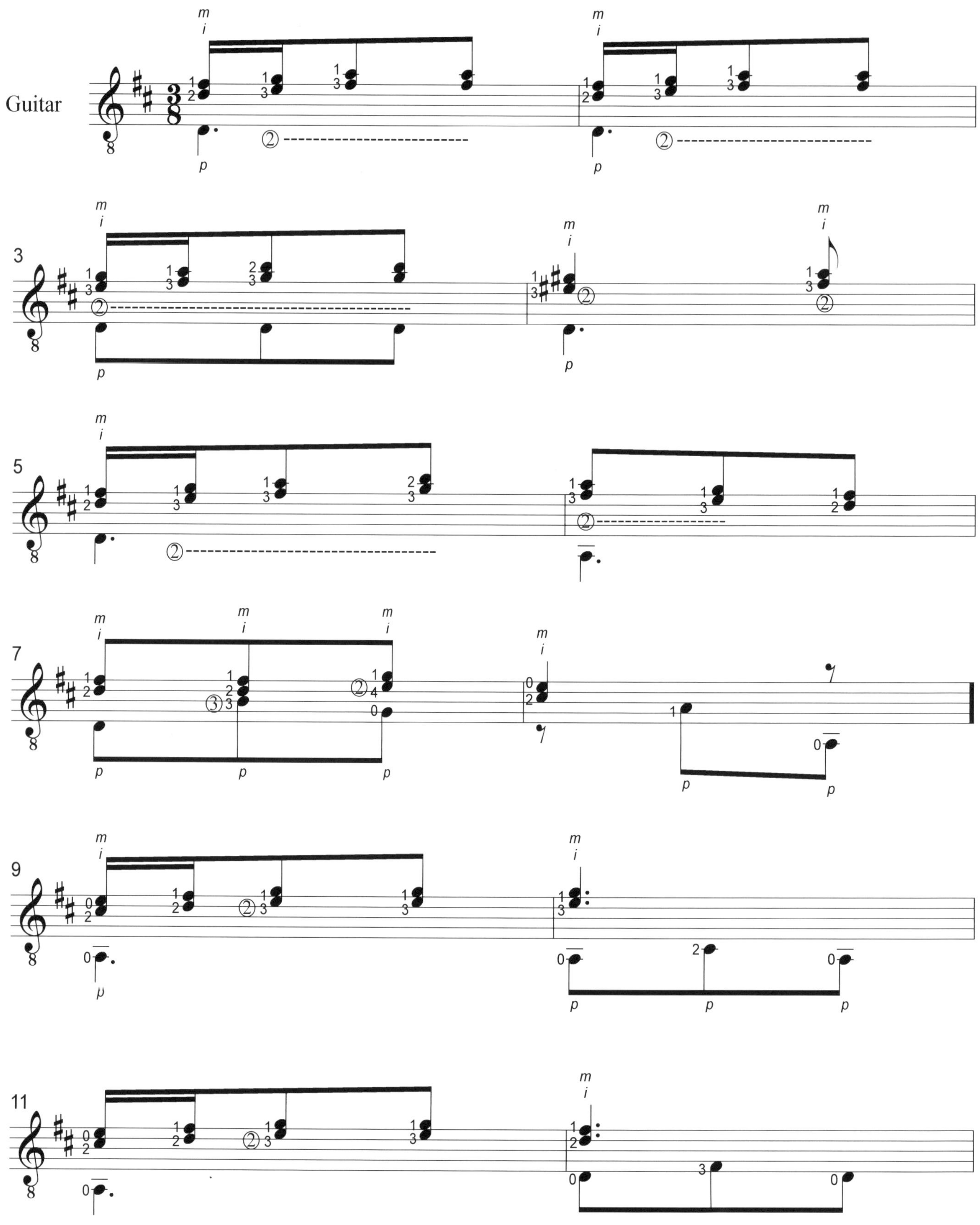

Guitar

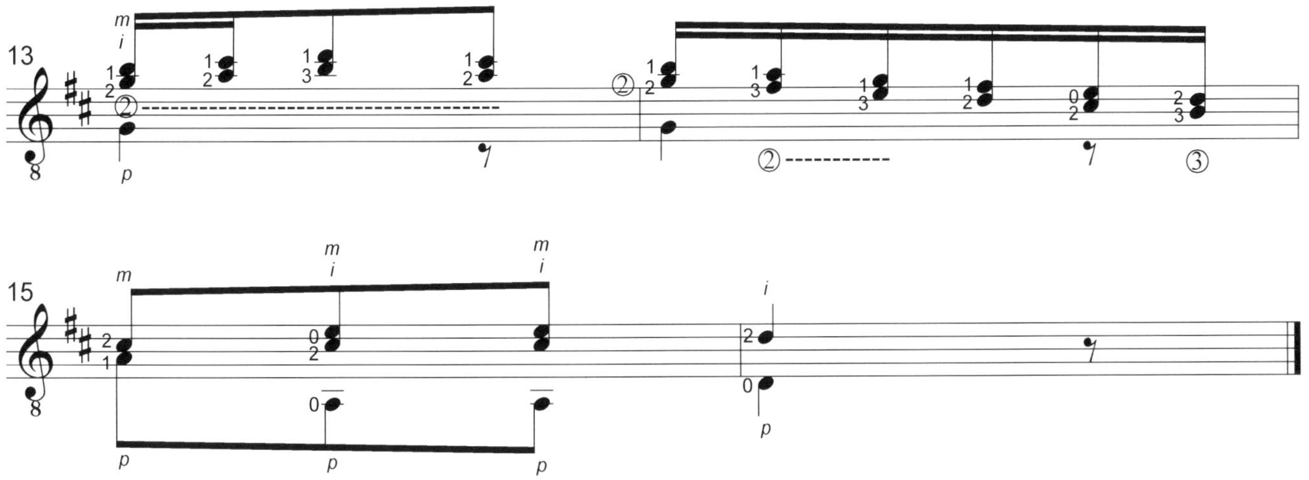

Performance notes:

1) Use "tirando" or free strokes with the right hand.

2) Play the melodic voice or treble voice (stems up) louder by pressing inward toward the soundboard with "m."

3) When a L.H. finger is repeated on the same string, keep the "guide finger" on the string when shifting.

4) In 3/8 meter, the eighth-note duration represents the beat. Beat one is strong, beats two and three are weaker.

5) For "rhythmic" phrasing, place the emphasis on the first beat of each measure.

6) For "melodic" phrasing place the emphasis on beats two and three of each measure.

7) Measures 8, 10, 12, and 16 should be interpreted with "rhythmic" phrasing, placing emphasis on beat one.

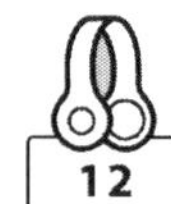

Exercise in Thirds, No. 5

Fernando Sor and Napoleon Coste
Edited by Corey Whitehead

Performance Notes

1) Use tirando or free strokes imitating the sound of apoyando.
2) Emphasize the upper voice (stems up).
3) Play slurs lightly, with the second note softer than the first.

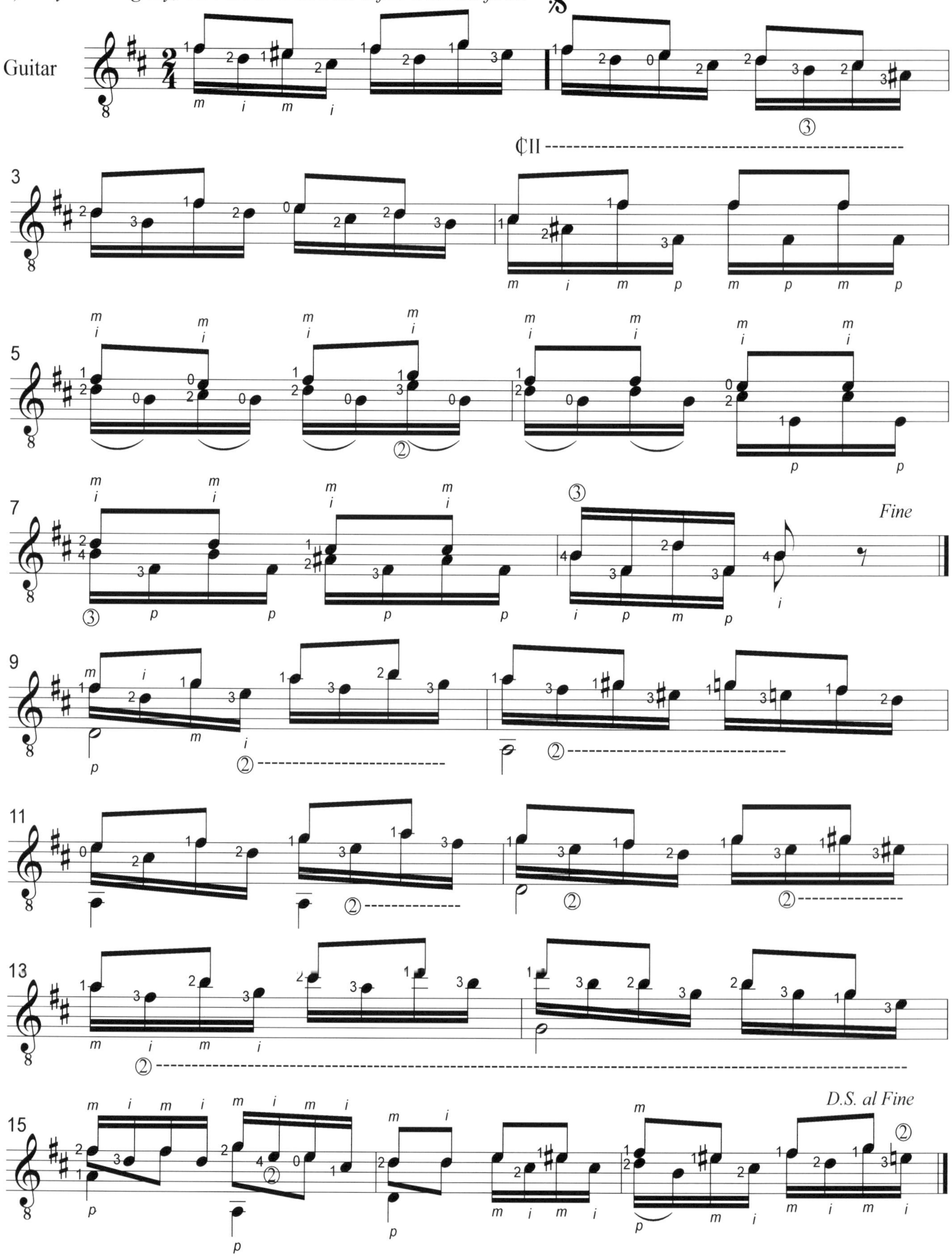

Guitar

Fine

D.S. al Fine

Exercise in Thirds, No.6

Fernando Sor and Napoleon Coste
Edited by Corey Whitehead

Performance Notes 13

1) Use tirando or free strokes imitating the sound of apoyando.
2) Emphasize the upper voice (stems up).
3) Right-hand fingers "p-i" may be used as an alternative to "m-i."

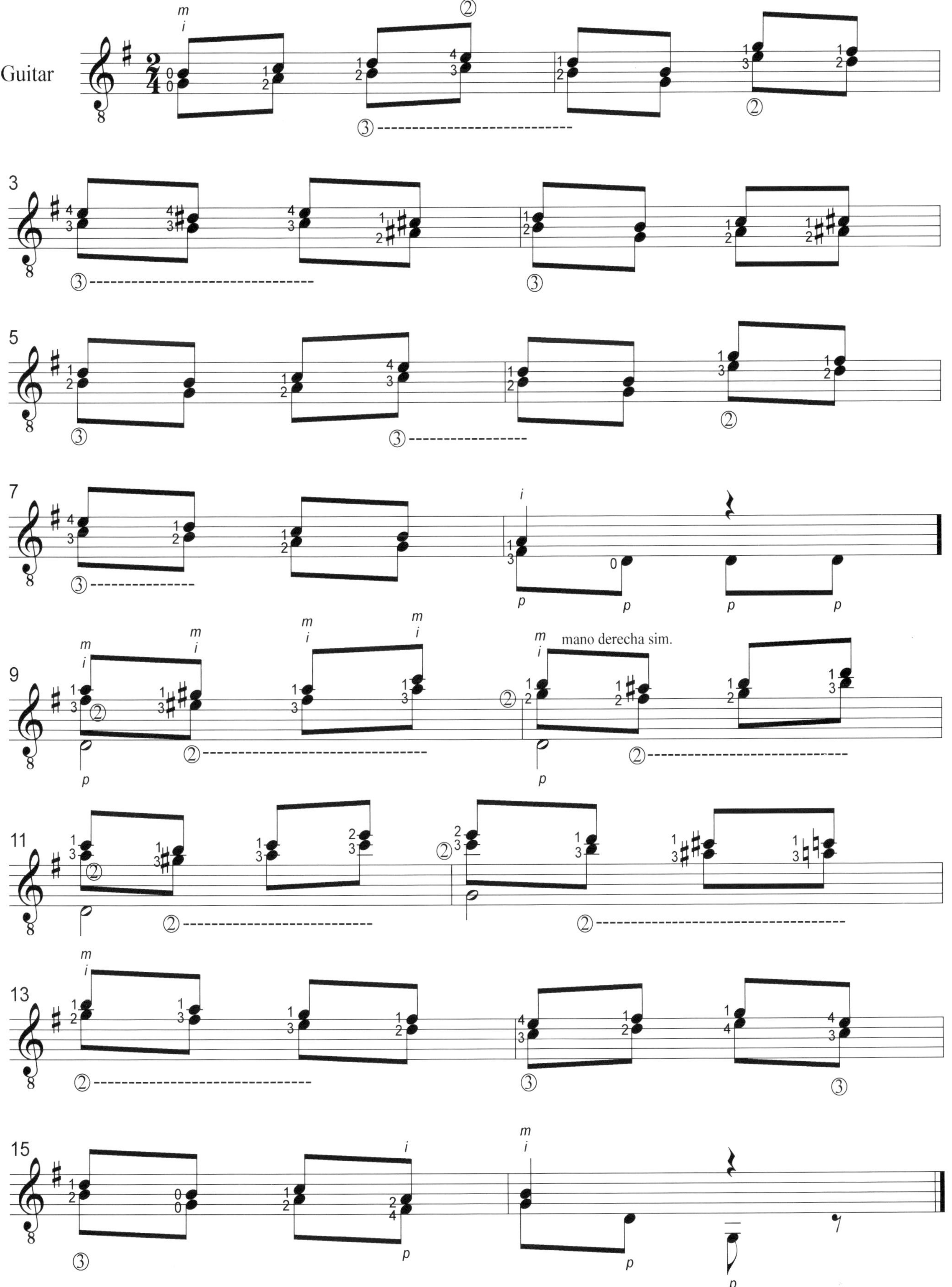

Exercise in Sixths, No. 1

Fernando Sor and Napoleon Coste
Edited by Corey Whitehead

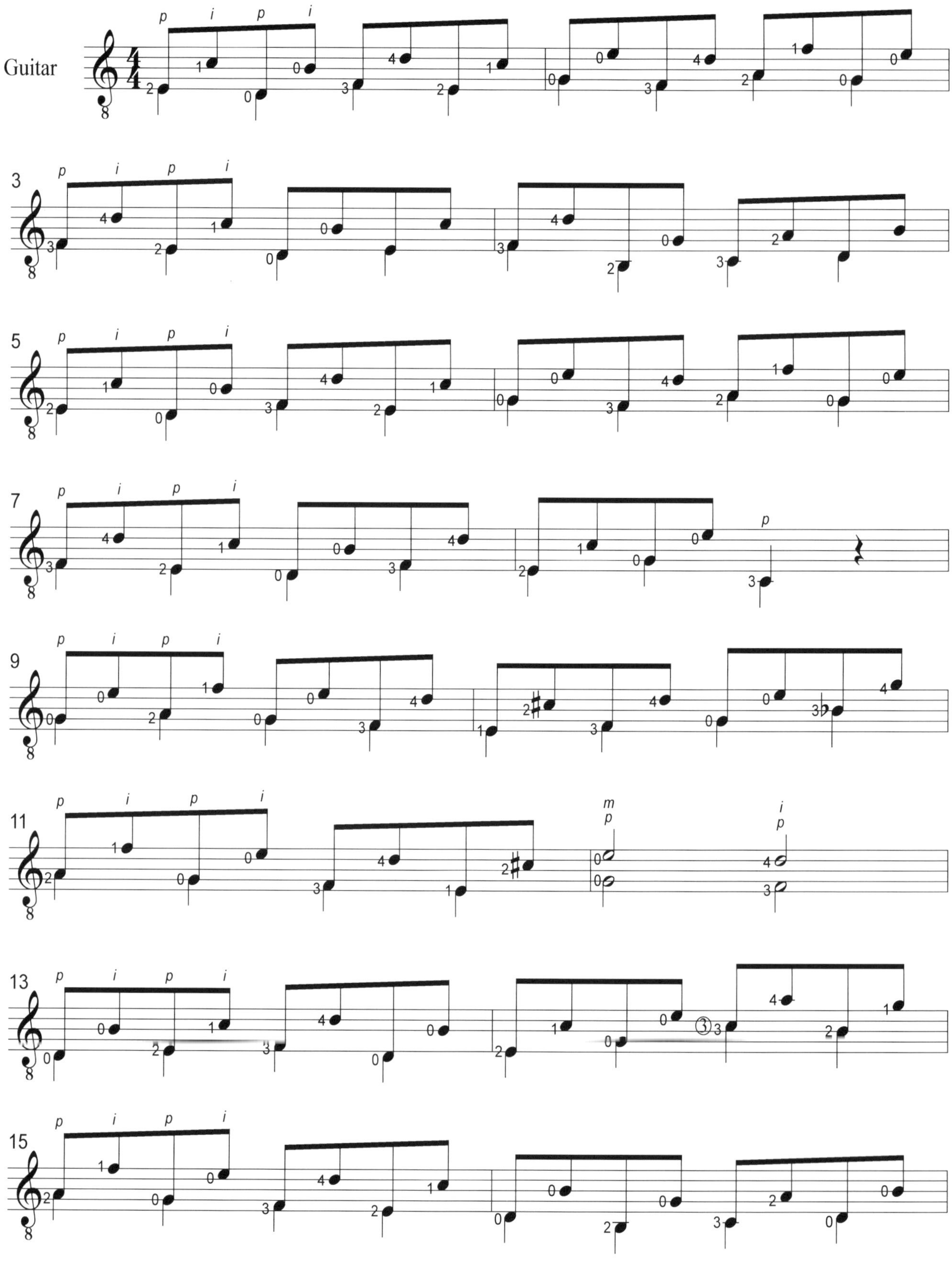

Guitar

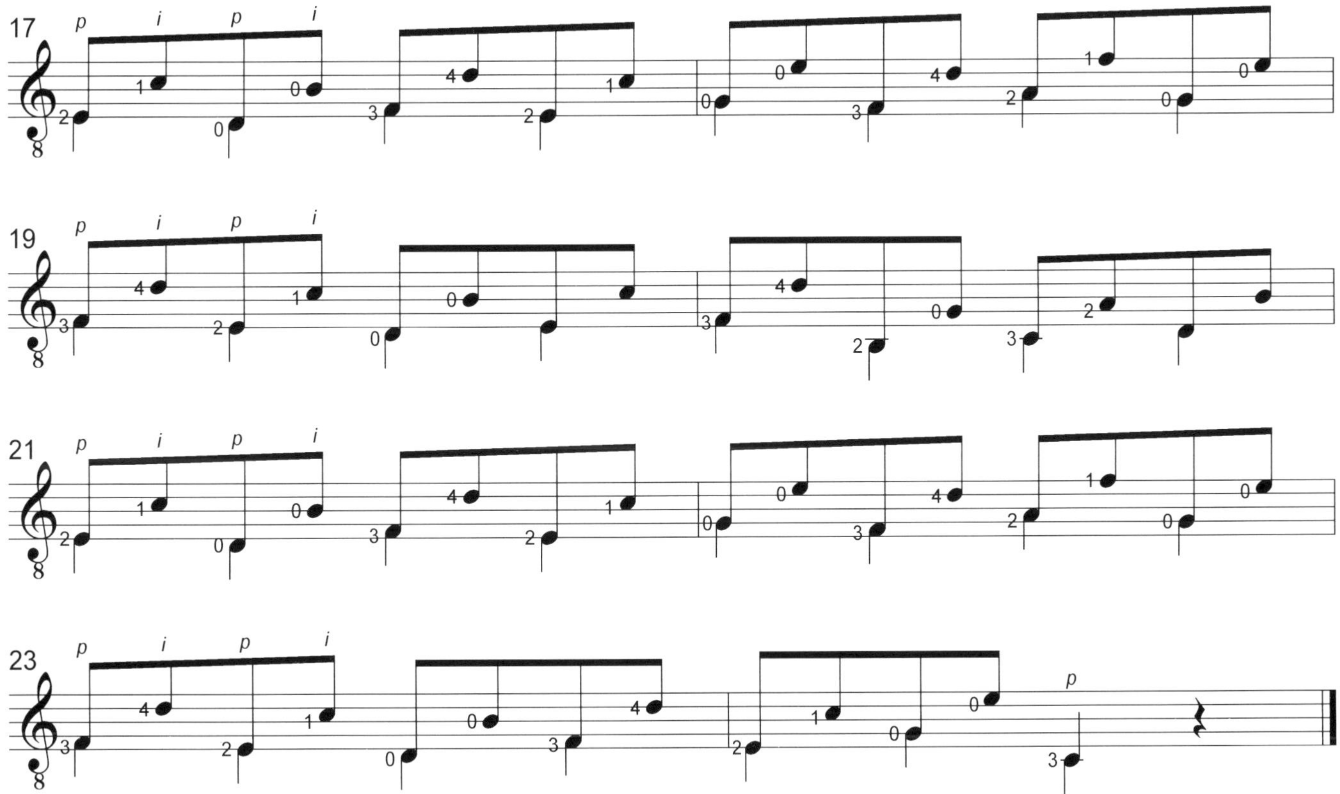

Performance Notes

1) Use tirando or free strokes in the bass (melodic) voice imitating the sound of "apoyando."

2) Emphasize the lower voice (stems down).

3) You could play "apoyando" or rest stroke in the bass voice instead of free stroke.

4) In 4/4 meter or "common time," the first and third beats are strong, with the first beat being stronger.

5) Beats two and four are weaker relative to beats one and three.

*6) For **melodic phrasing**, place the emphasis on beats two, three and four.*

*7) For **rhythmic phrasing**, place the emphasis on beat one.*

Exercise in Sixths, No. 2

Fernando Sor and Napoleon Coste
Edited by Corey Whitehead

Performance Notes
1) Use tirando or free strokes.
2) Emphasize the upper voice (stems up).

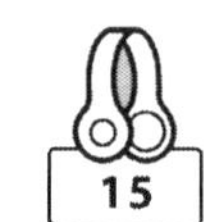

Guitar

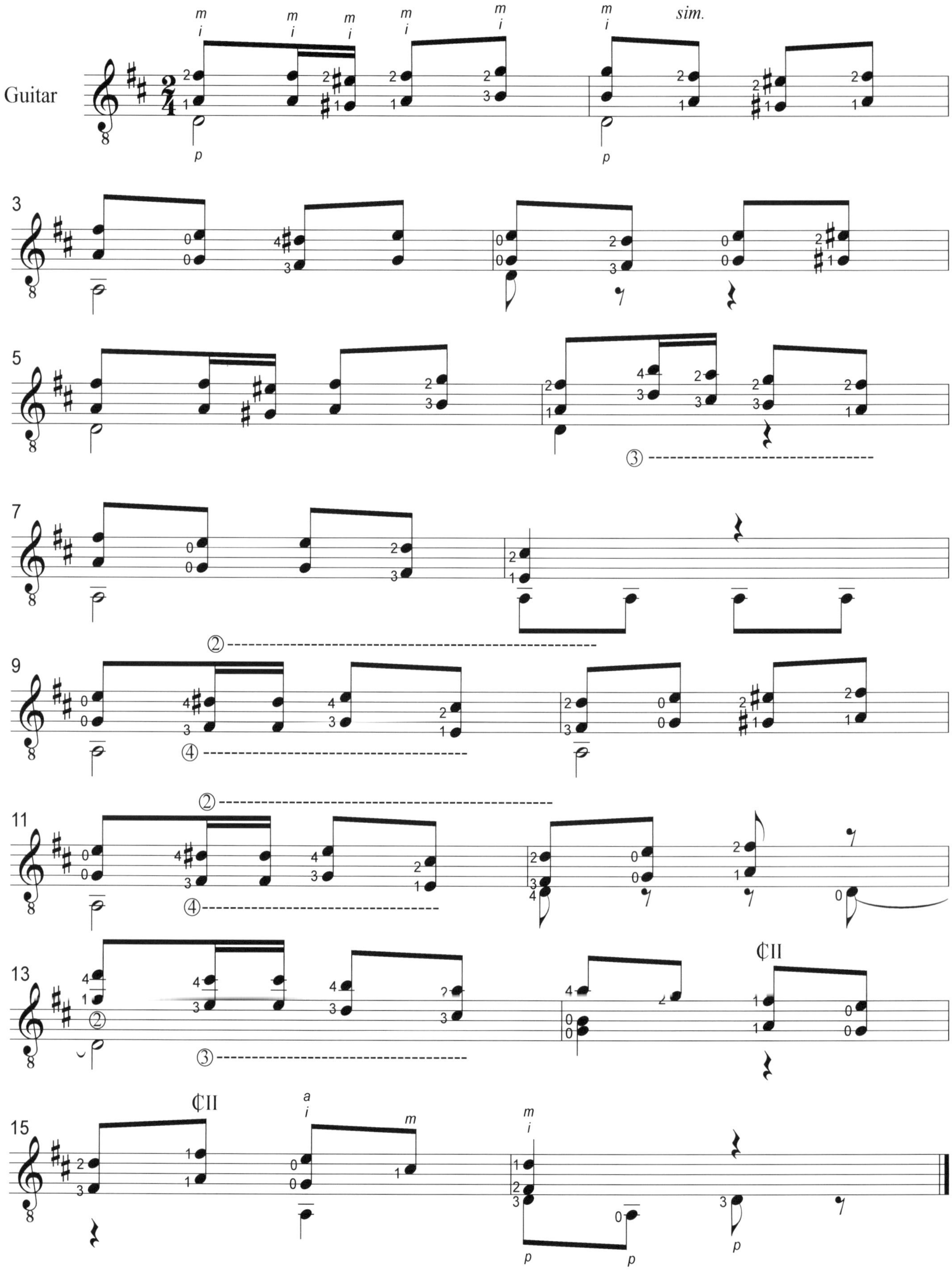

Performance Notes 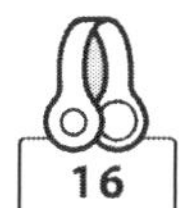

Exercise in Sixths, No. 3

Fernando Sor and Napoleon Coste
Edited by Corey Whitehead

1) Use tirando or free strokes imitating the sound of "apoyando."
2) Emphasize the lower voice (stems down).
3) Observe fingering in m. 14, use guide fingers for "portamento."

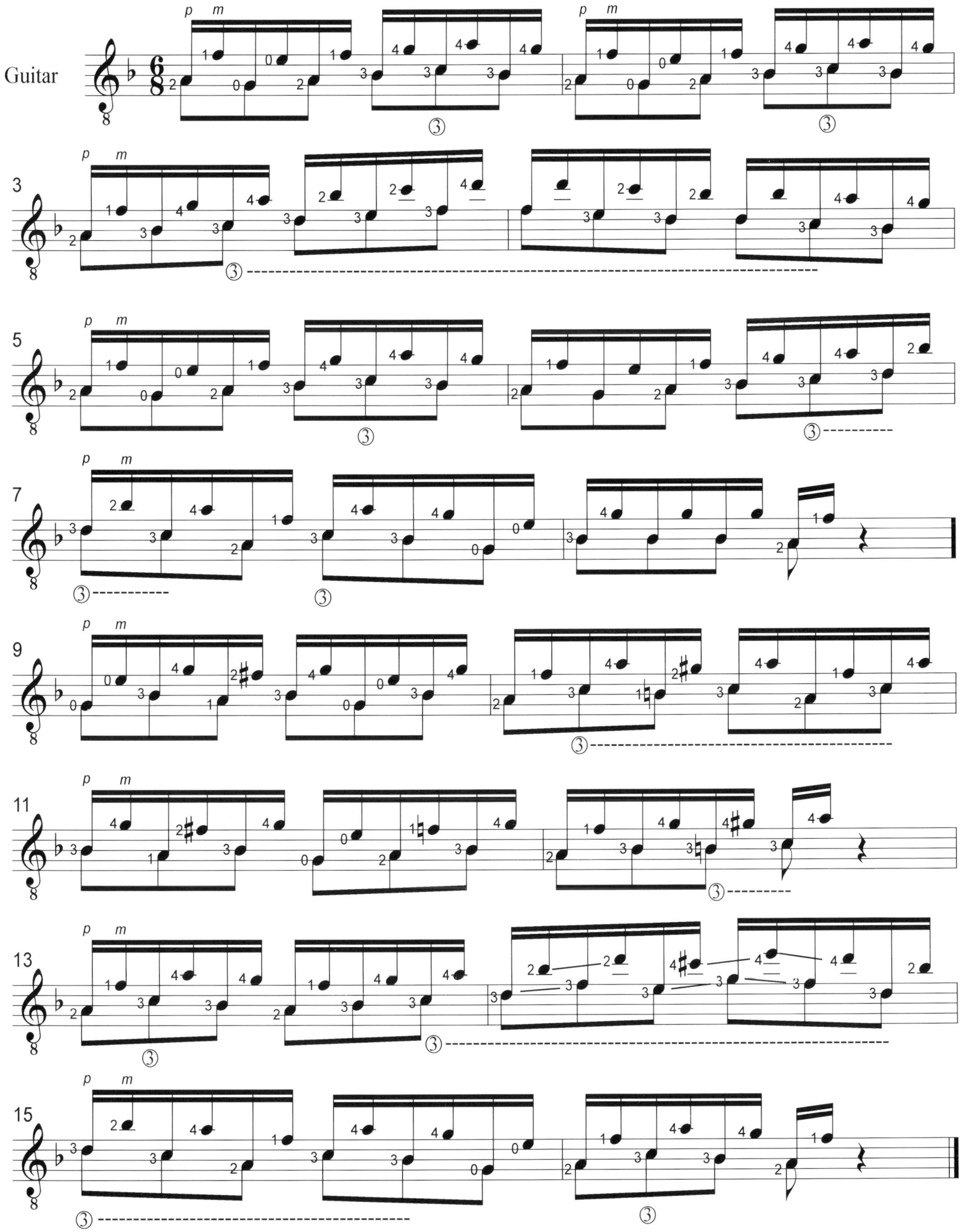

Guitar

Exercise in Sixths, No. 4

Fernando Sor and Napoleon Coste
Edited by Corey Whitehead

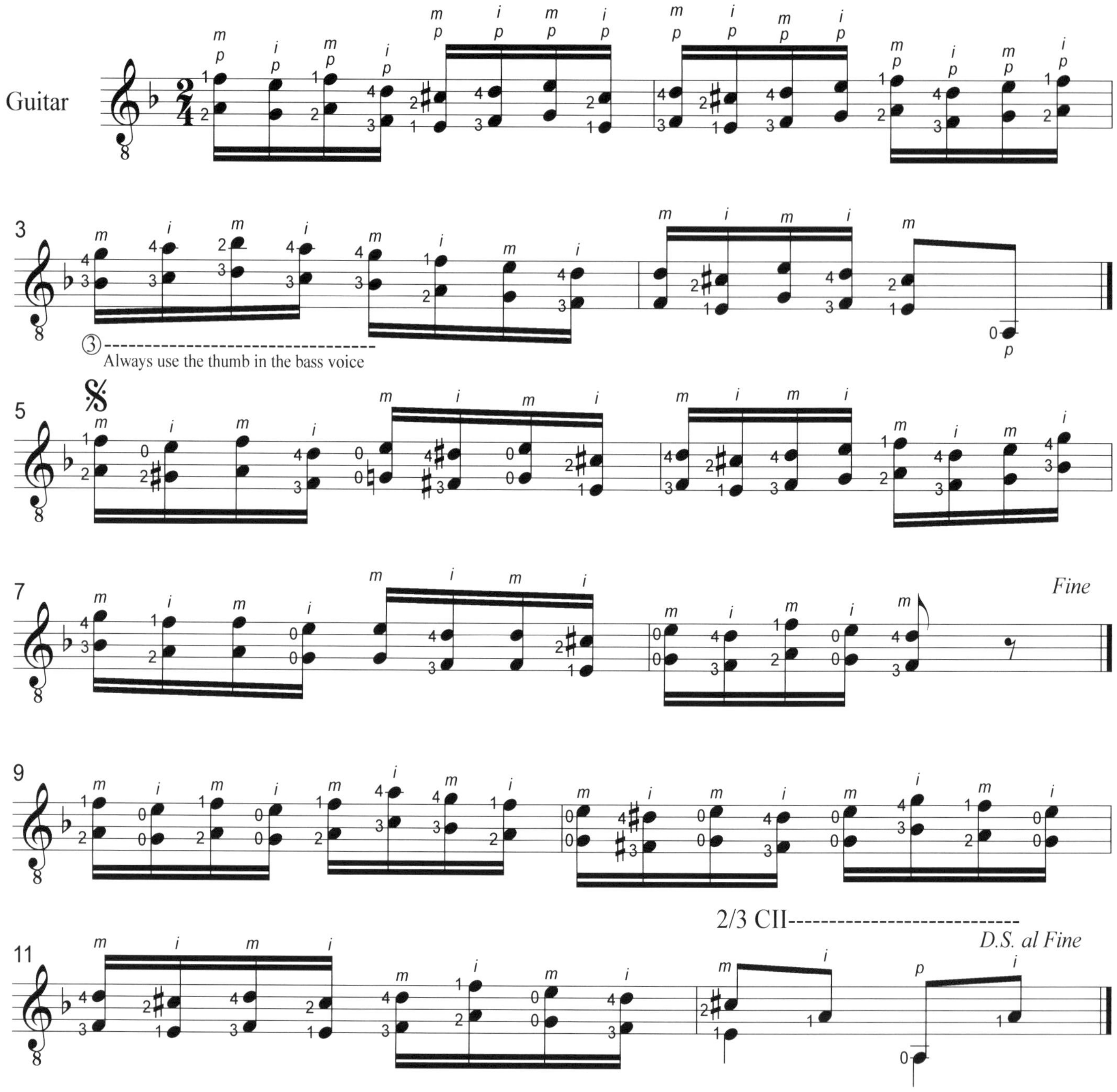

Guitar

Always use the thumb in the bass voice

Fine

2/3 CII

D.S. al Fine

Performance Notes

1) Use tirando or free strokes imitating the sound of "apoyando."
2) Emphasize the upper voice.
3) You can use right-hand fingers "i-a" instead of "p-m" or "p-i."
4) Separate stems are indicated for the bass voice only in the final measure as in the original edition.
5) Consider the lower voice to be the accompaniment throughout.
6) Emphasize the first note of each group of four sixteenth notes.
7) In 2/4 meter, beat one is strong and beat two is relatively weaker.

This page has been left blank to avoid an awkward page turn.

Exercise in Sixths, No. 5

Fernando Sor and Napoleon Coste
Edited by Corey Whitehead

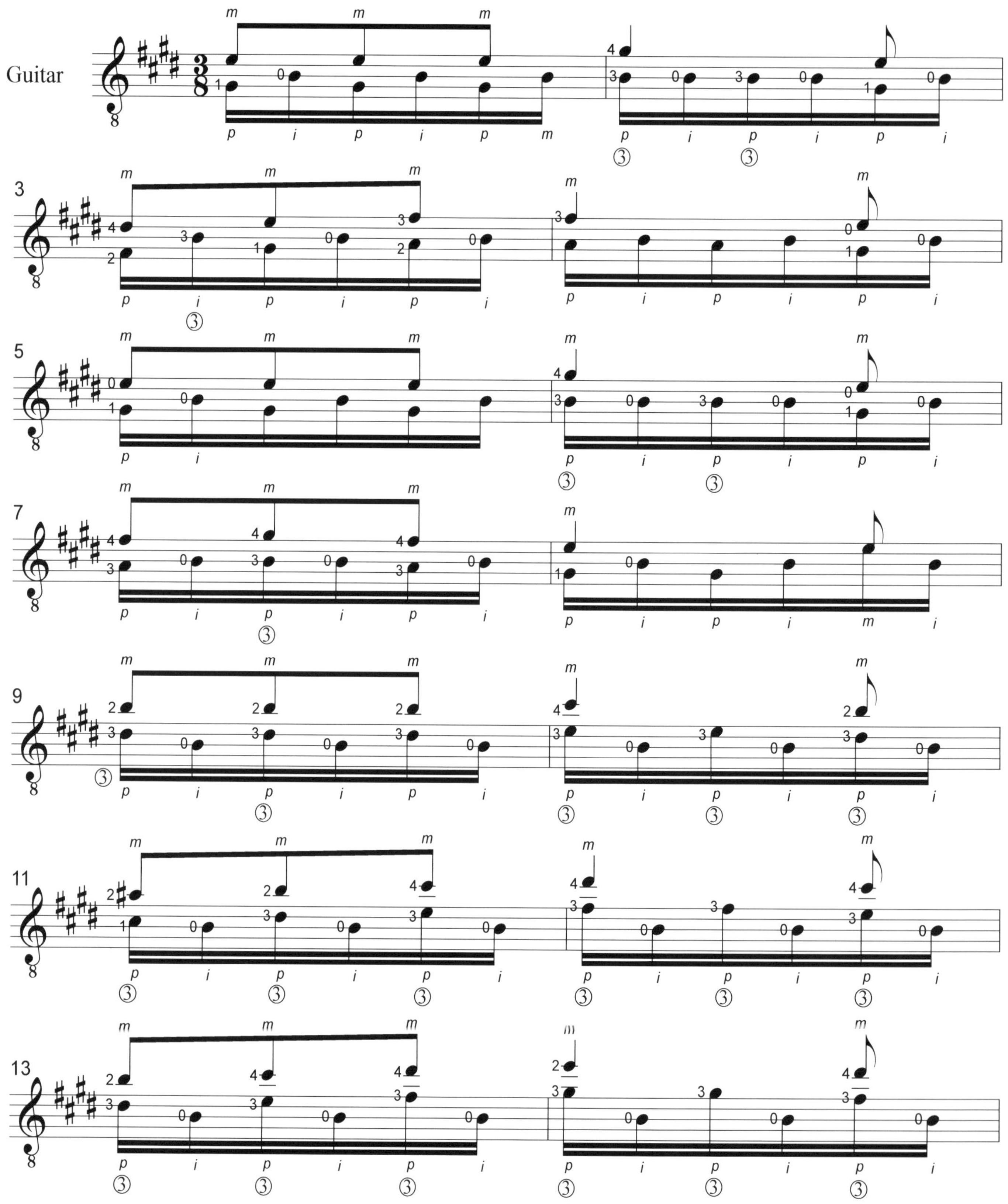

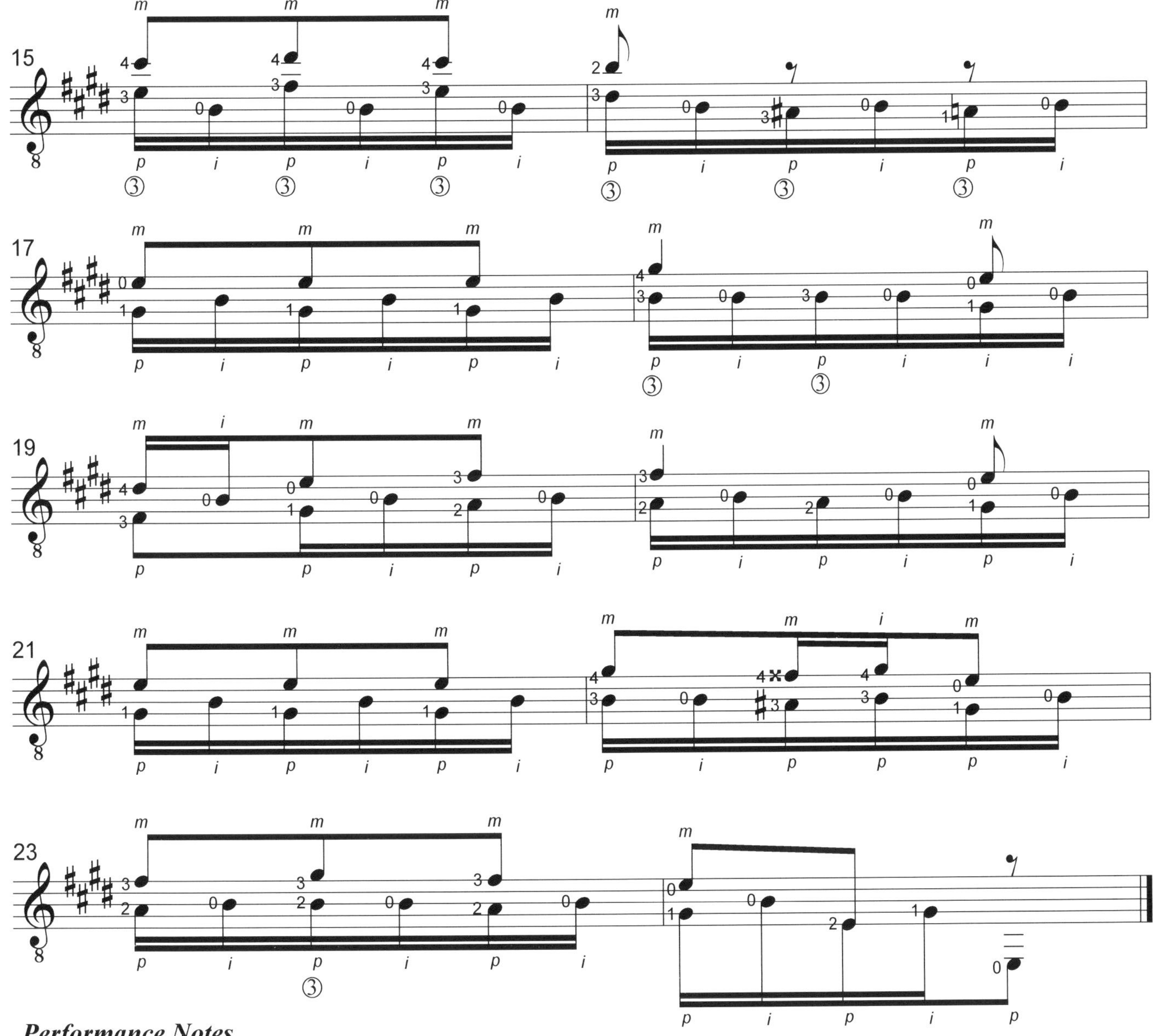

Performance Notes

1) Use tirando or free strokes imitating the sound of apoyando.

2) Emphasize the upper voice (stems up).

3) Keep L.H. fingers on the strings if repeated in a shift: Measures 7, 11-12, 13, 15, 22, and 23.

4) Play the open B softly as open strings are naturally loud.

5) Strive for a legato connection in the melodic voice (stems up).

6) Improvise your own dynamics as no dynamics are indicated by the composer.

7) Dissonances should be emphasized and resolved to relatively weaker consonances.

Exercise in Sixths, No. 6

Fernando Sor and Napoleon Coste
Edited by Corey Whitehead

Play the middle voice on 3rd string, except for the occaisional open B.

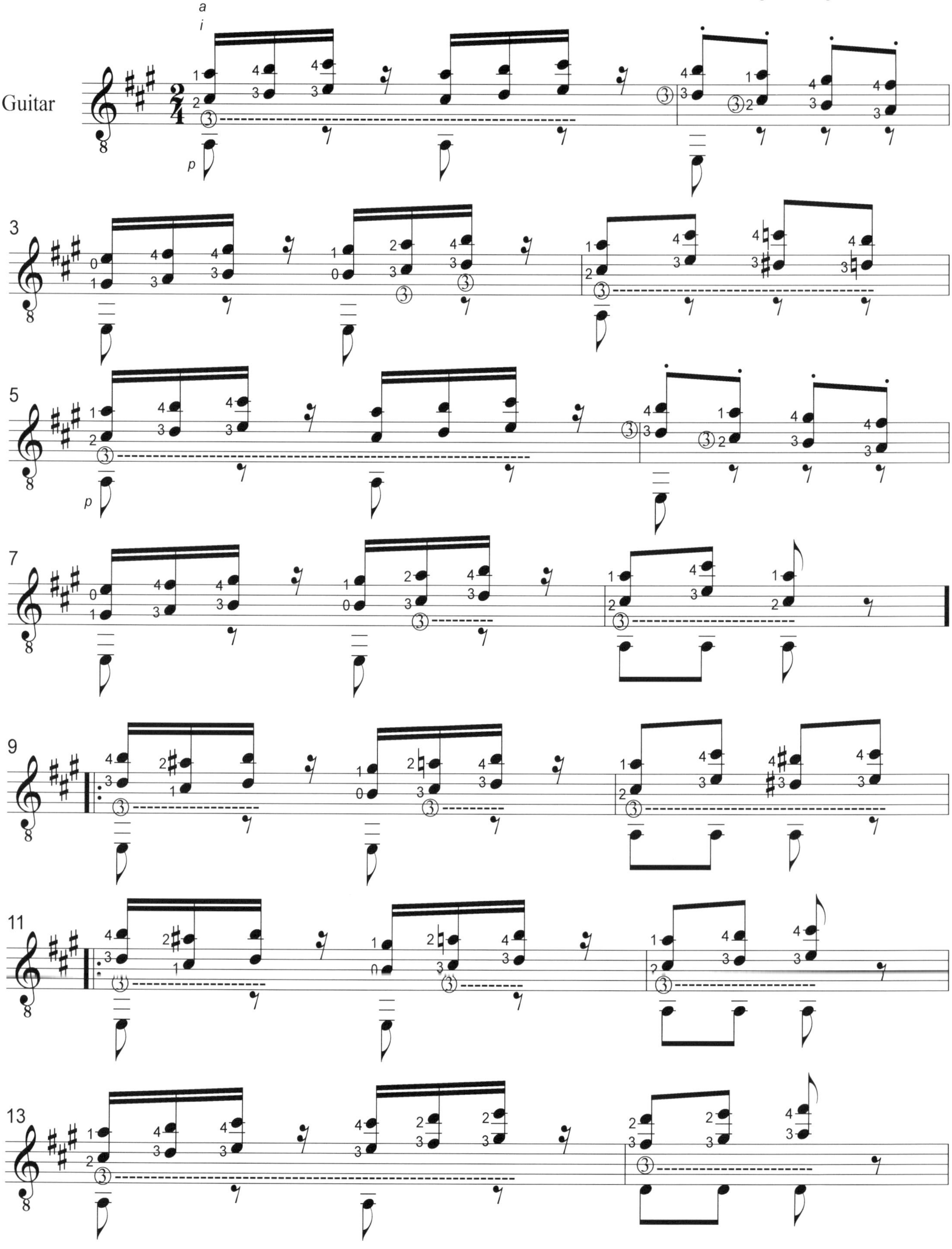

Guitar

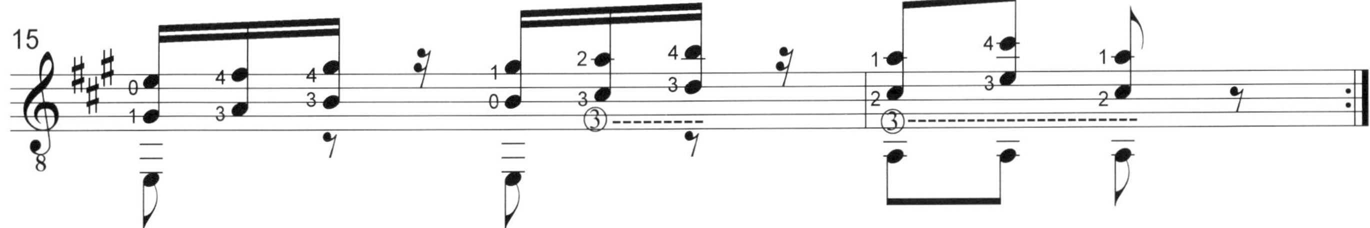

Performance Notes

1) Use tirando or free strokes imitating the sound of apoyando.

2) Emphasize the highest voice.

3) Use L.H. fingers as guide fingers if repeated in a shift.

4) You can use "p-i-m" as an alternative right-hand fingering.

5) Strive for a legato connection in the upper voices.

6) Improvise your own dynamics as no dynamics are indicated by the composer.

7) Dissonances should be emphasized and resolved to relatively softer consonances.

8) Interpret the articulation indication "staccato" as "light."

9) Usually "staccato" means "short and detached," but here, it can also be interpreted as "light."

10) When playing notes above the 12th fret, place the heel of the left hand on the upper bout while maintaining arched fingers.

11) When placing the L.H. heel against the edge of the upper bout, the L.H. thumb can be placed against the fingerboard for maximum extension of the left-hand fingers.

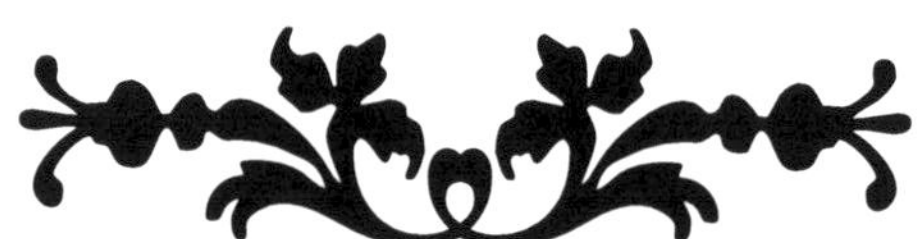

Classical Studies
Part 1/Unit 3

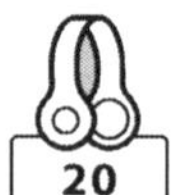

Op. 60 No. 2

Mateo Carcassi
Edited by Corey Whitehead

Moderato con espressivo ♩ = 100

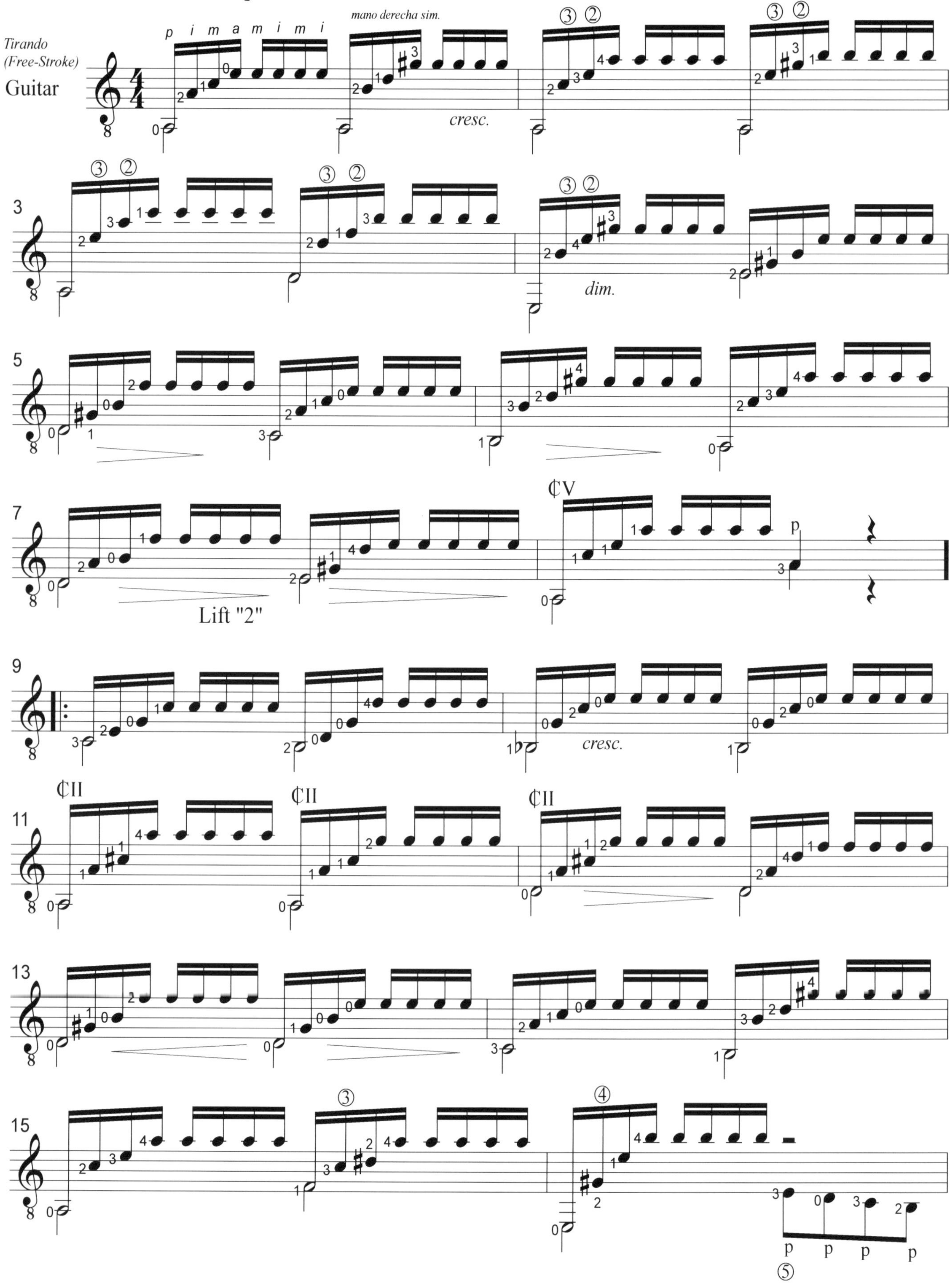

Tirando (Free-Stroke)
Guitar

p i m a m i m i

mano derecha sim.

cresc.

dim.

Lift "2"

¢V

¢II

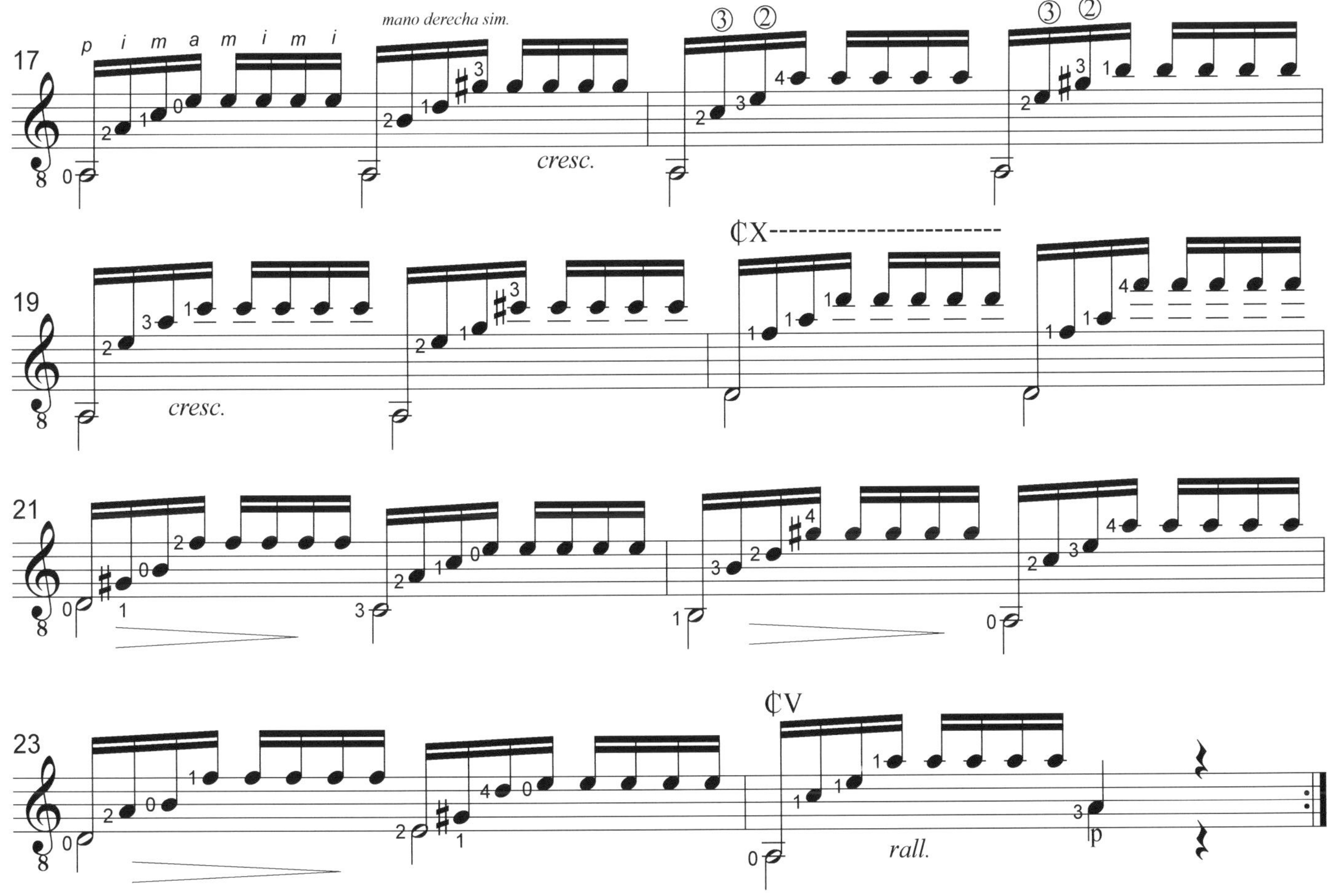

Performance Notes

1) Use tirando strokes imitating the sound of apoyando.

2) Emphasize the bass voice (stems down) as if it is a stone hitting a pond, and the resulting tones are ripples.

3) Allow bass notes to ring for their full duration.

4) Allow voices within a measure to sustain and blend together when they are consonant. This concept is called "finger pedal" in the notation of music for harpsichord.

5) Strive for a legato connection between measures.

6) Improvise your own dynamics where no dynamics are indicated by the composer.

7) Dissonances should be emphasized and resolved to relatively softer consonances.

8) Dissonances often result from ***accidentals****; i.e., sharps or flats not included in the key signature.*

9) The key signature here is A minor with no sharps or flats, but the piece uses many accidentals to "tonicize" other notes.

10) "Tonicization" of a note other than the root of the scale (A) requires a temporary key change.

11) F-sharp and G-sharp are diatonic scale tones in A melodic minor even though they appear as accidentals in this piece.

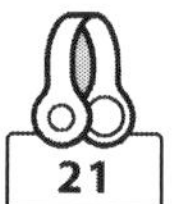

Op. 60 No. 3

Mateo Carcassi
Edited by Corey Whitehead

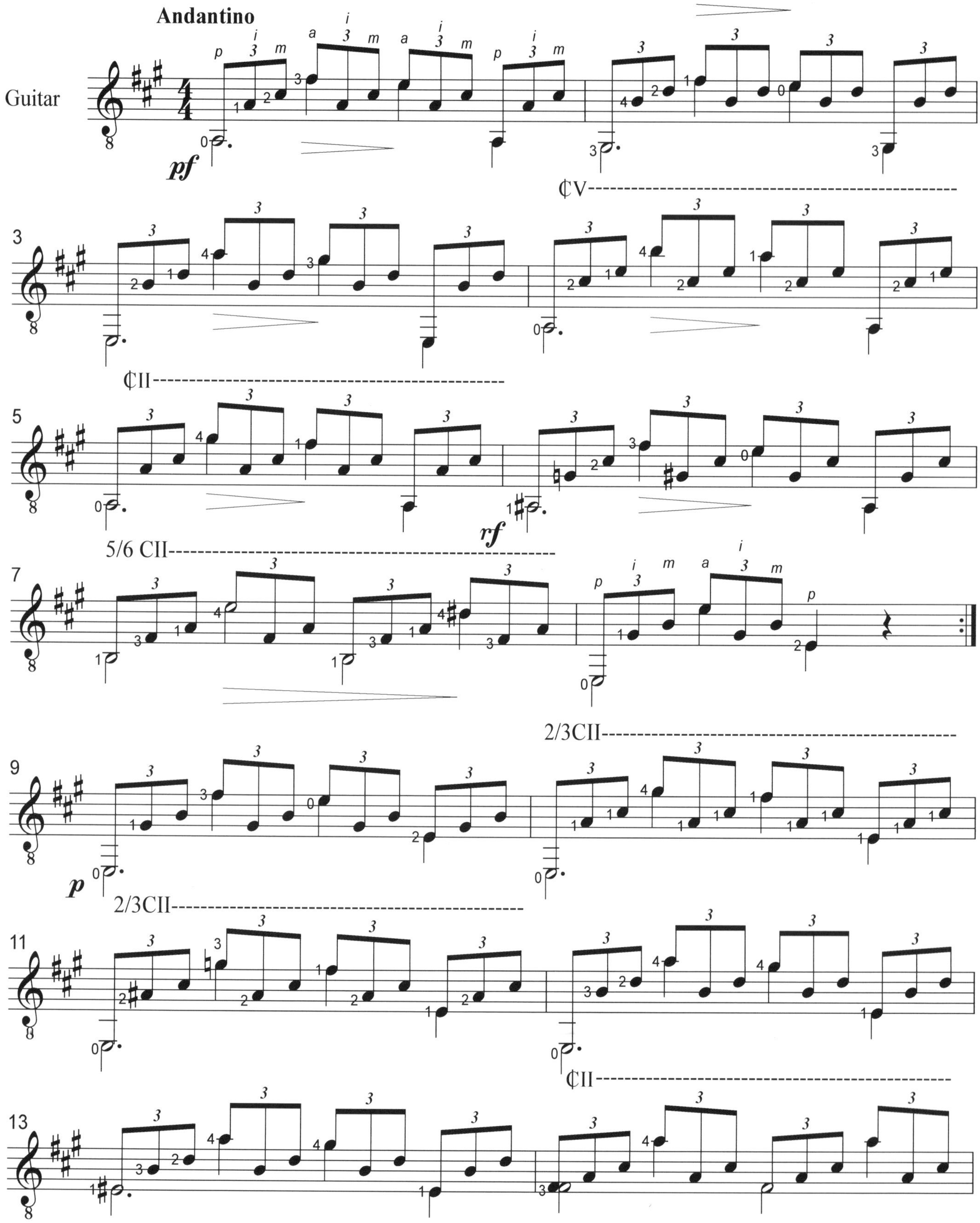

Andantino

Guitar

pf

¢V

¢II

rf

5/6 CII

2/3CII

p

2/3CII

¢II

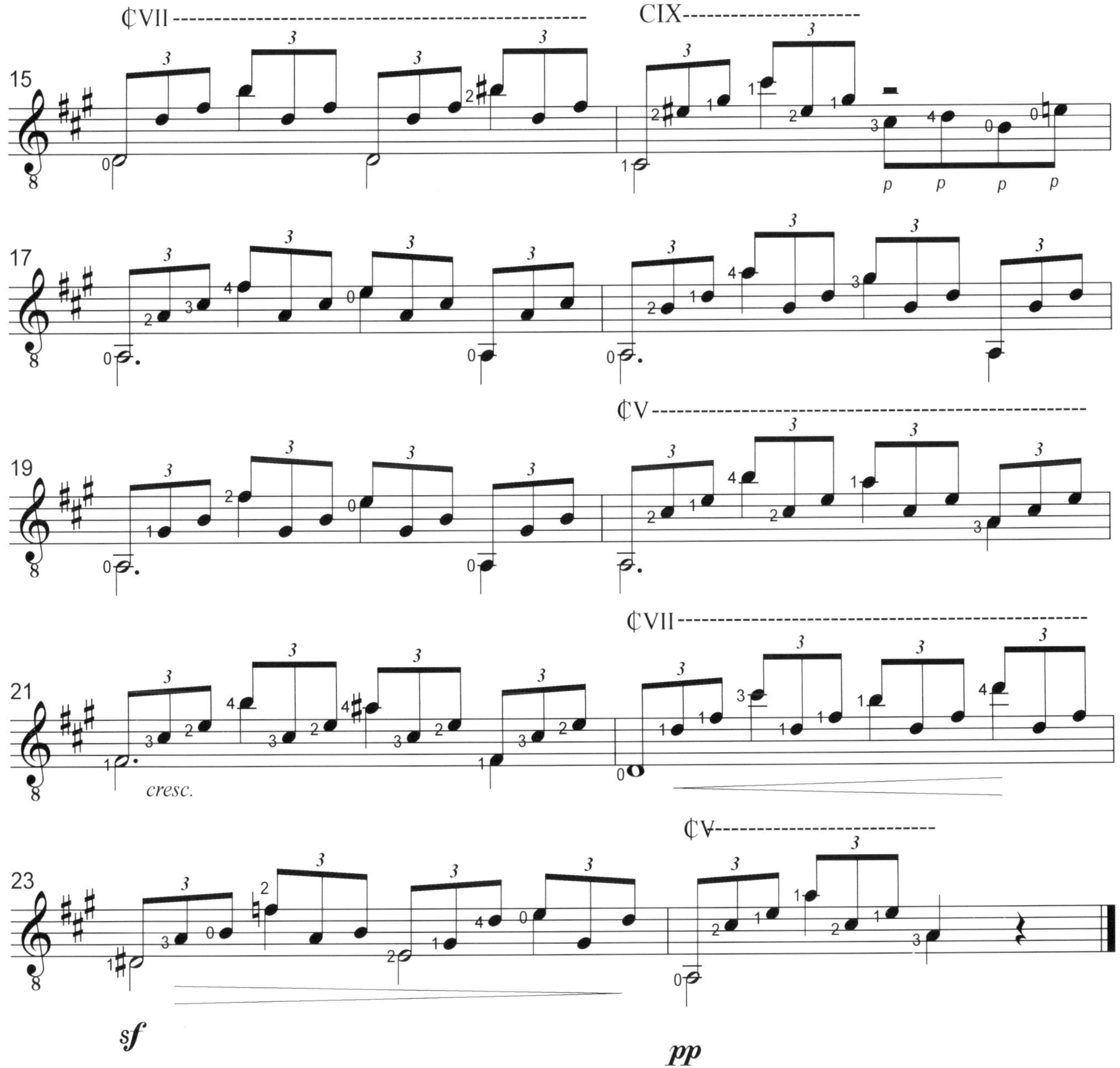

Performance Notes

1) *Use apoyando on the melody which is the first note of each triplet on beats two and three.*

2) *Emphasize the lower voice (stems down) on beats one and four.*

3) *Allow bass notes to ring for their full duration.*

4) *Allow voices within the measure to ring together when they are consonant.*

5) *Strive for a legato connection in the melodic and bass voices.*

6) *The dynamic* ***pf*** *is used in 19th-century guitar music and indicates that following the initial soft dynamic, one then plays following the soft downbeat.*

Op. 60 No. 6

Matteo Carcassi
Edited by Corey Whitehead

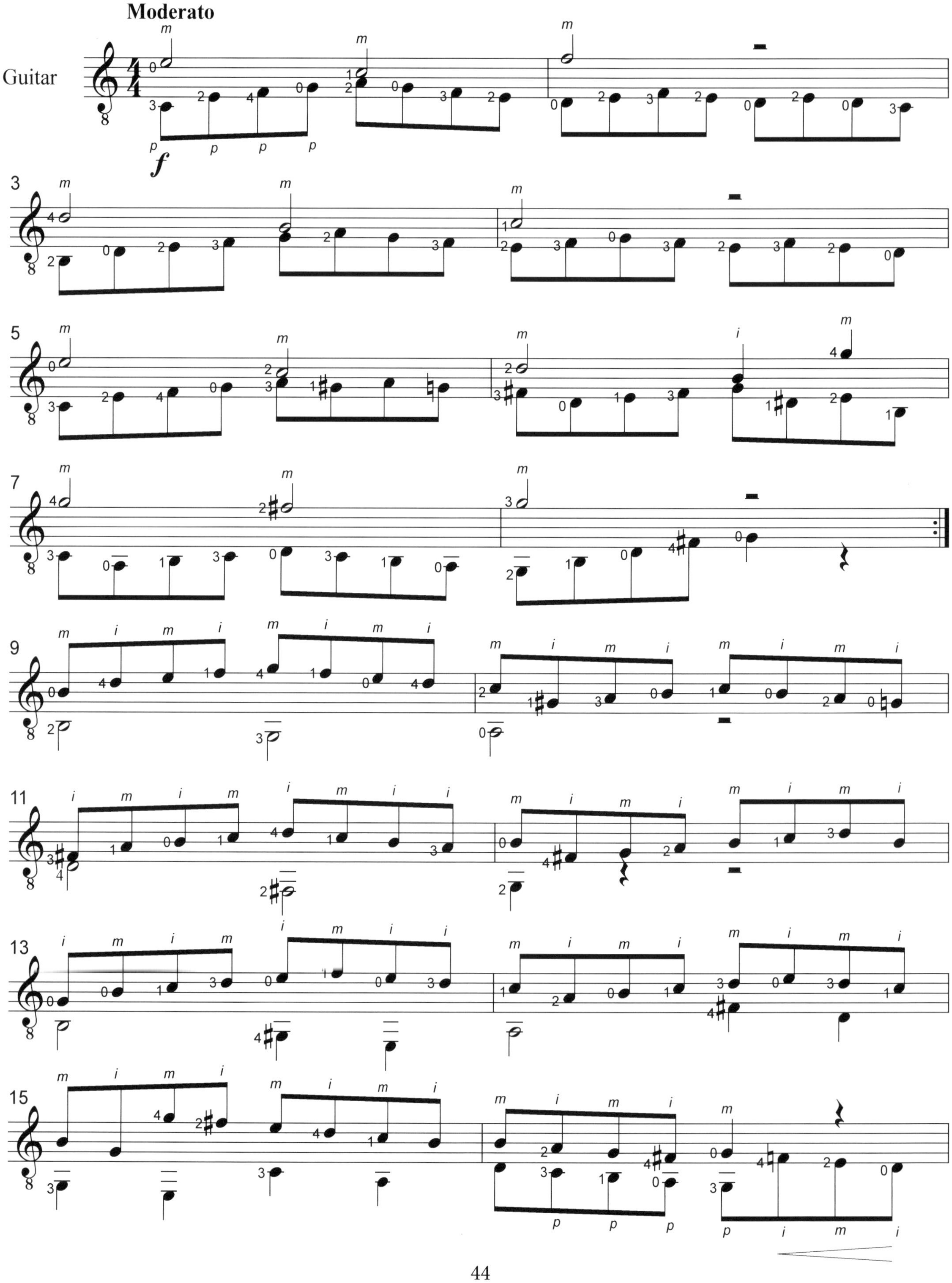

Moderato

Guitar

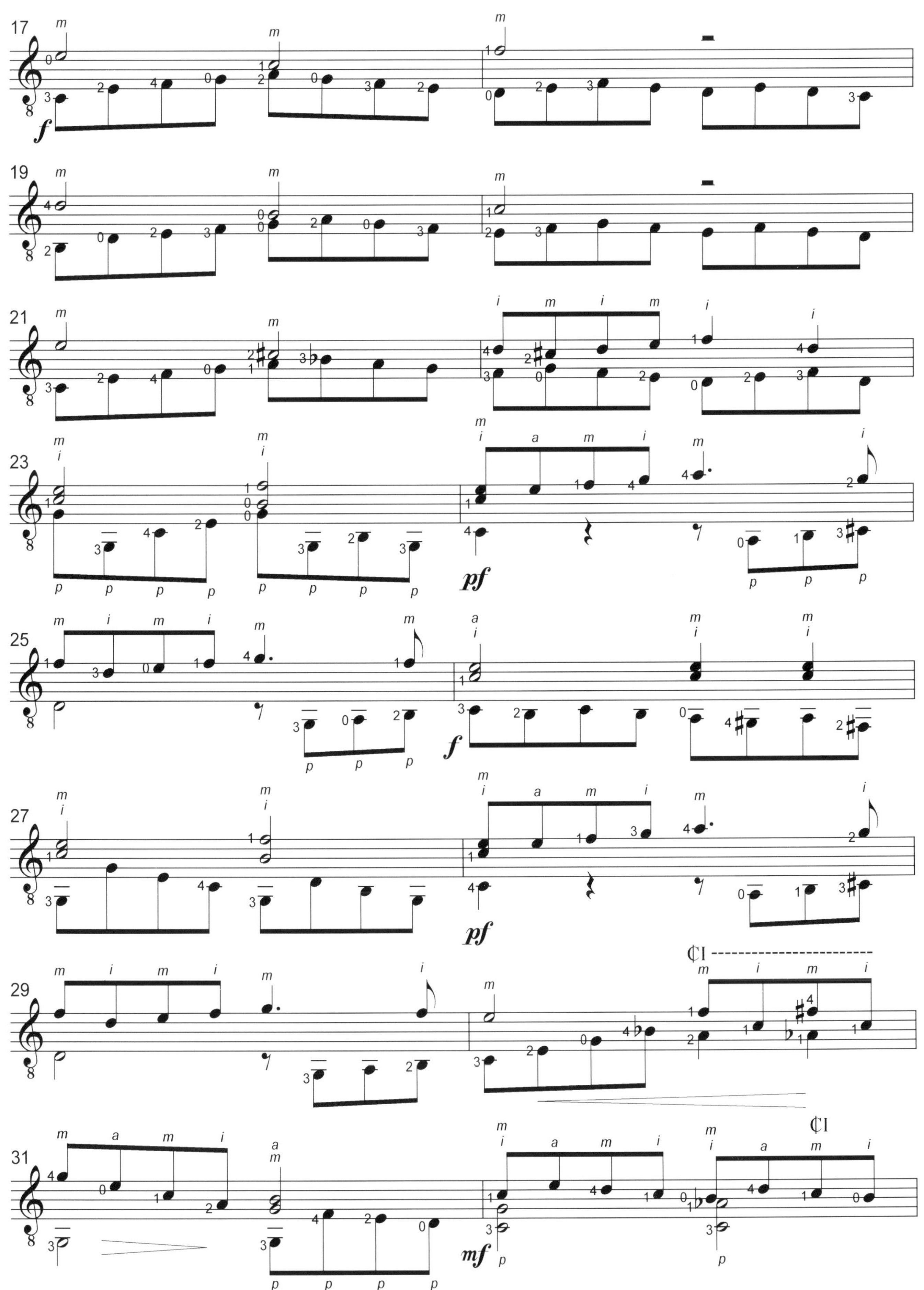
17
f
19
21
23
pf
25
f
27
pf
29
CI
31
mf
CI

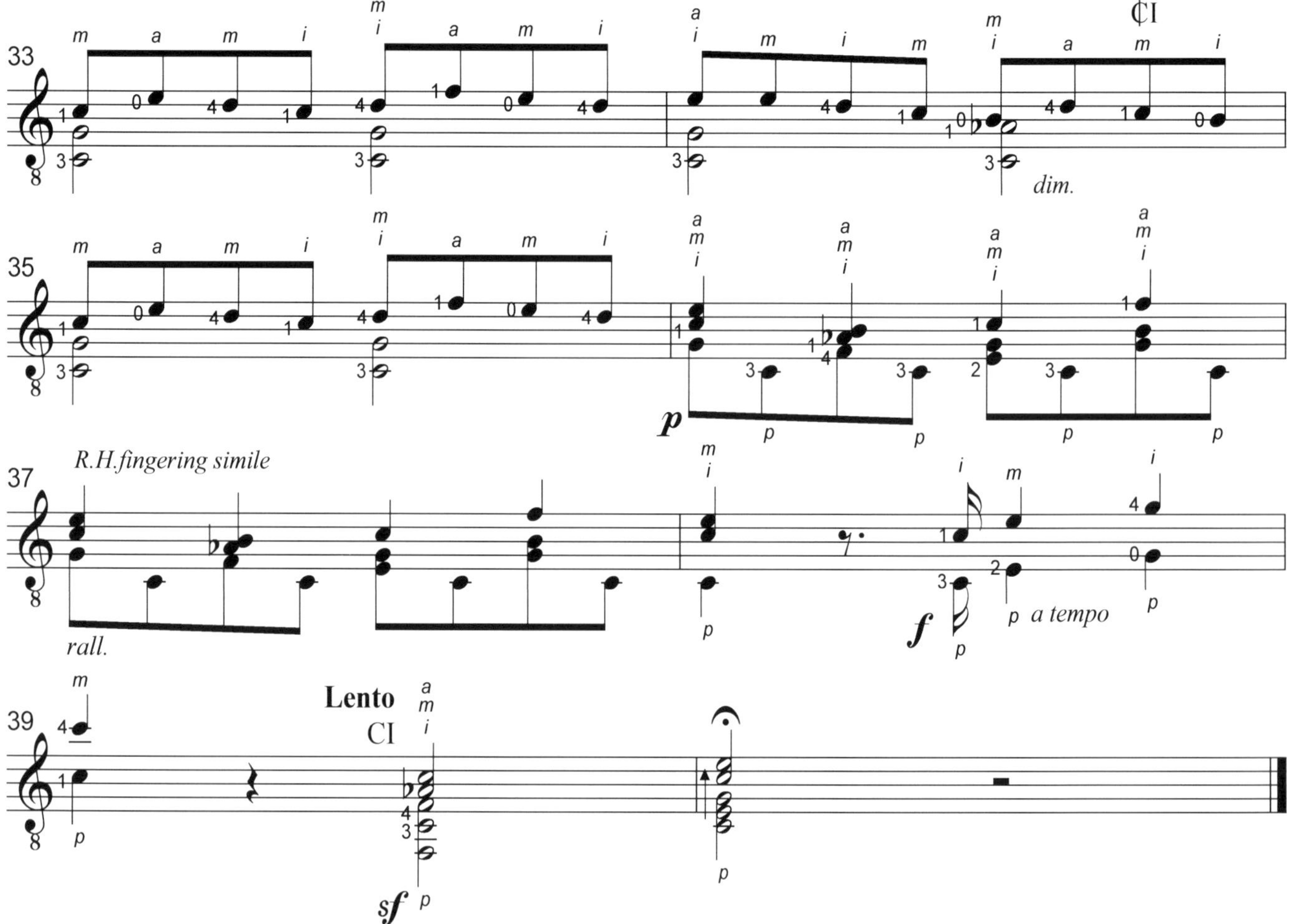

Performance Notes

1) Use apoyando or tirando strokes imitating the sound of apoyando.

2) Emphasize the upper voice (stems up).

3) Allow bass notes to ring for their full duration.

4) Allow voices within the measure to blend together when they are consonant.

5) Strive for legato connections in general.

6) Improvise your own dynamics where no dynamics are indicated by the composer.

7) Dissonances should be emphasized and resolved to relatively softer consonances.

8) Often, dissonances appear as accidentals, i.e., sharps or flats not included in the key signature.

9) The key signature is C Major with no sharps or flats, but the piece uses many accidentals to "tonicize" other notes.

10) "Tonicization" of a note other than the root of the scale (C) requires a temporary key change.

*11) The dynamic **pf** is used in 19th-century guitar music and indicates that following the initial soft dynamic, one then plays following the soft downbeat.*

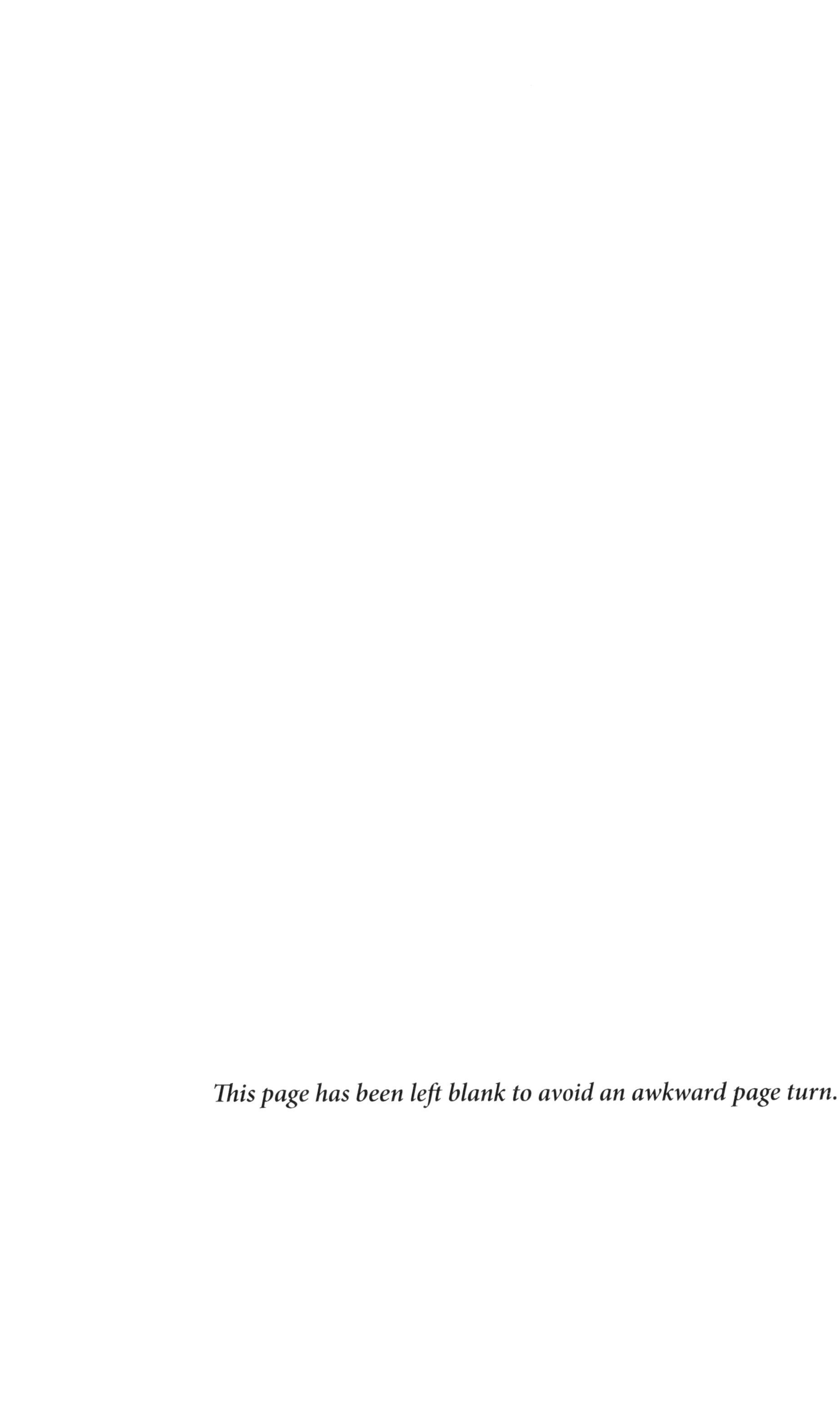

This page has been left blank to avoid an awkward page turn.

Op. 60 No. 7

Mateo Carcassi
Edited by Corey Whitehead

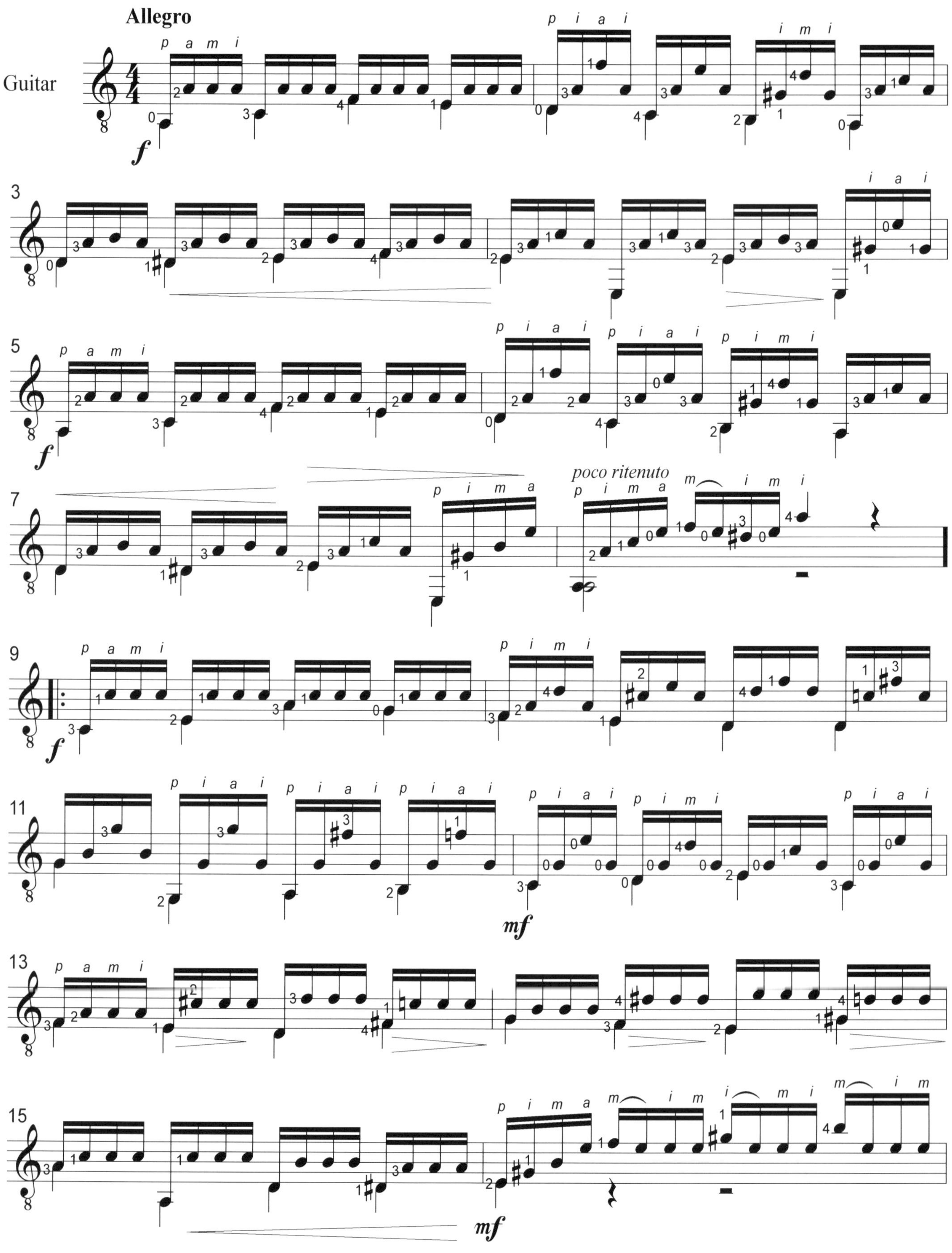

Allegro

Guitar

poco ritenuto

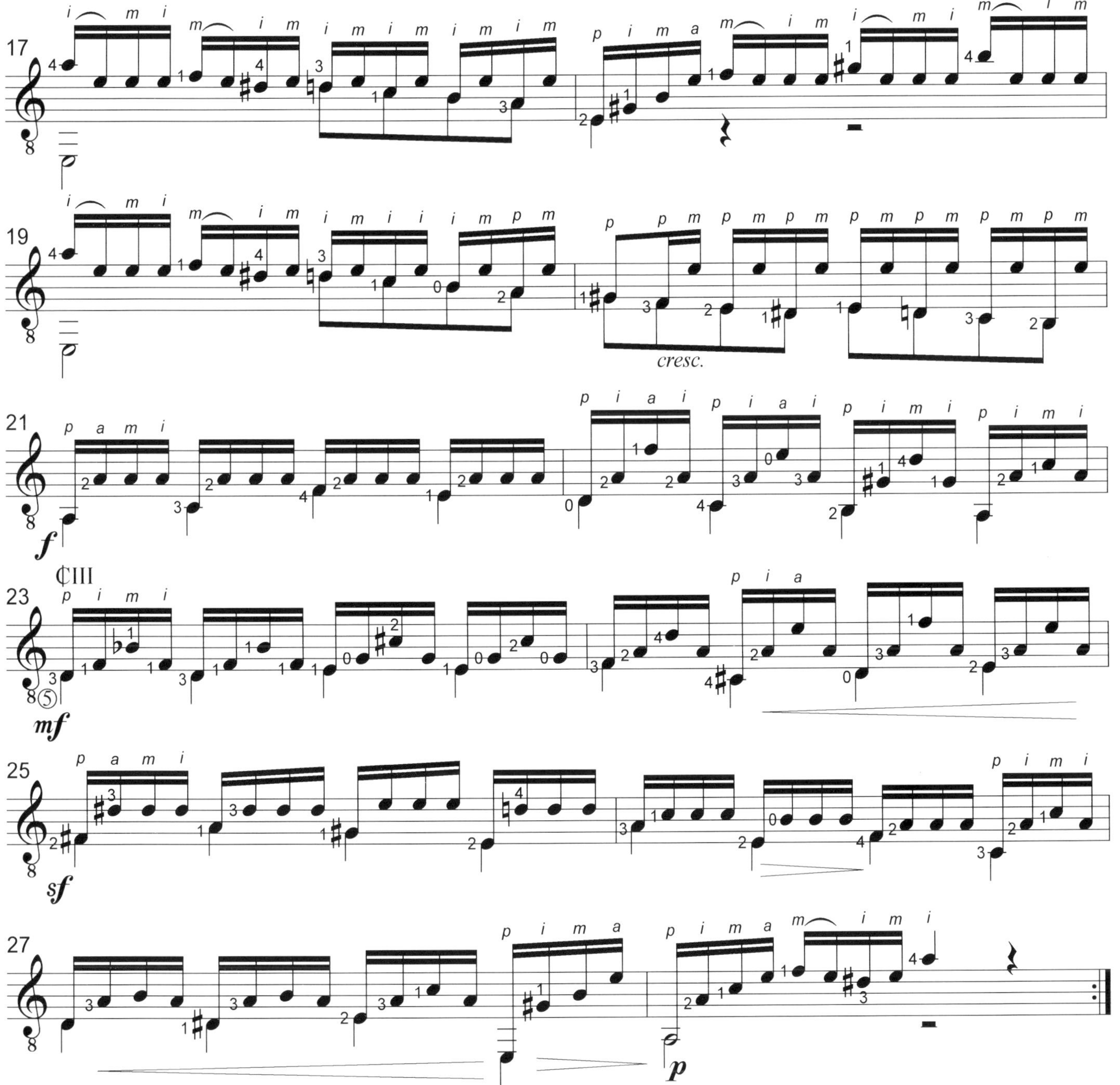

Performance Notes

1) Use tirando strokes imitating the sound of apoyando.

2) Emphasize the bass voice (stems down).

3) Allow bass notes to ring for their full duration.

4) Allow voices within the measure to blend together when consonant.

5) As an alternative to (p-a-m-i), one may use (p-i-m-i) to play the trémolo.

6) Use apoyando on beats two and three of measure 8.

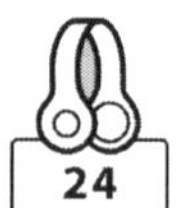

Op. 60 No. 8

Mateo Carcassi
Edited by Corey Whitehead

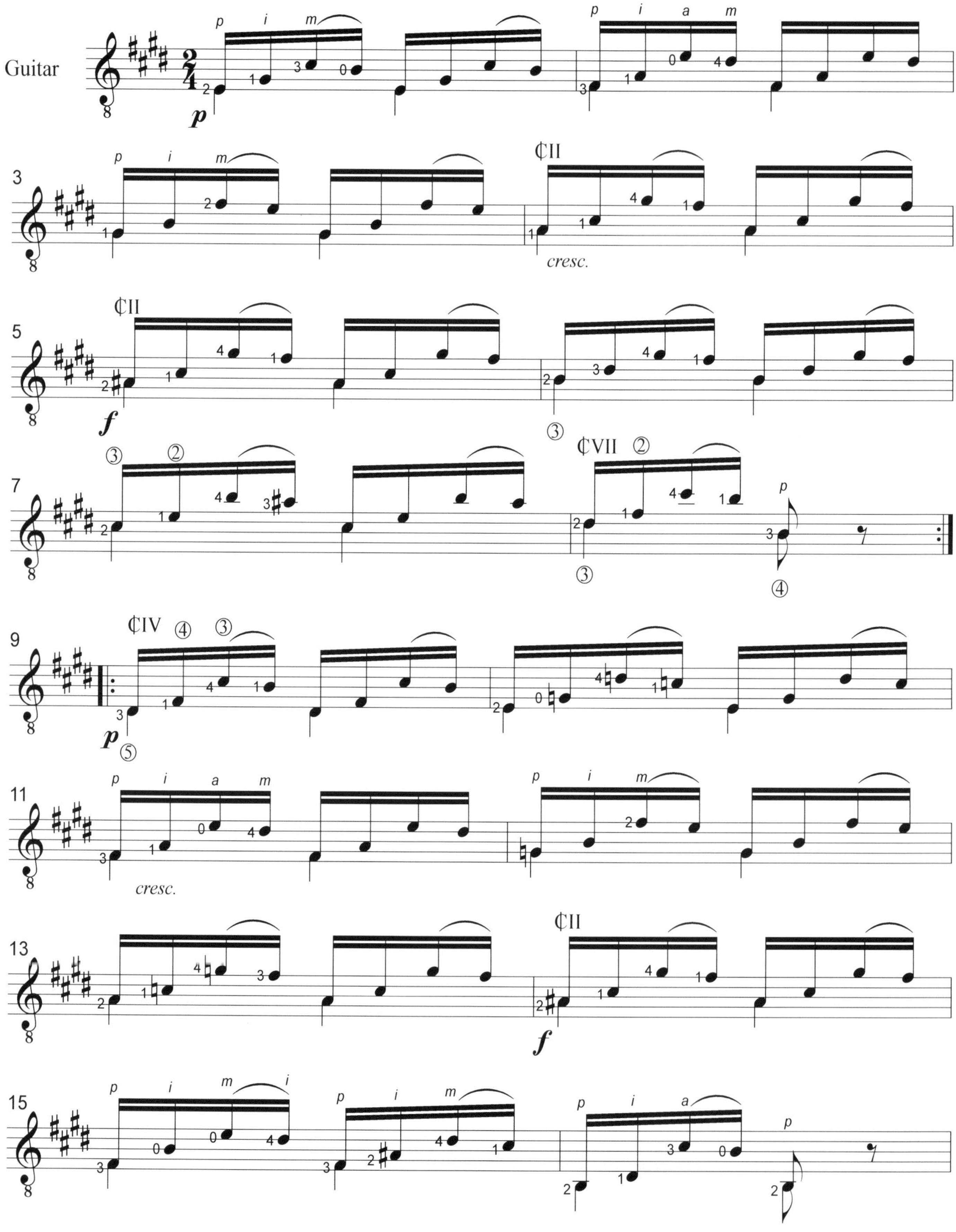

Guitar

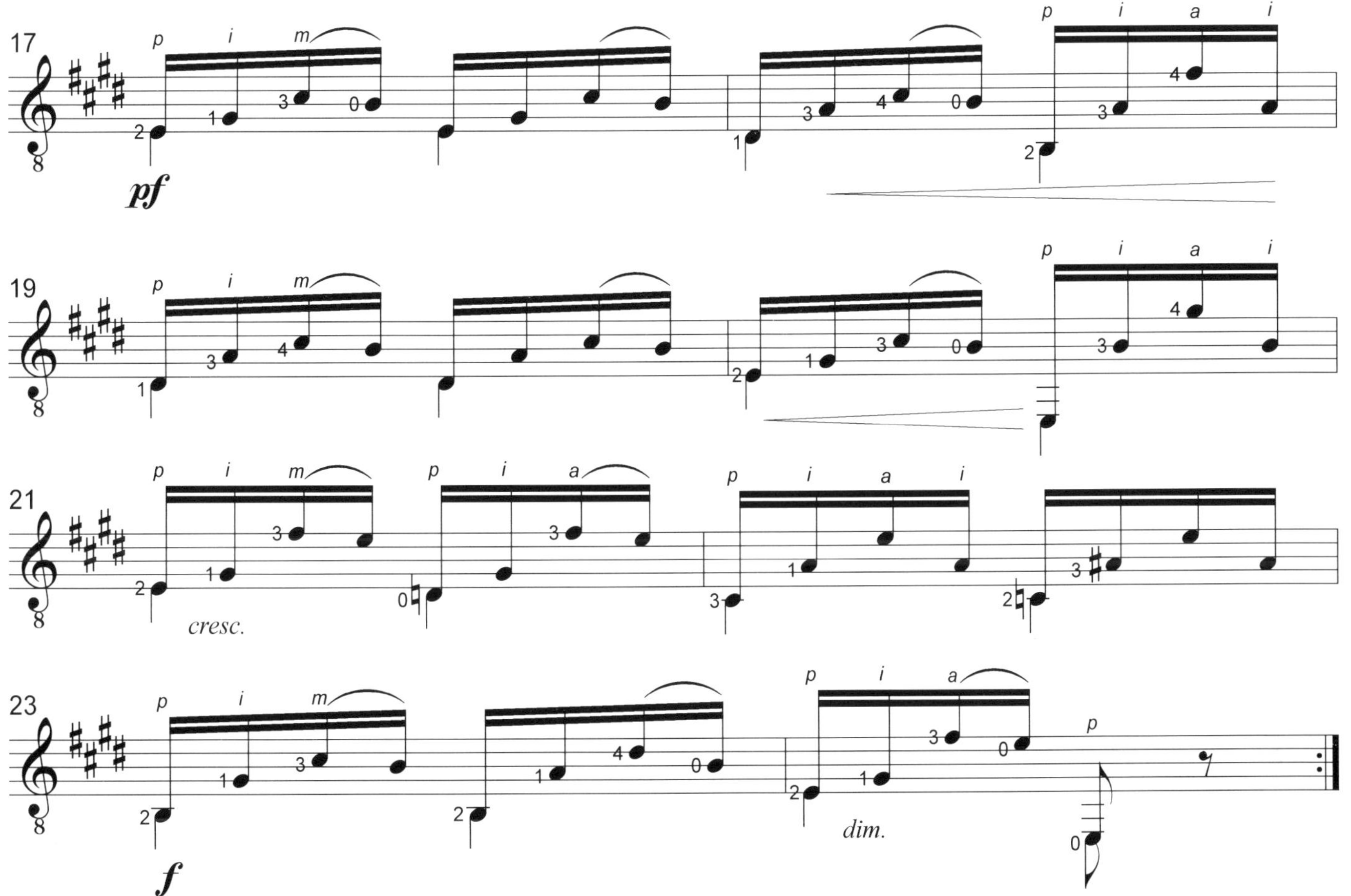

Performance Notes

1) Use tirando strokes to emulate the sound of apoyando.

2) Emphasize the upper voice (stems up).

3) Allow bass notes to ring for their full duration.

4) Allow voices within the measure to sound together when they are consonant.

5) The slur in measure 15 is a "cross-string" slur. Both notes are played with the R.H. and sound together consecutively.

6) Improvise your own dynamics where no dynamics are indicated by the composer.

7) Dissonances should be emphasized and resolved to relatively softer consonances.

8) Dissonances often appear as accidentals - sharps and flats not included in the key signature.

9) The key signature for E Major has four sharps but this piece uses many accidentals to "tonicize" other notes.

10) "Tonicization" of a note other than the root of the scale (E) requires a temporary key change

*11) The dynamic **pf** is used in 19th-century guitar music and indicates that following the initial soft dynamic, one then plays following the soft downbeat.*

Op. 60 No. 13

Mateo Carcassi
Edited by Corey Whitehead

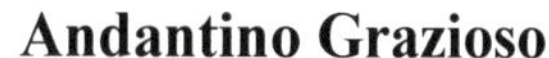

Tirando (Free-Stroke)

Guitar

pf

mano derecha sim.

f

mf

mano derecha sim.

mano derecha sim.

mano derecha sim.

mano derecha sim.

mano derecha sim.

mano derecha sim.

f

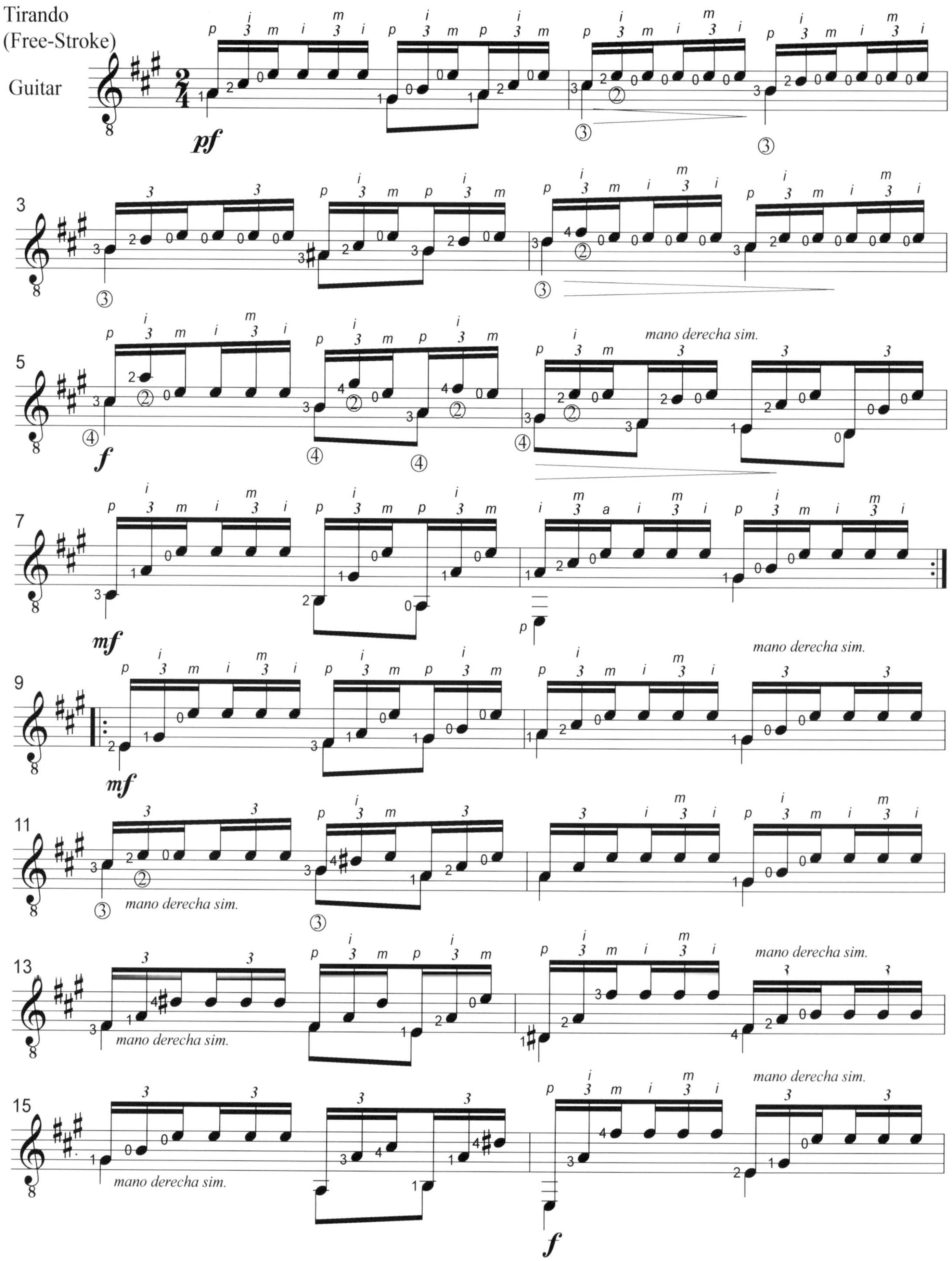

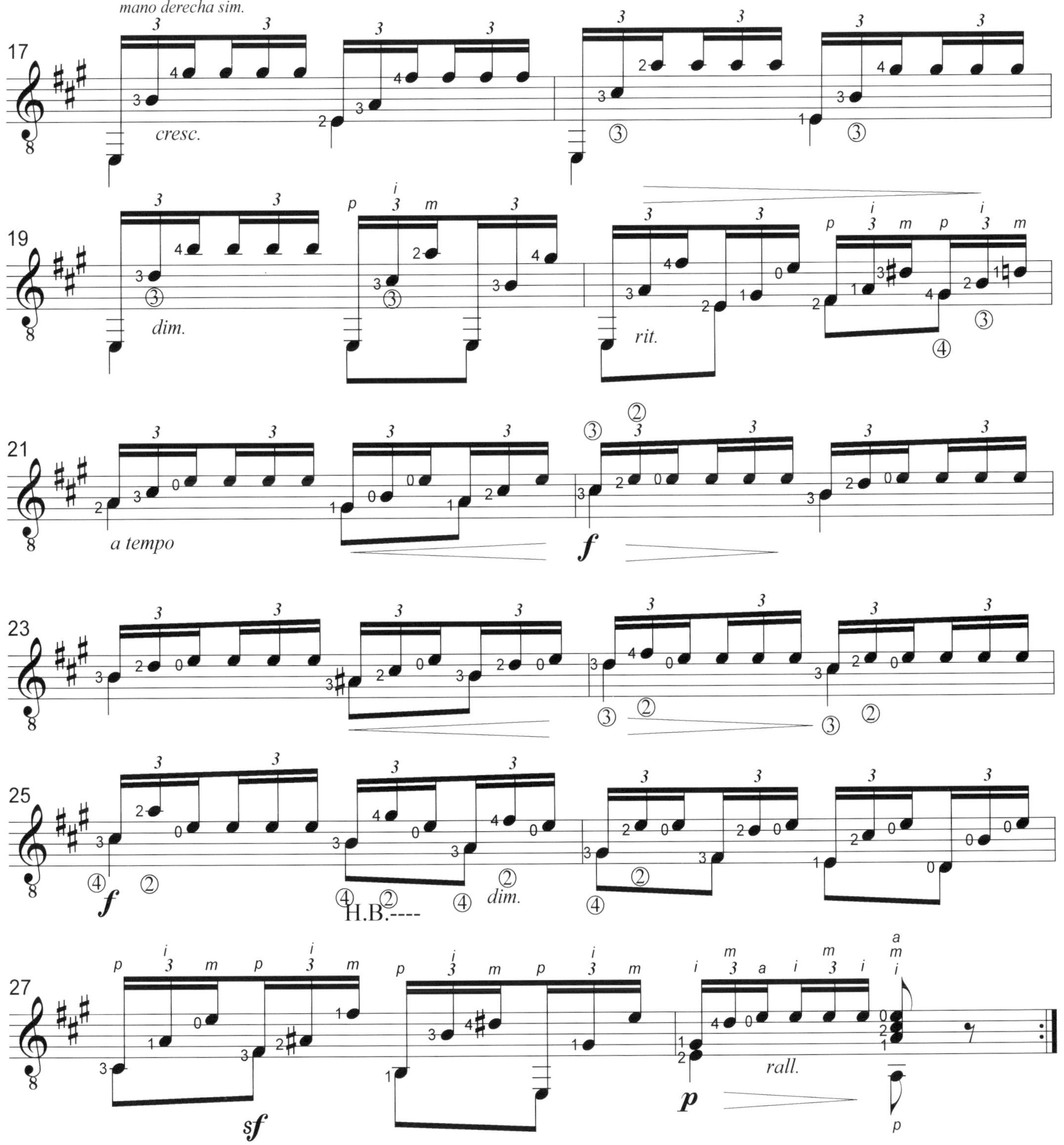

Performance Notes

1) Use tirando strokes imitating the sound of apoyando.
2) Emphasize the lower voice (stems down).
3) Allow voices within the measure to sound together when they are consonant.
5) Strive for a legato feel in general.
6) Improvise your own dynamics where no dynamics are indicated by the composer.
7) Dissonances should be emphasized and resolved to relatively softer consonances.
8) Often, the dissonances appear as accidentals, i.e., sharps or flats not included in the key signature.
9) The key signature for A Major has three sharps, but this piece uses many accidentals to "tonicize" other notes.
10) "Tonicization" of a note other than the root of the scale (A) requires a temporary key change.
11) H.B. indicates a hinge barré.
*12) The dynamic **pf** is used in 19th-century guitar music and indicates that following the initial soft dynamic, one then plays following the soft downbeat.*

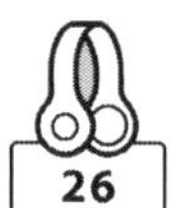

Op. 60 No.16

Mateo Carcassi
Edited by Corey Whitehead

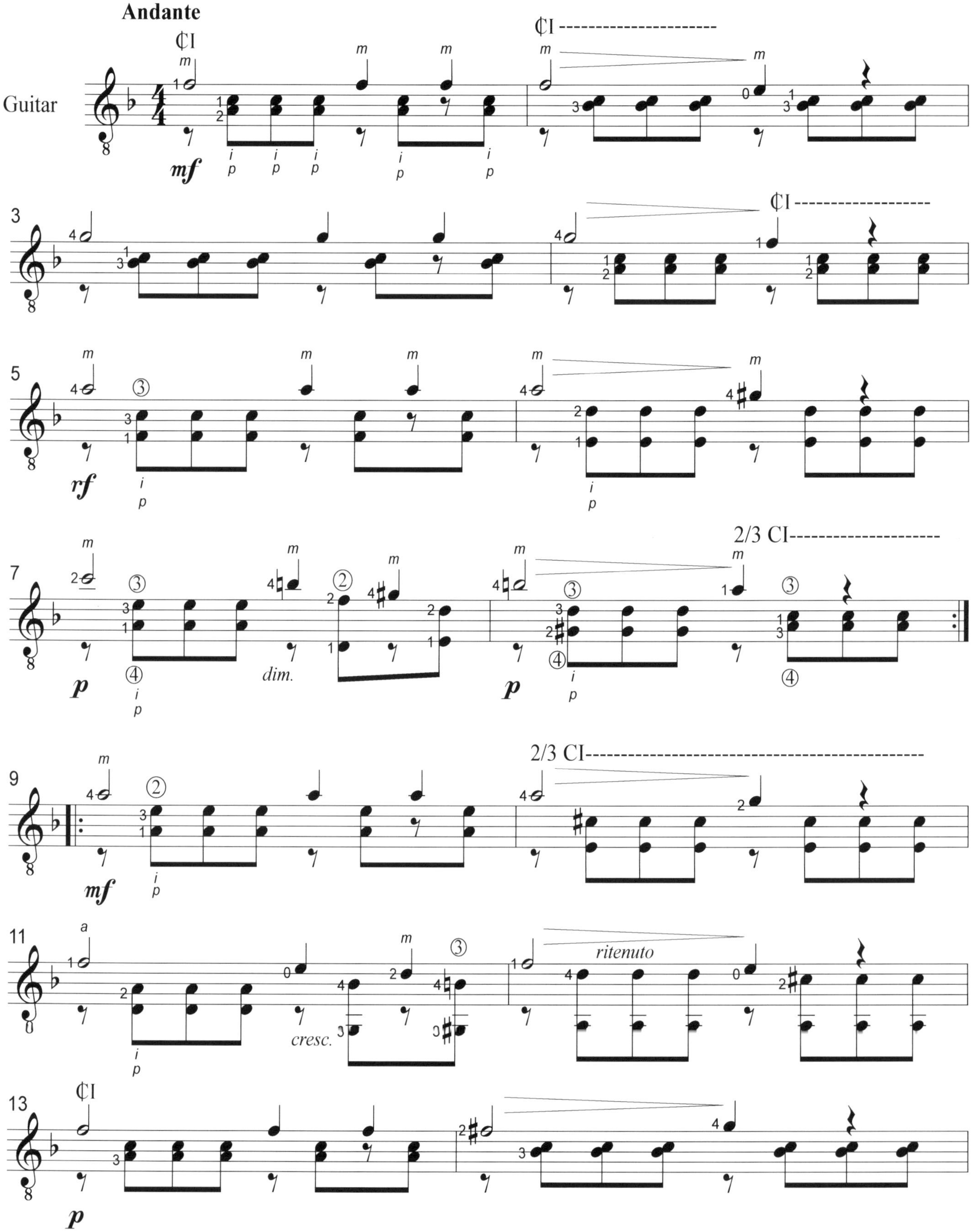

Andante

Guitar

mf *rf* *p* *dim.* *p* *mf* *cresc.* *ritenuto* *p*

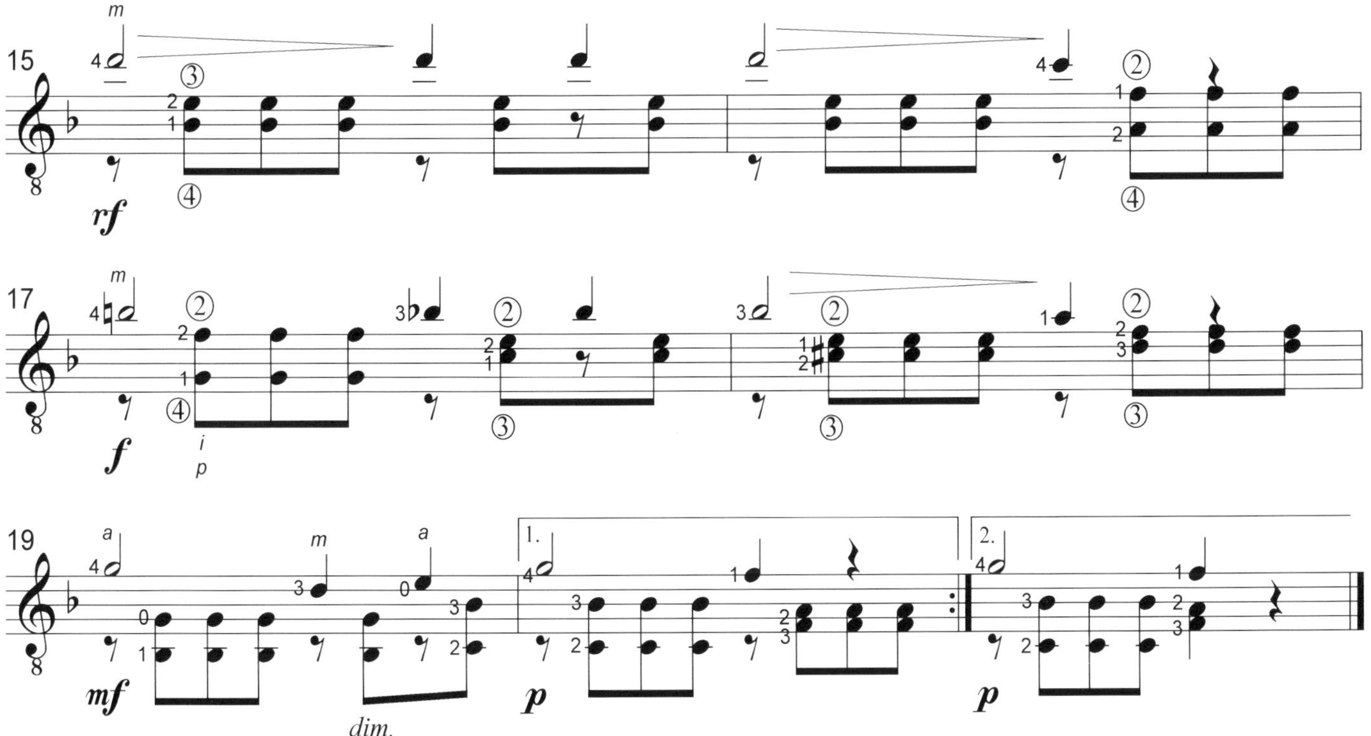

Performance Notes

1) Use apoyando to emphasize the upper melodic voice (stems up).

2) Stop the bass notes with the right hand where rests are indicated.

3) Allow voices within the measure to ring together when consonant.

4) Strive for a legato connection in the melodic voice (stems up).

5) Improvise your own dynamics where no dynamics are indicated by the composer.

6) Dissonances should be emphasized and resolved to relatively softer consonances.

7) Often, the dissonances appear as accidentals, i.e., sharps or flats not included in the key signature.

8) F Major has one flat but this piece uses many accidentals to "tonicize" other notes.

9) "Tonicization" of a note other than the root of the scale (F) requires a temporary key change.

Op. 60 No. 19

Mateo Carcassi
Edited by Corey Whitehead

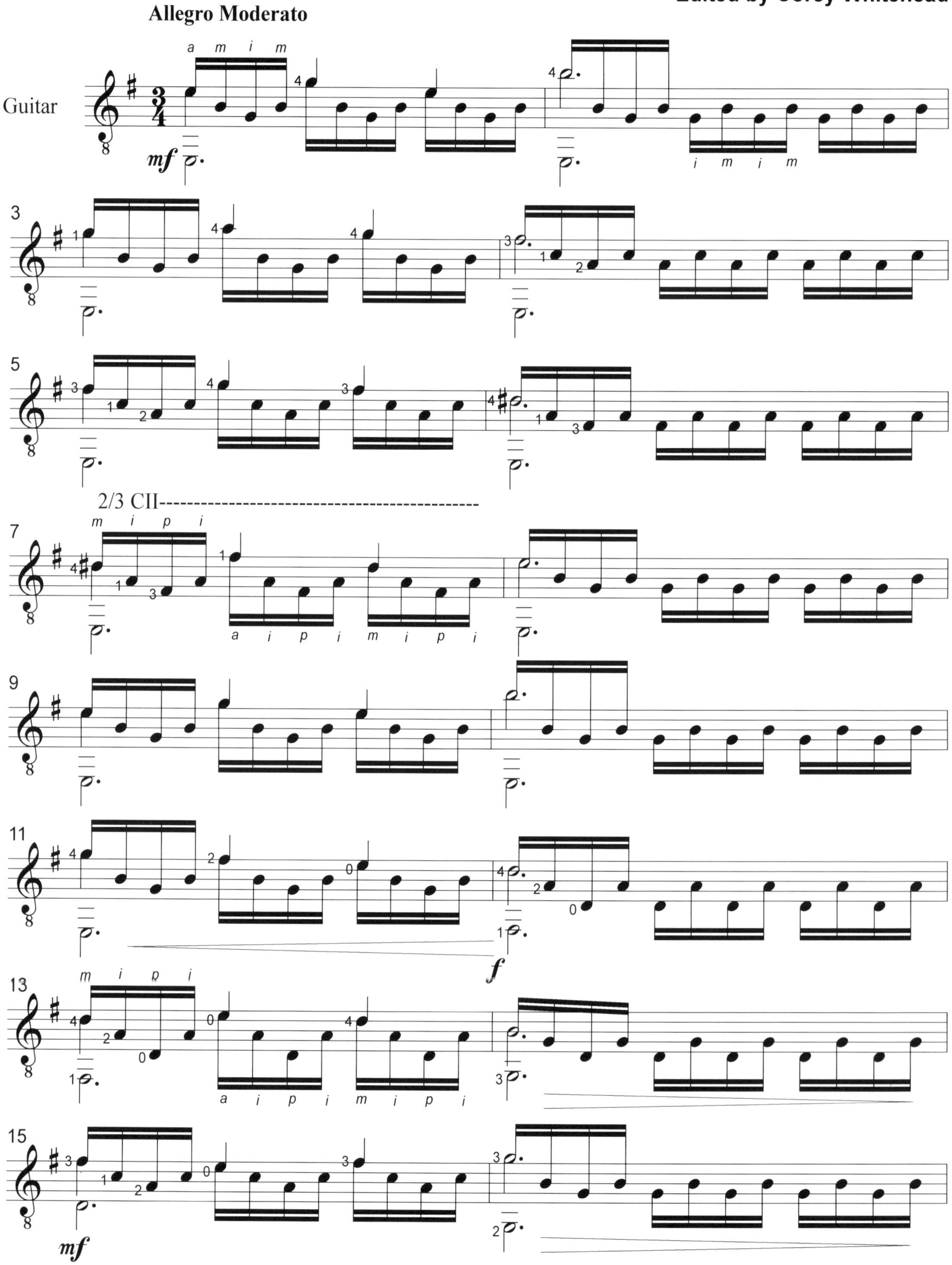

Allegro Moderato

Guitar

2/3 CII

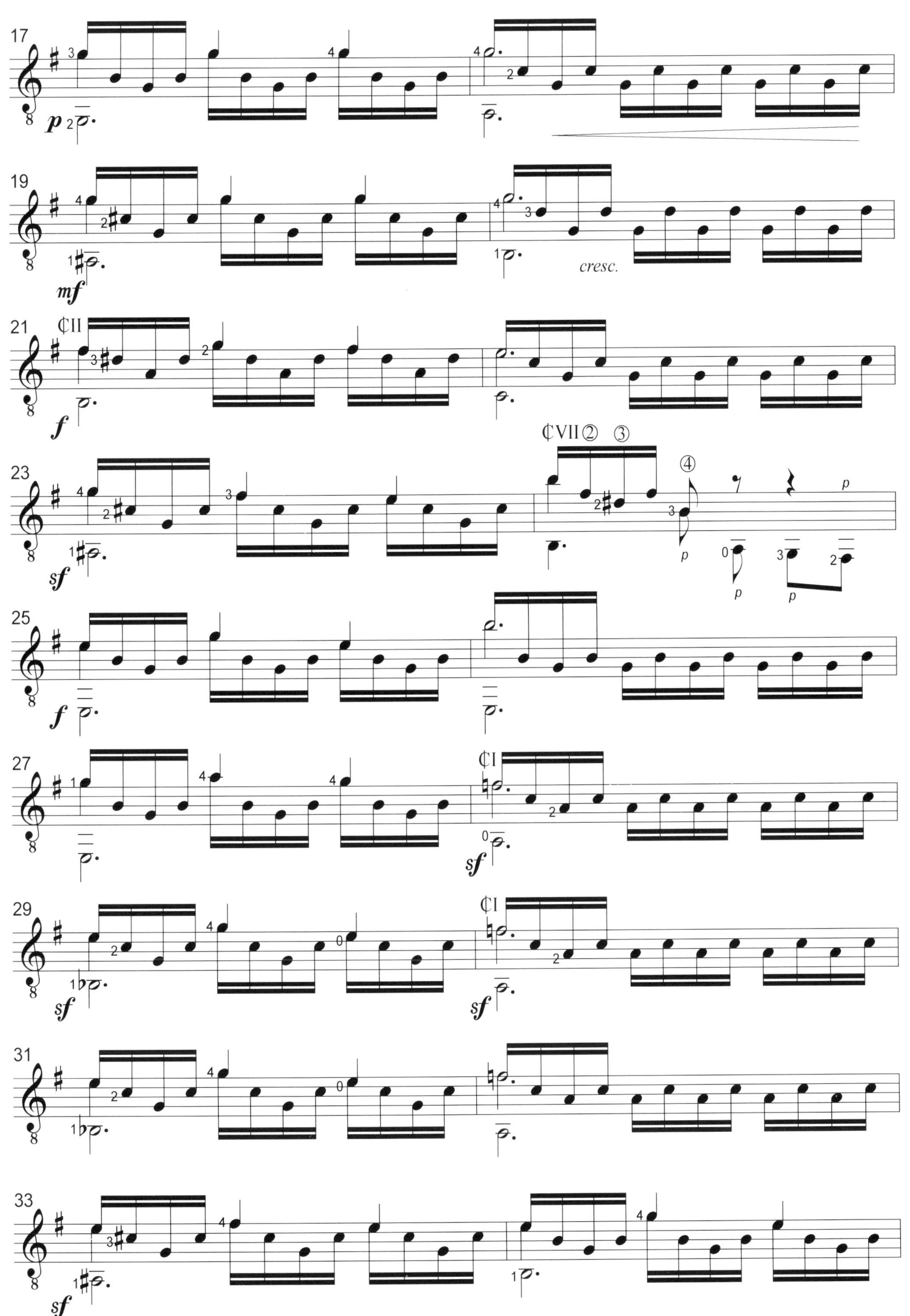
cresc.
CII
CVII ② ③
④
CI
CI

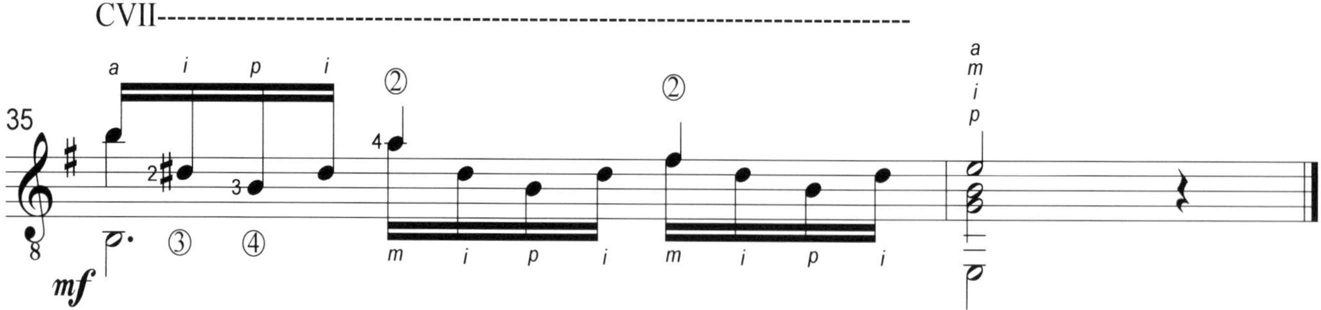

Performance Notes

1) Use apoyando or tirando strokes imitating the sound of "apoyando" on the melodic voice (stems up).

2) Emphasize the upper voice (stems up).

3) Allow bass notes to ring their full value.

4) Allow voices within the measure to sound together when they are consonant.

5) Strive for a legato feel in the melodic voice (stems up).

6) Improvise your own dynamics where no dynamics are indicated by the composer.

7) Dissonances should be emphasized and resolved to relatively softer consonances.

8) Often, the dissonances appear as accidentals, i.e., sharps or flats not included in the key signature.

9) E minor has one sharp but this piece uses many accidentals to "tonicize" other notes.

10) "Tonicization" of a note other than the root of the scale (E) requires a temporary key change.

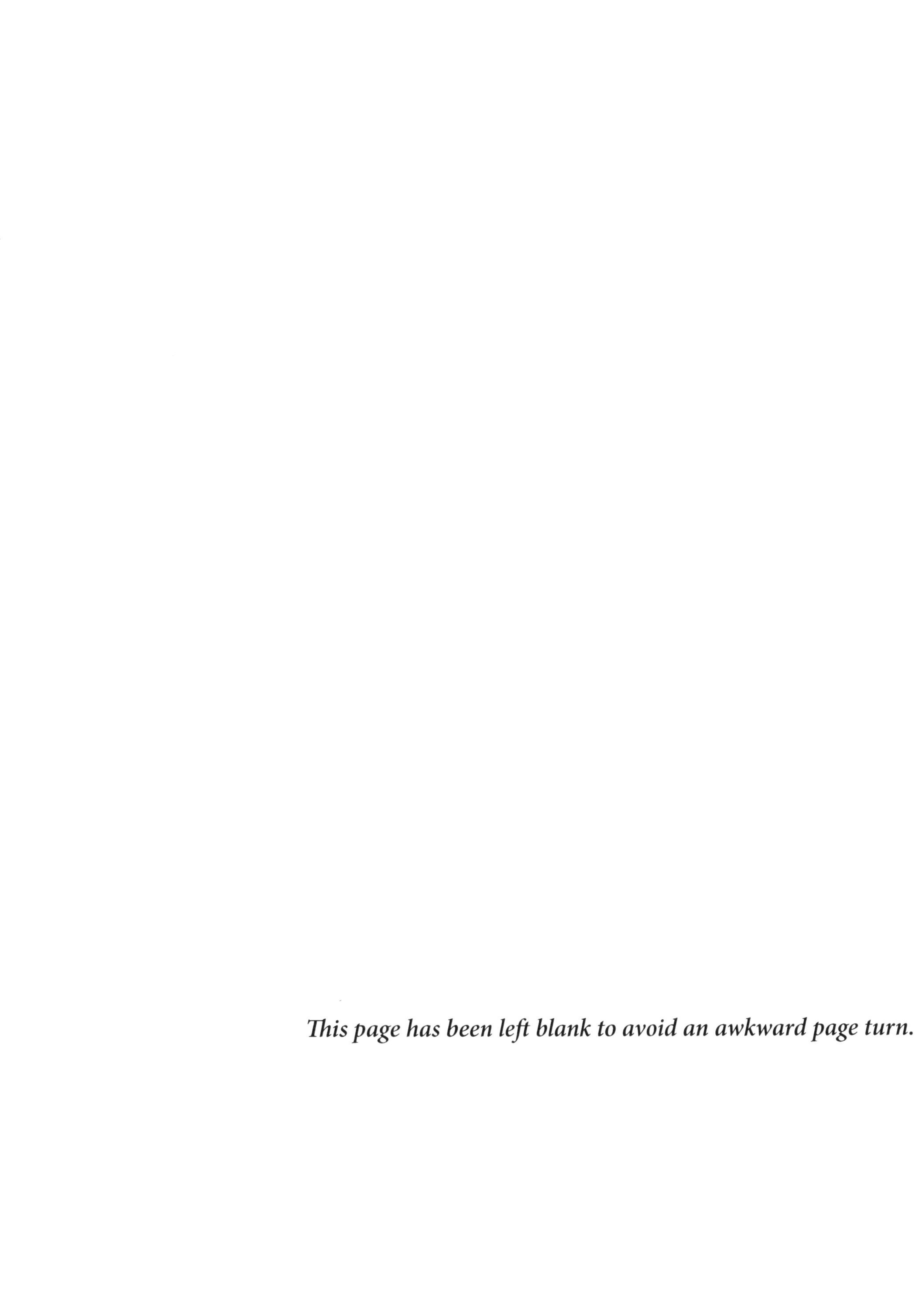

This page has been left blank to avoid an awkward page turn.

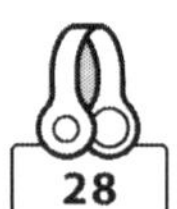

Estudio en Re Menor

Fernando Sor y Napoleon Coste
Edited by Corey Whitehead

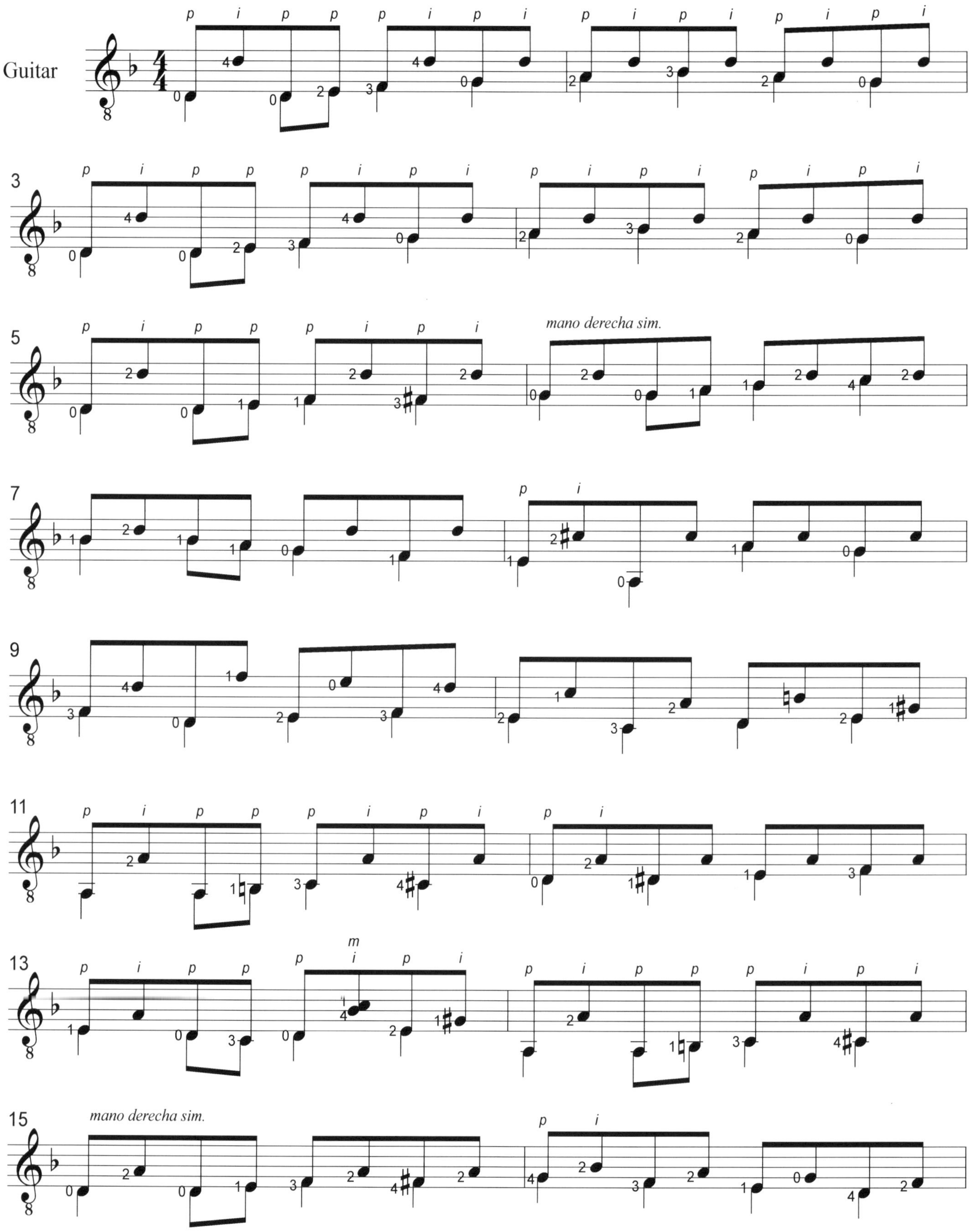

Guitar

p i p p p i p i p i p i p i p i

3 p i p p p i p i p i p i p i p i

5 p i p p p i p i *mano derecha sim.*

7 p i

9

11 p i p p p i p i p i

13 p i p p p m i p i p i p p p i p i

15 *mano derecha sim.* p i

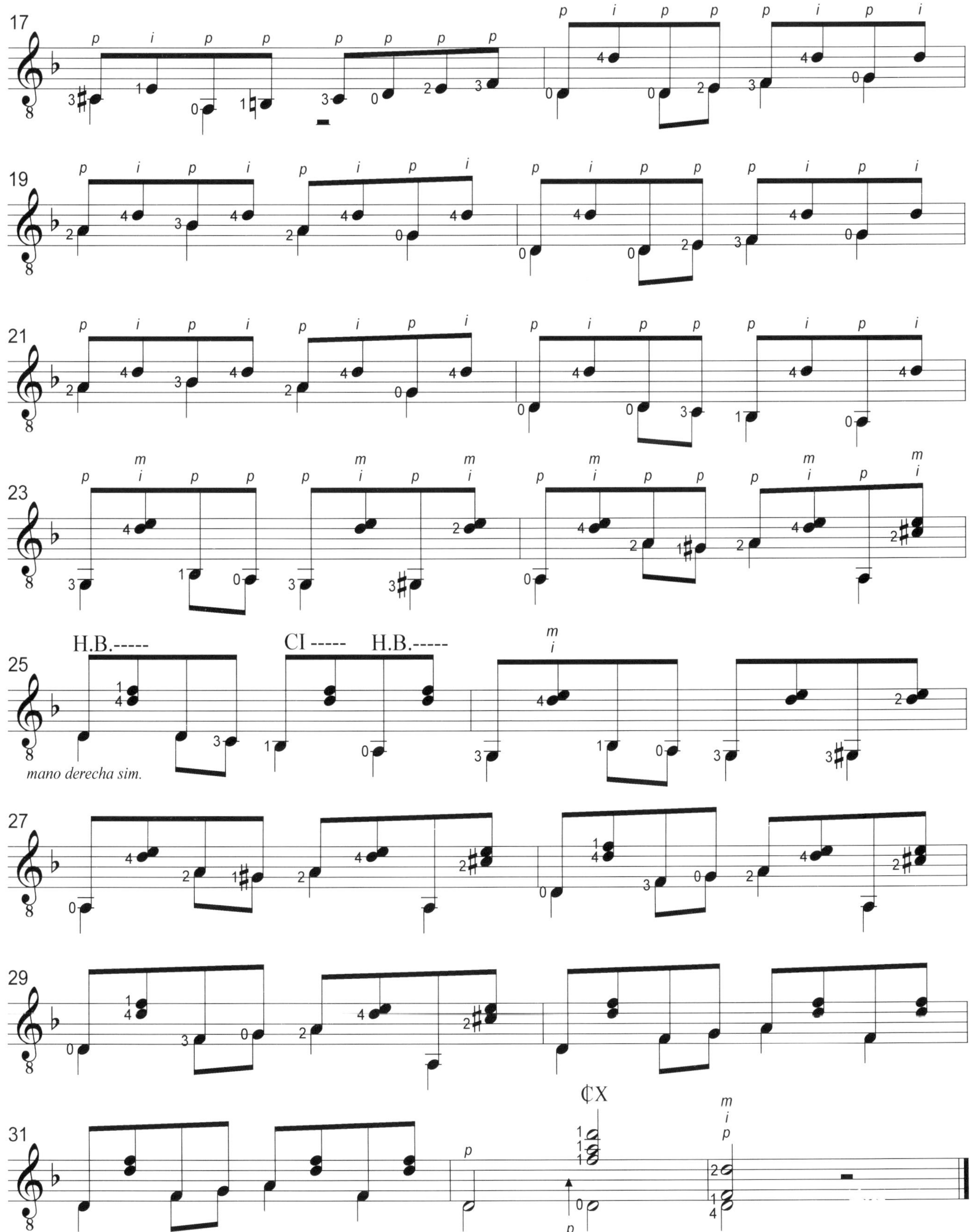

Performance Notes

1) The key is D minor with one flat; emphasize the chords/harmonies that use accidentals.

2) Use free strokes.

3) Emphasize the bass voice (stems down).

4) H.B. = hinge barré, barring only the first string for now, but "opening" in m. 26.

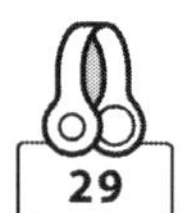

Della tenuto de tuono: Estudio No. 1

Mauro Giuliani
Edited by Corey Whitehead

Performance Notes

1) Use free strokes (tirando).

2) The symbol "H.B." means "hinge-barré," i.e., press the first string only with the barré finger.

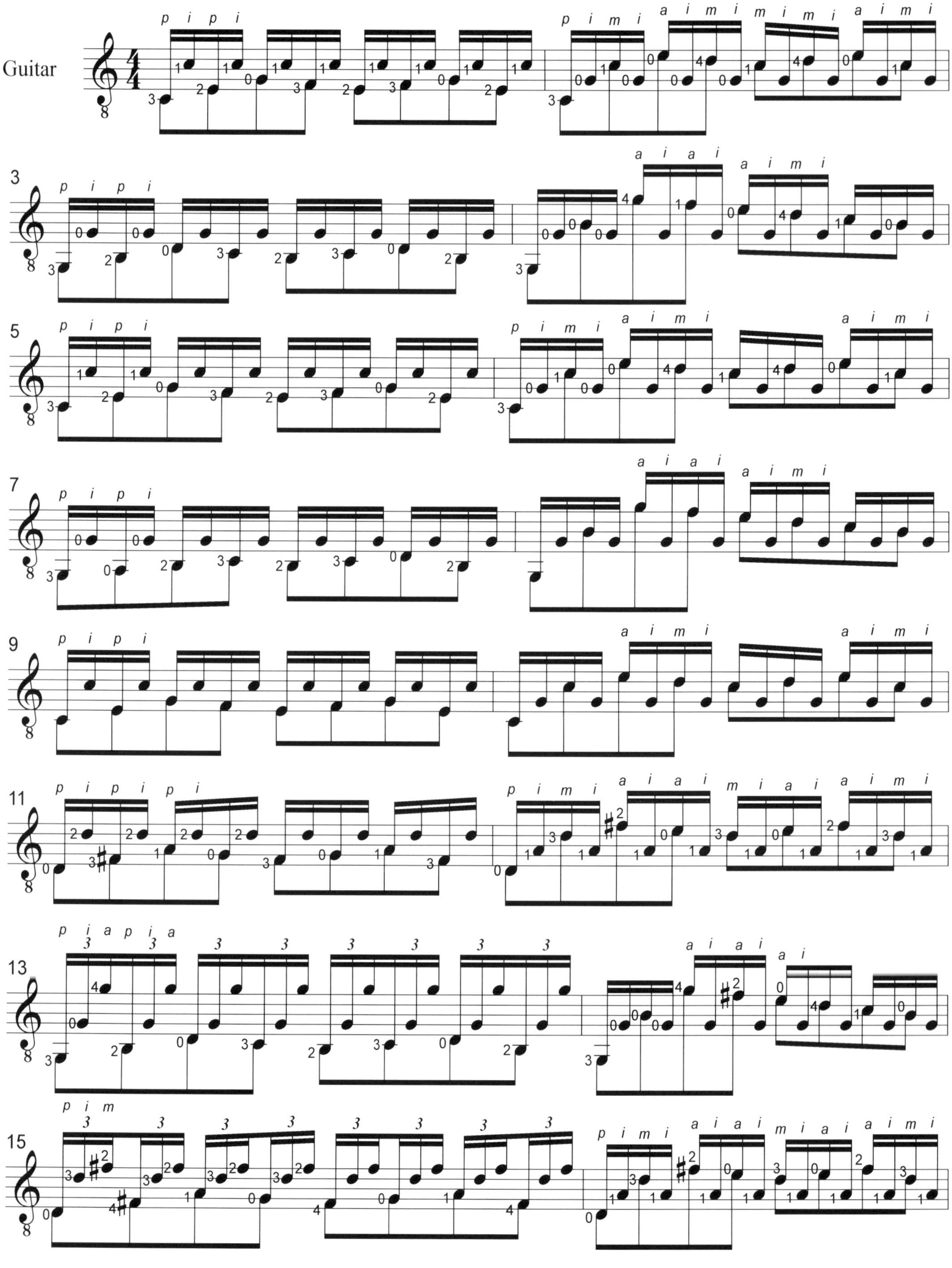

Guitar

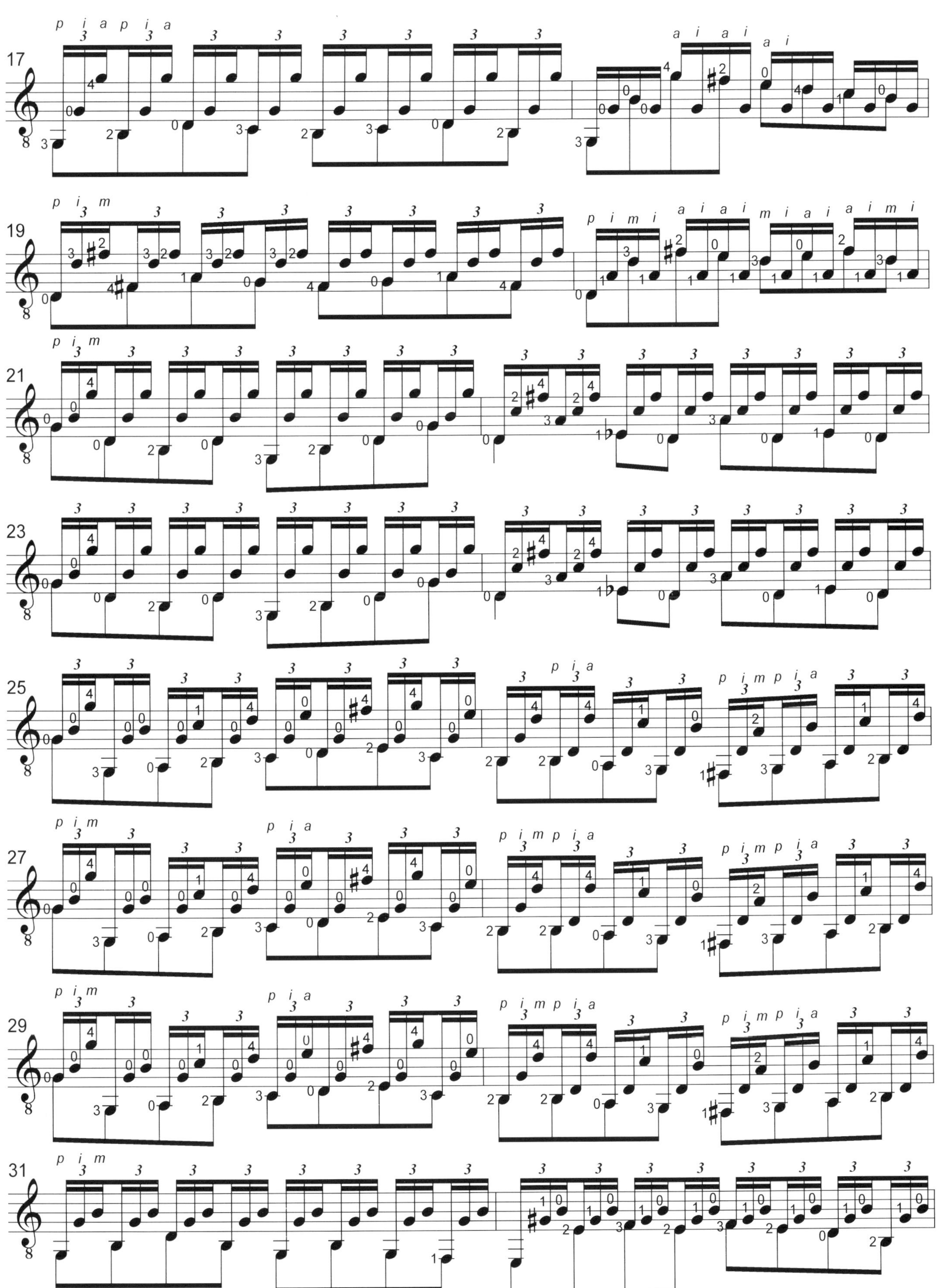

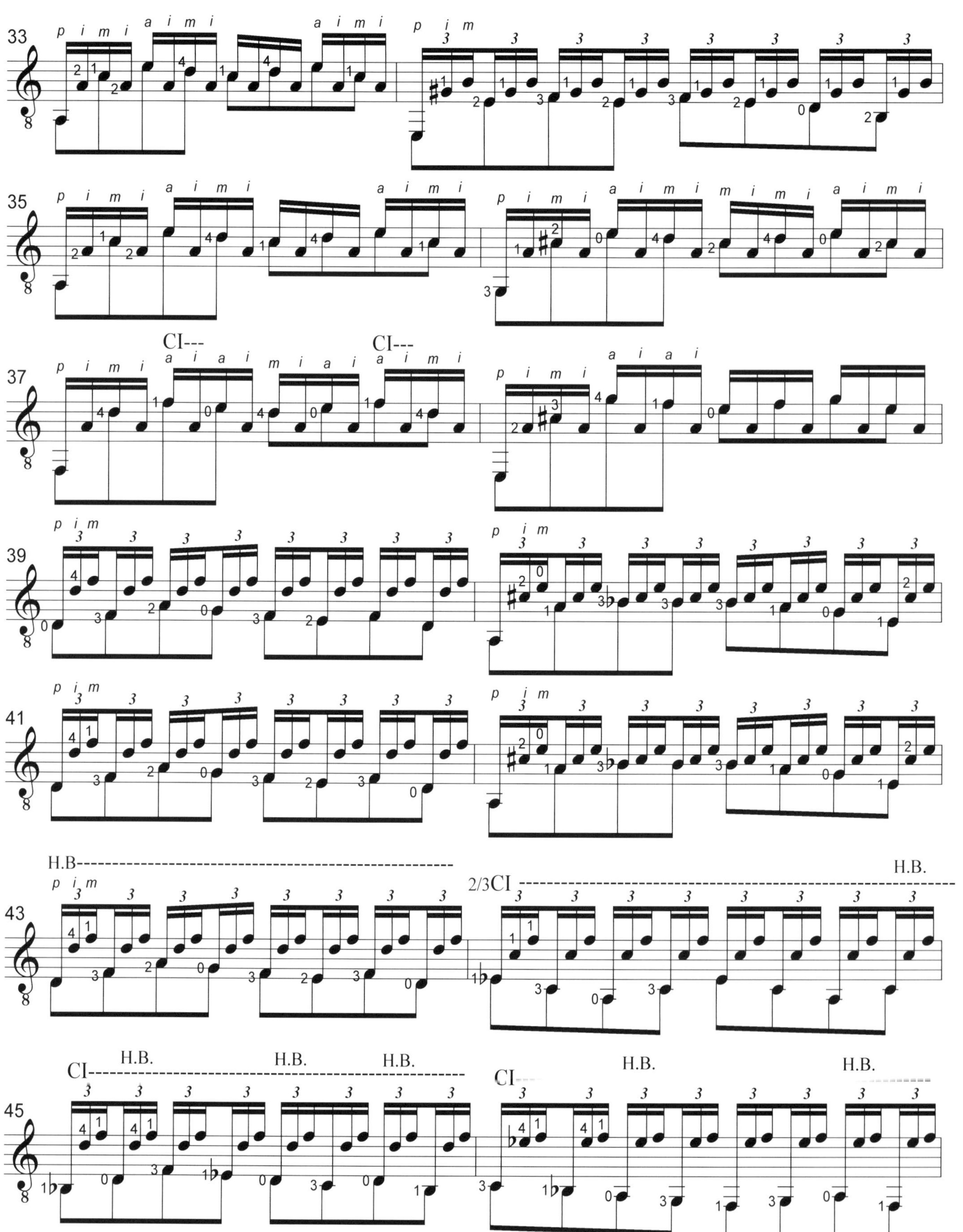
33
35
37
39
41
43
45
CI---
H.B.
2/3CI

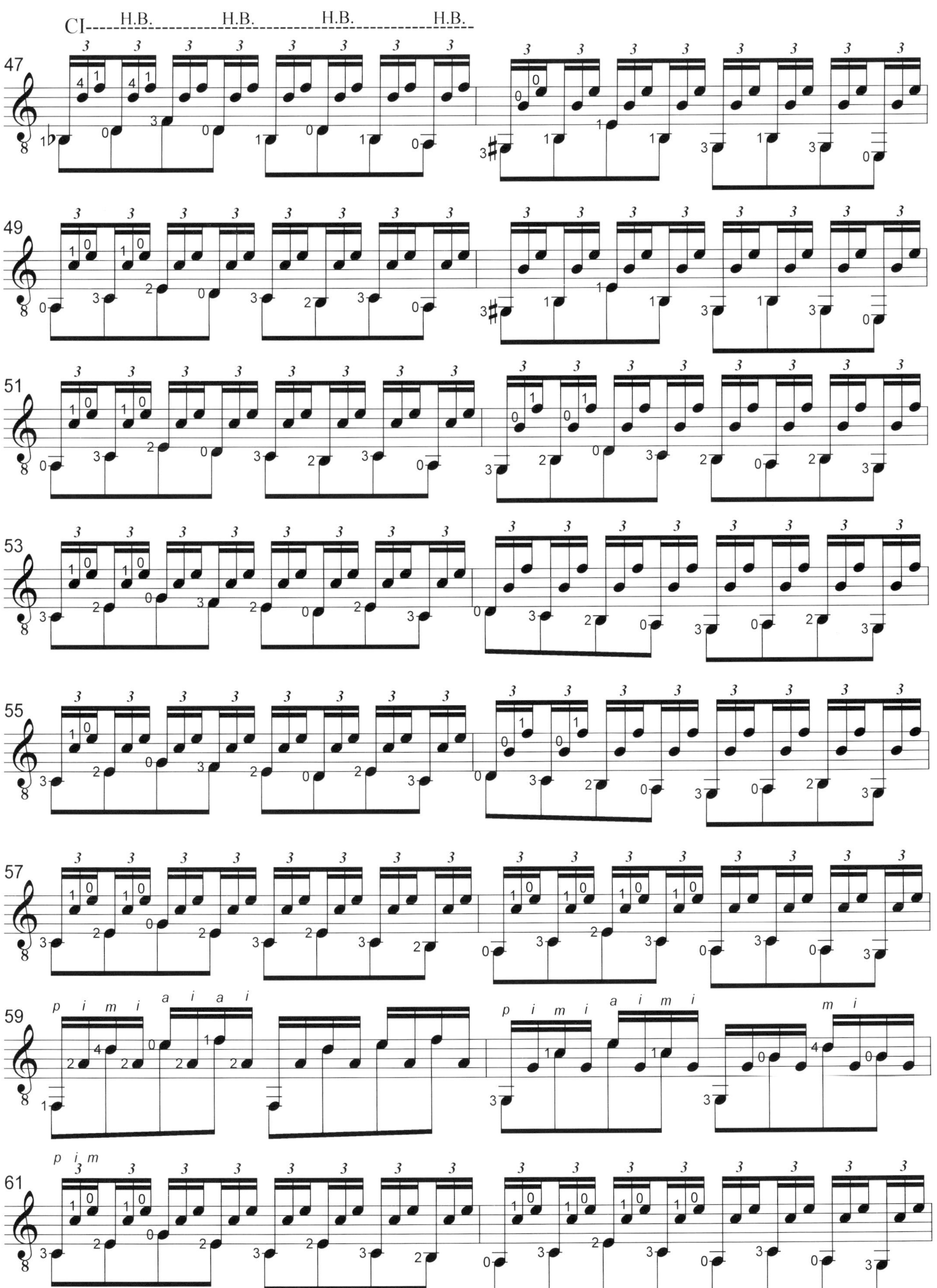
CI
H.B.
H.B.
H.B.
H.B.
47
49
51
53
55
57
59
p i m i a i a i
p i m i a i m i
m i
61
p i m

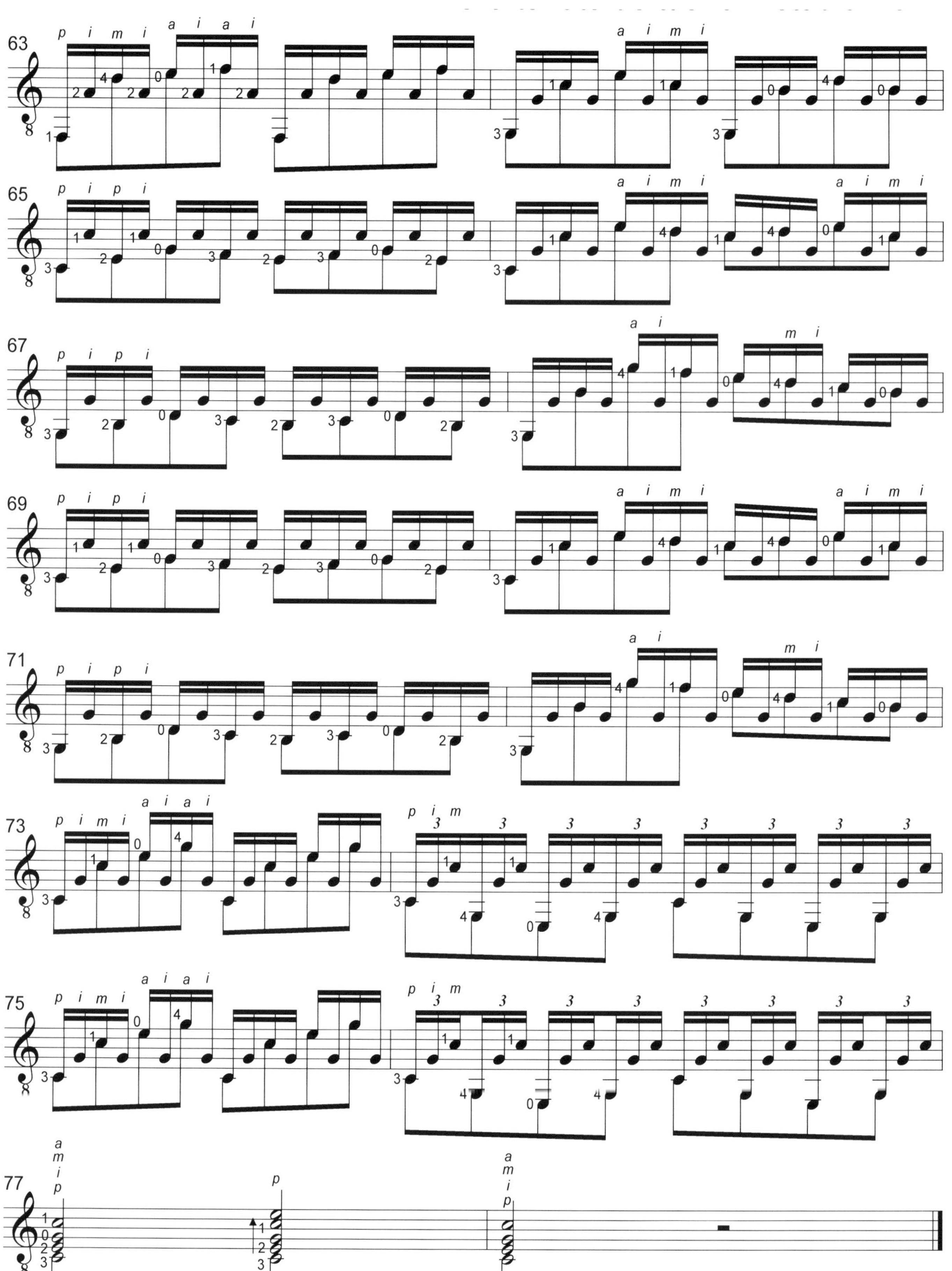
63
65
67
69
71
73
75
77

Flamenco Studies
Part 2/Unit 1

Pic1/T1. Alegrías silencio

Richard Marlow
Edited by Corey Whitehead

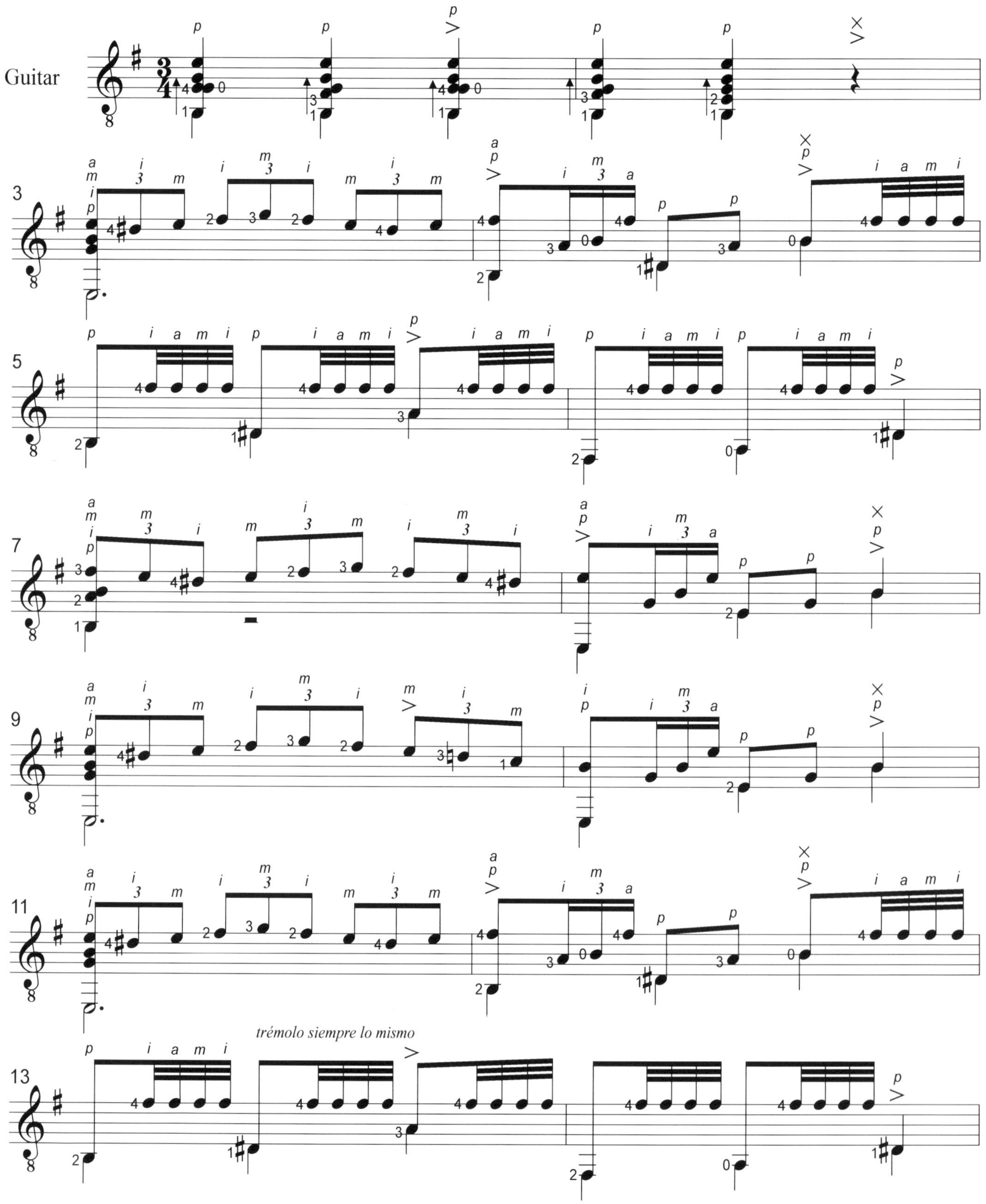

Guitar

trémolo siempre lo mismo

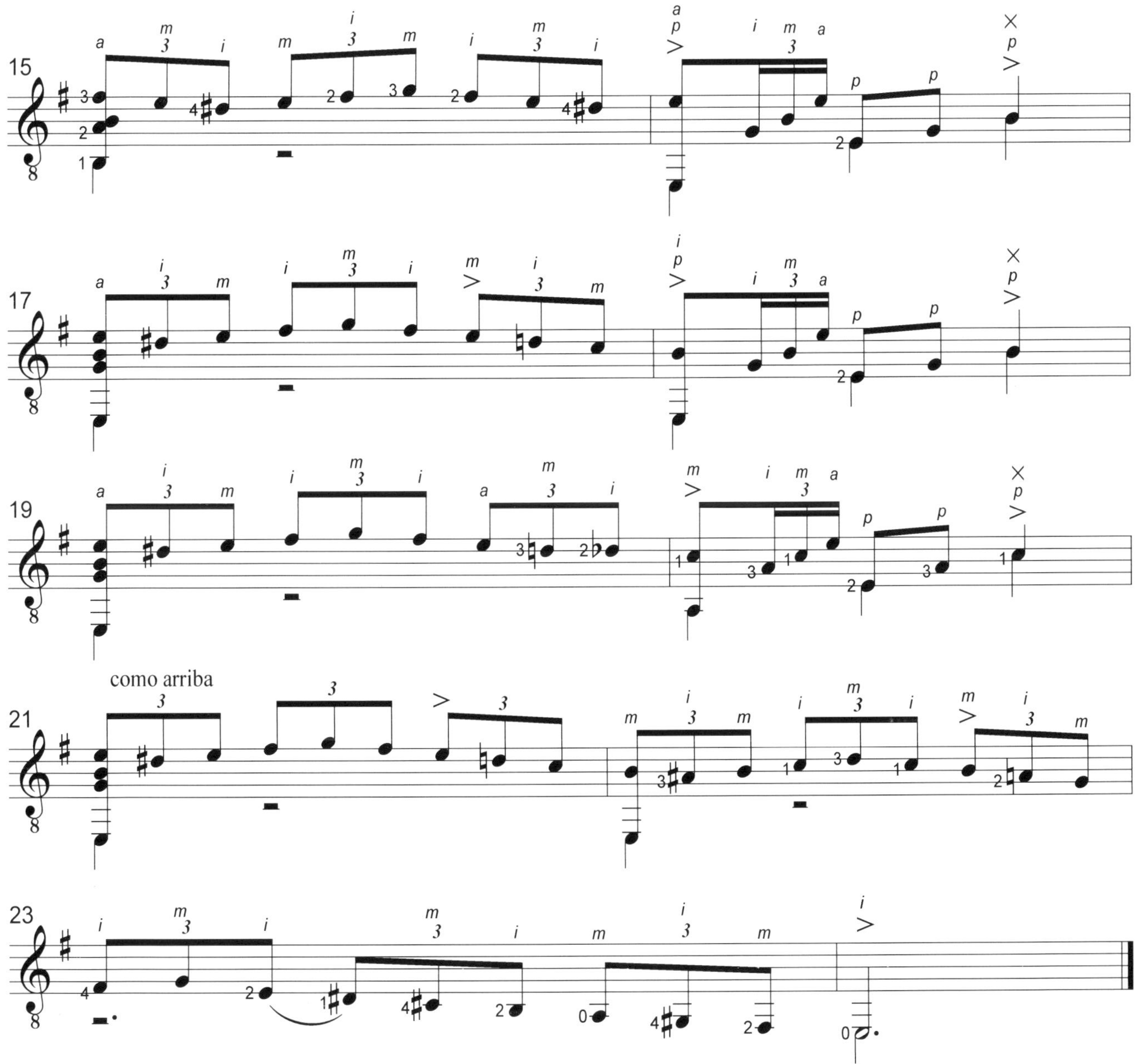

Performance Notes

1) The "silencio" is a part of the form of the "Alegrías para baile" for the accompaniment of dance.
2) The meter as shown in 3/4 follows the chord progression. The chords generally change in each measure.
3) The actual "meter" of the "palo" begins on "beat 12" of the 4-measure phrase, one beat before measure one.
4) The next metric cycle begins on the next "beat 12" on measure 4, beat 3.
5) The accent pattern is noted with accent marks and golpes on beats 12, 3, 6, and 10.
6) Counting the beats is customary at first, but later the meter is "felt" as described below.
7) The accent pattern above produces the following amalgam of meters: 3/4, 3/4, 4/4, 2/4
*8) When the "beats" are counted, they follow this pattern: un-dos-**Trés**-quatro-cinco-**Seis**-siete-ocho-nueve-**Díez**-un-**Dos***

un	dos	**Trés**	quatro	cinco	**Seis**	siete	ocho	nueve	**Díez**	un	**Dos**
1	*2*	***3***	*4*	*5*	***6***	*7*	*8*	*9*	***10***	*1*	***2***

9) "1-2" is used again at the end rather than "11-12."
10) The form of the Alegrías consists of the Llamada, Salida, Desplante, Falseta, Paseo, Escobilla, Ida, and Bulerías.
Llamada: This opening "call" is also used as a transition between sections and for accelerando.
Salida: The moment the dancer begins to dance.
Desplante: the dancer performs "contratiempos" and improv, moving to the rear of the stage (atrás), and raising his/her arms.
Silencio/Falseta: An artistic demonstration of arm movements, as the guitarist demonstrates various techniques.
Paseo: To "stroll" or walk stage left to stage right and vice-versa, marking the accents with foot stomps.
Escobilla: Also called "Zapateado," dancers display virtuosity to complex arpeggio accompaniment.
Ida: To "take leave" from the Alegrías and transition to the faster "Bulerías."
11) The trémolo (i a m i) is played using free strokes and the bass notes are played with the thumb (p) using rest stroke.
12) x = golpe/tap

R1. Soleá rasgueado

Richard Marlow
Edited by Corey Whitehead

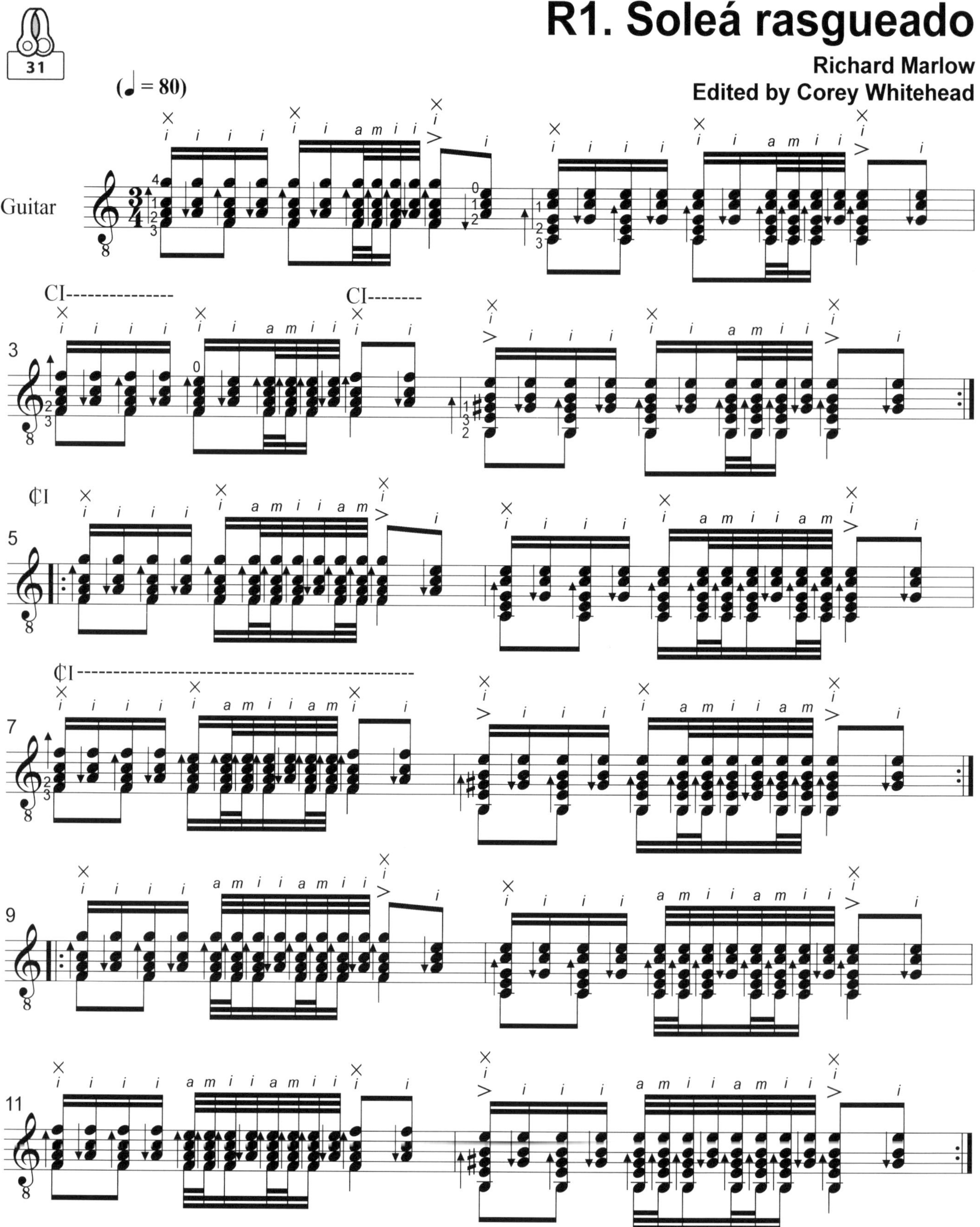

Performance Notes

1) Anchor the thumb (pulgar) on the sixth string throughout.
2) The "x" symbol signifies a "golpe" with the "a" finger simultaneously as the "i" finger strums downward.
3) The R.H. fingers "a-m-i" should touch the "p" or pulgar *lightly before strumming downward.*

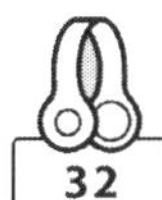

A1. Soleá arpegios

Richard Marlow
Edited by Corey Whitehead

(♩ = 100)

Play rest stroke with the thumb whenever possible.

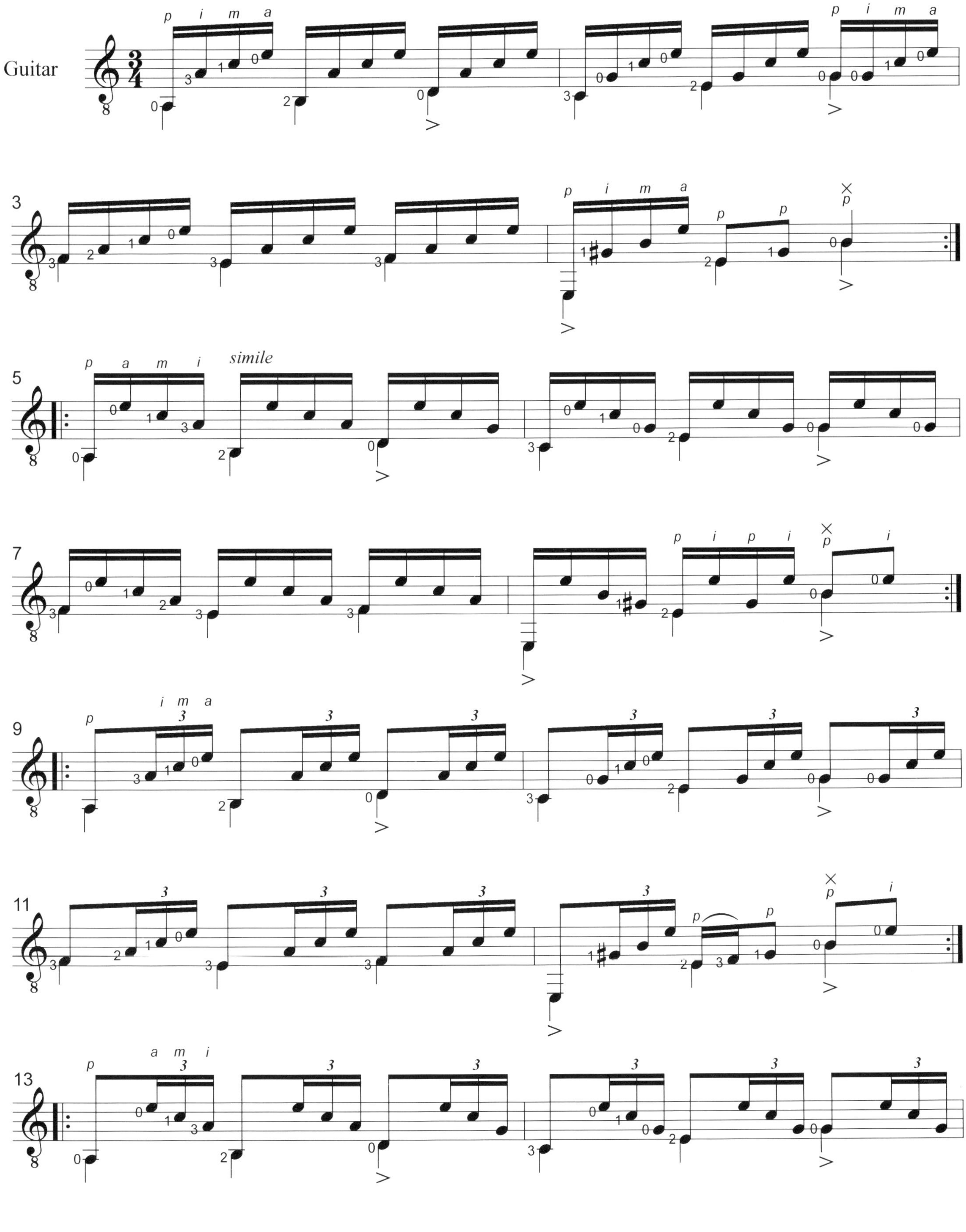

Guitar

simile

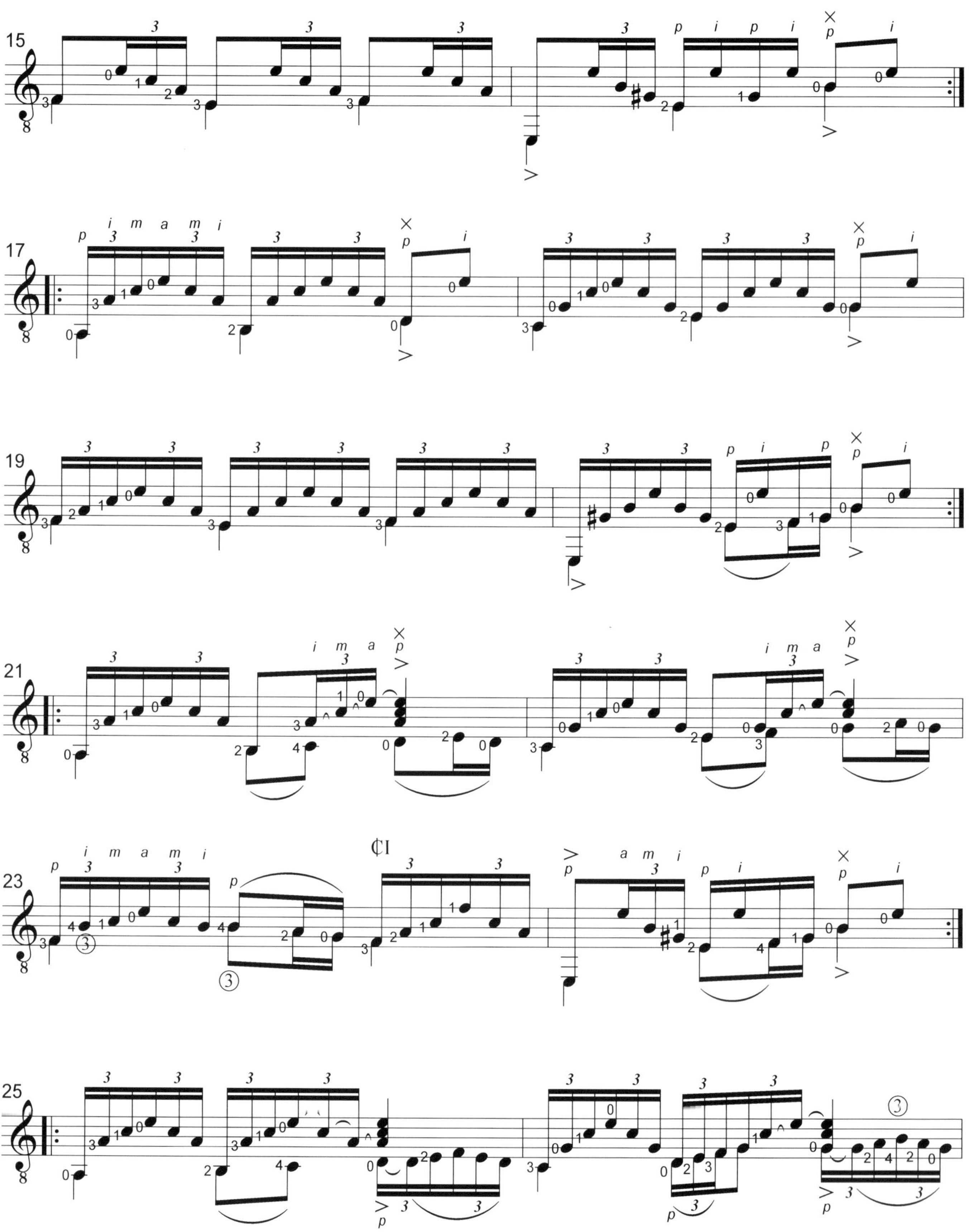

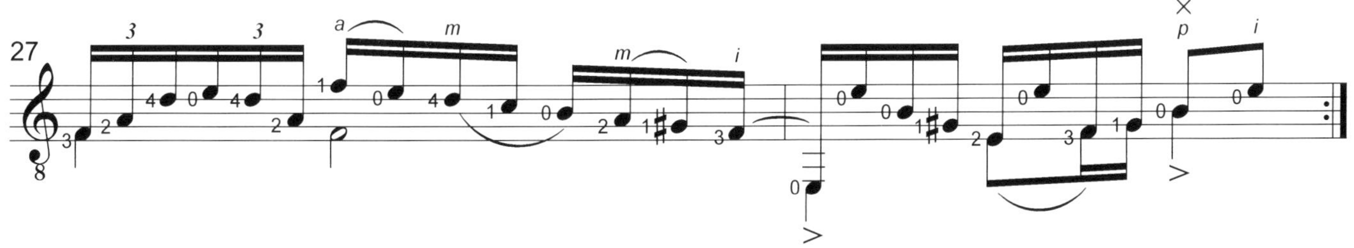

Performance Notes

1) Hold down common fingers within the measure to create harmony, even when dissonant.

2) Tie (hold) the "F" (Fa) over the barline in measures 3-4, 7-8, 11-12, 15-16, 19-20, 23-24, 27-28.

3) On repeats, you may change the composite rhythm between the bass and treble voices to create four sixteenth notes in measures 21-22.

4) The technique of "dragging" the same right-hand finger between two consecutive notes is called "retraste" as in measure 27.

5) Pulgar *(thumb) plays* apoyando *whenever possible.*

6) There are five patterns and two mixed variations of this part of the Soleá form known by the root note of the chords: Am-C-F-E (La-Do-Fa-Mi).

The naming classification system for the flamenco studies in this book makes for easy reference in two ways. The Arabic numeral denotes the difficulty level of the study. The letters refer to the type of technique:

A = Arpeggio
R = Rasgueado
P = Pulgar (thumb)
Pic. = Picado
T = Trémolo

For example, A1 is the easiest level study for arpeggios, and A2 would be the next level of difficulty for arpeggios and so on.

x = *golpe* or to hit the soundboard on the tap-plate *(golpeador)* with the "*a*" and/or "*m*."

These technical elements are phrases that are combined to create larger flamenco works. For example, one could combine the various studies in the *Soleá* form *(palo)* and create a guitar accompaniment for dancers, or a solo composition. Guitarists personalize these standard phrases to create variations. The way a guitarist personalizes these standard phrases in variations is what leads to an artist having their own "voice" within the framework of standard rhythms and chord progressions. The blues is similar to flamenco in the sense that the chord progressions and rhythms are standard, ubiquitous and predictable, but each artist makes the blues form their own musically. Another form of variation is writing different lyrics for the same melody, which occurs in many flamenco forms such as *Tientos, Tangos, Fandangos, Soleá* and more.

Notes with a diamond-shaped head indicate notes that are pressed by the left hand, but not played by the right hand.

P1. Tientos pulgar

Richard Marlow

Edited by Corey Whitehead

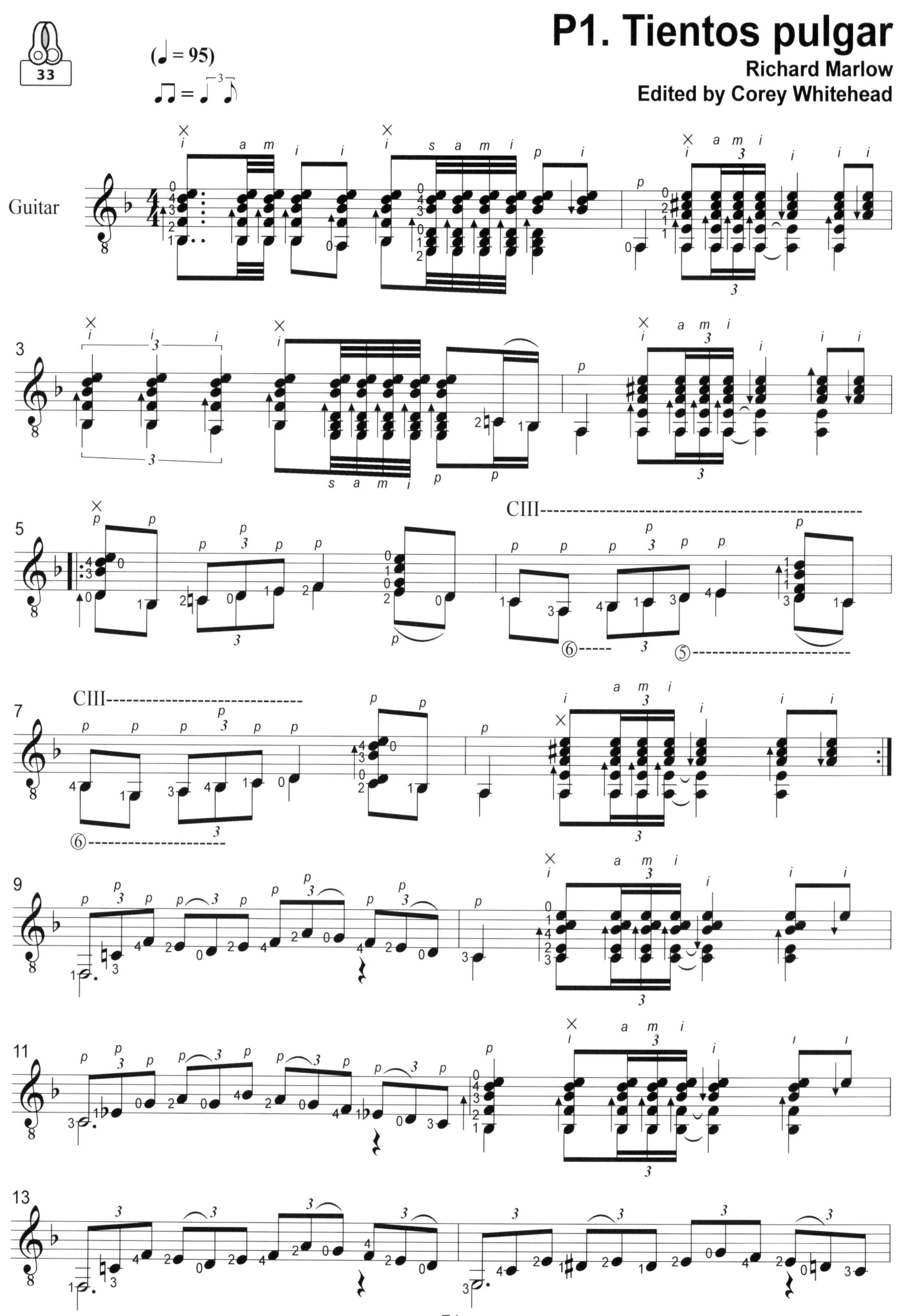

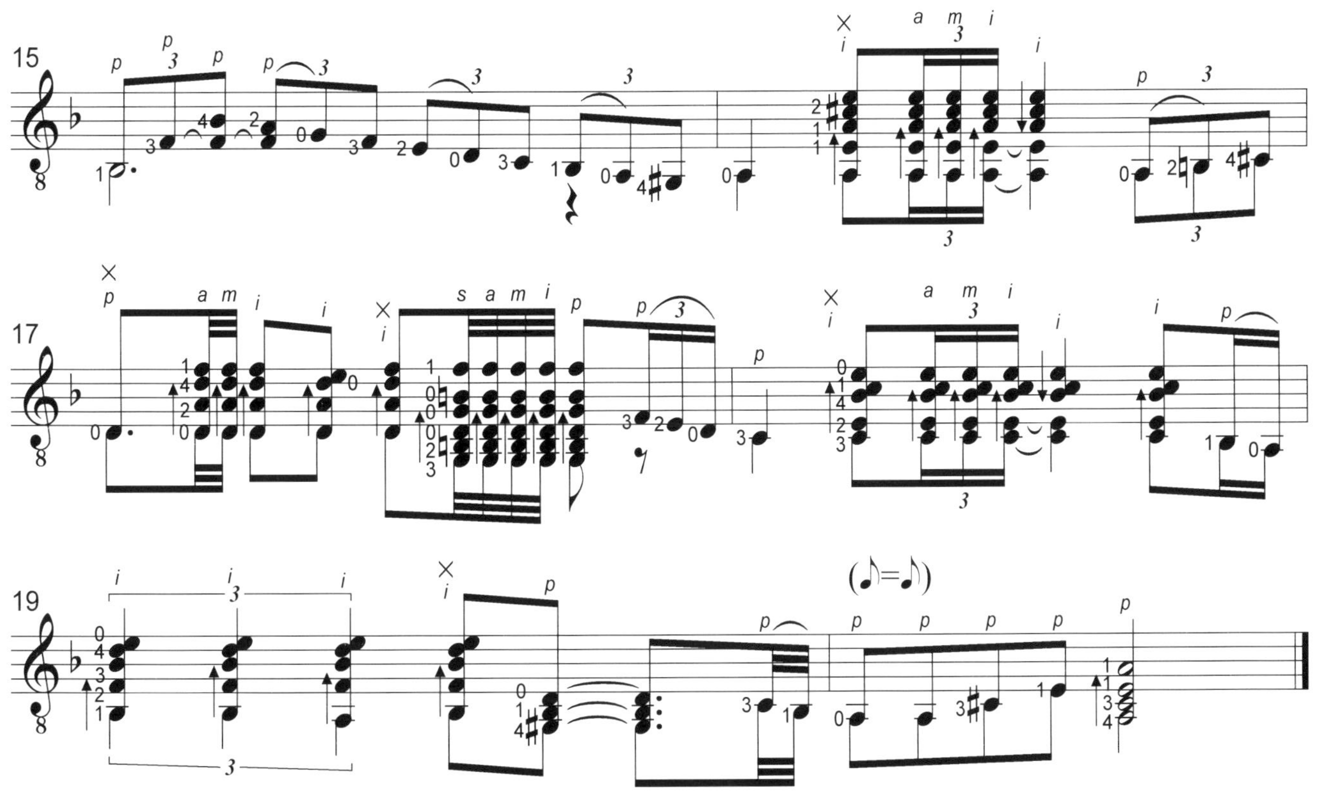

Performance Notes

1) Allow notes to ring together when possible using fixed fingers in measures 9, 11, 13, 14, and 15.

2) Except in the last measure, all eighth-notes are played as "swing eighths".

3) The second eighth-note of a beat is equivalent to 1/3 of the beat, or the last note of a triplet.

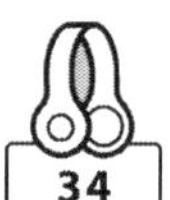

T1. Farruca trémolo

Corey E. Whitehead

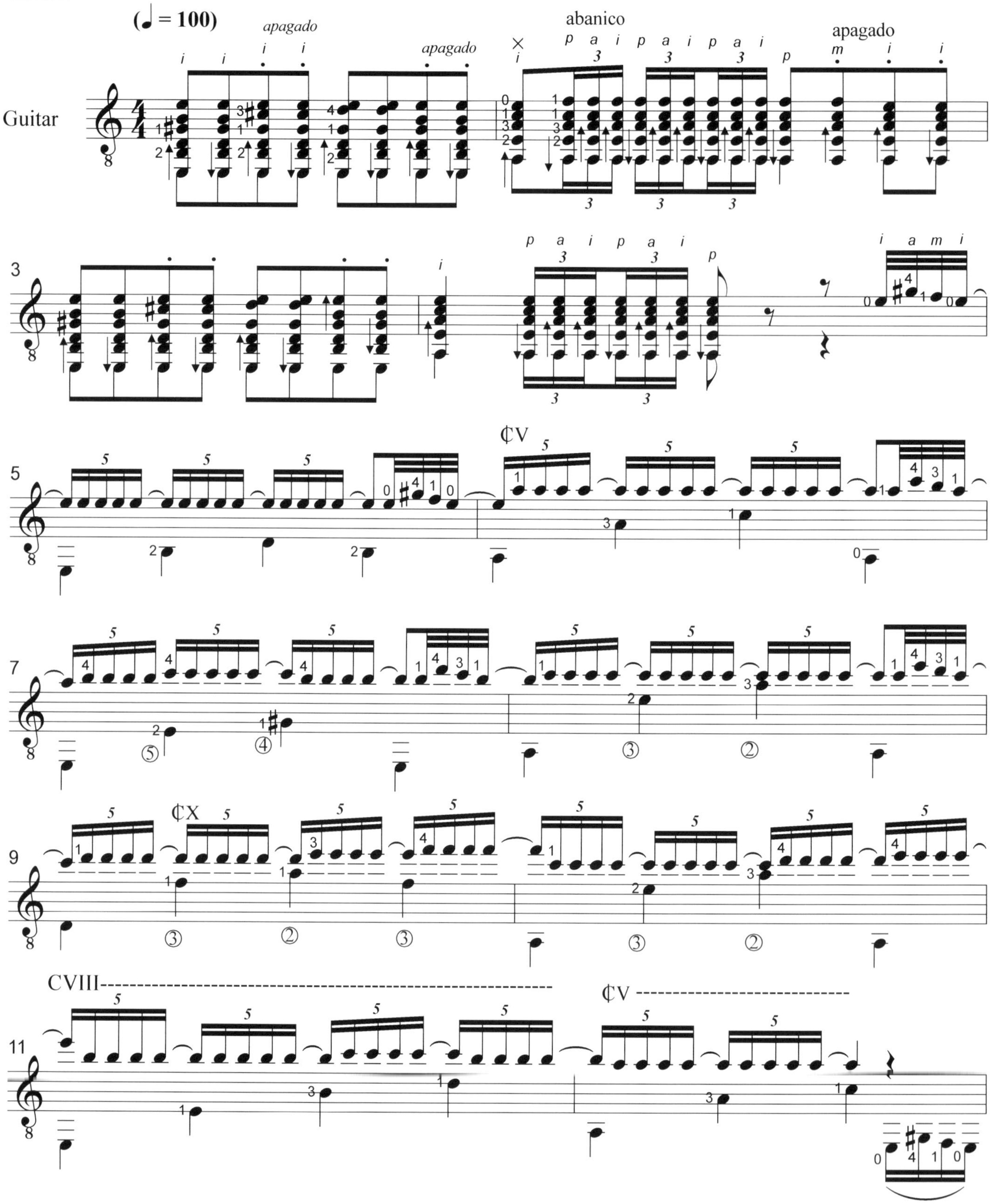

(♩ = 100)

apagado *apagado* abanico apagado

Guitar

CV

CX

CVIII

CV

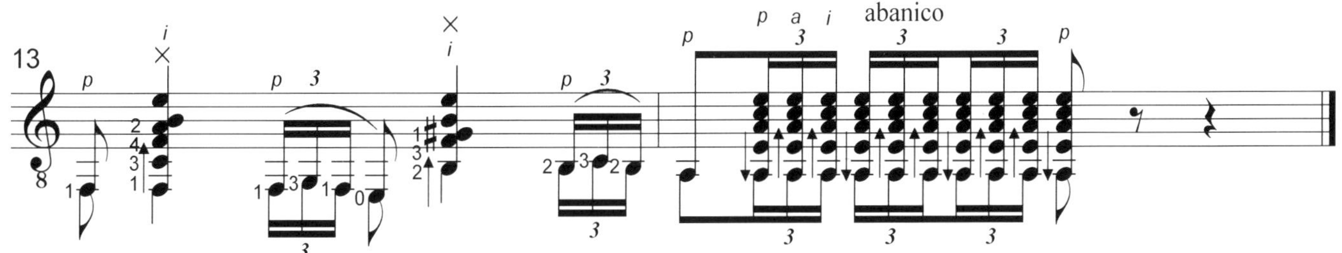

Performance Notes

1) The flamenco trémolo was first used in Granaínas as a group of four 32nd notes on the upbeat, followed by the thumb on the downbeat (i-a-m-i-p).

2) Later, the trémolo was alternatively used in a group of five 16th notes placed evenly to a beat (p-i-a-m-i).

3) In this example both rhythmic variations are used.

4) The trémolo is always played tirando (free stroke); the bass is played apoyando (rest stroke) when possible.

5) The term "abanico" (fan) refers to the (p-a-i) rasgueado having a motion simliar to using a fan to cool oneself. This technique may be executed with several different right-hand finger combinations. Each right-hand fingering has its own sound or "aire." The finger "p-a-i" was chosen here as it is a lighter sounding strum than using combninations of "p" with "m-a." The subsequent strum is also intentional in order to create a syncopation by accenting the second half of beat four.

6) The term "apagado" means muted or "turned off", i.e., stopping the sound of the strings with the left-hand pinky finger.

7) The apagdo technique is used to play the short and light "staccato" sound indicated by the dot (.) over the notes.

L1. Tarantas ligados

Corey E. Whitehead

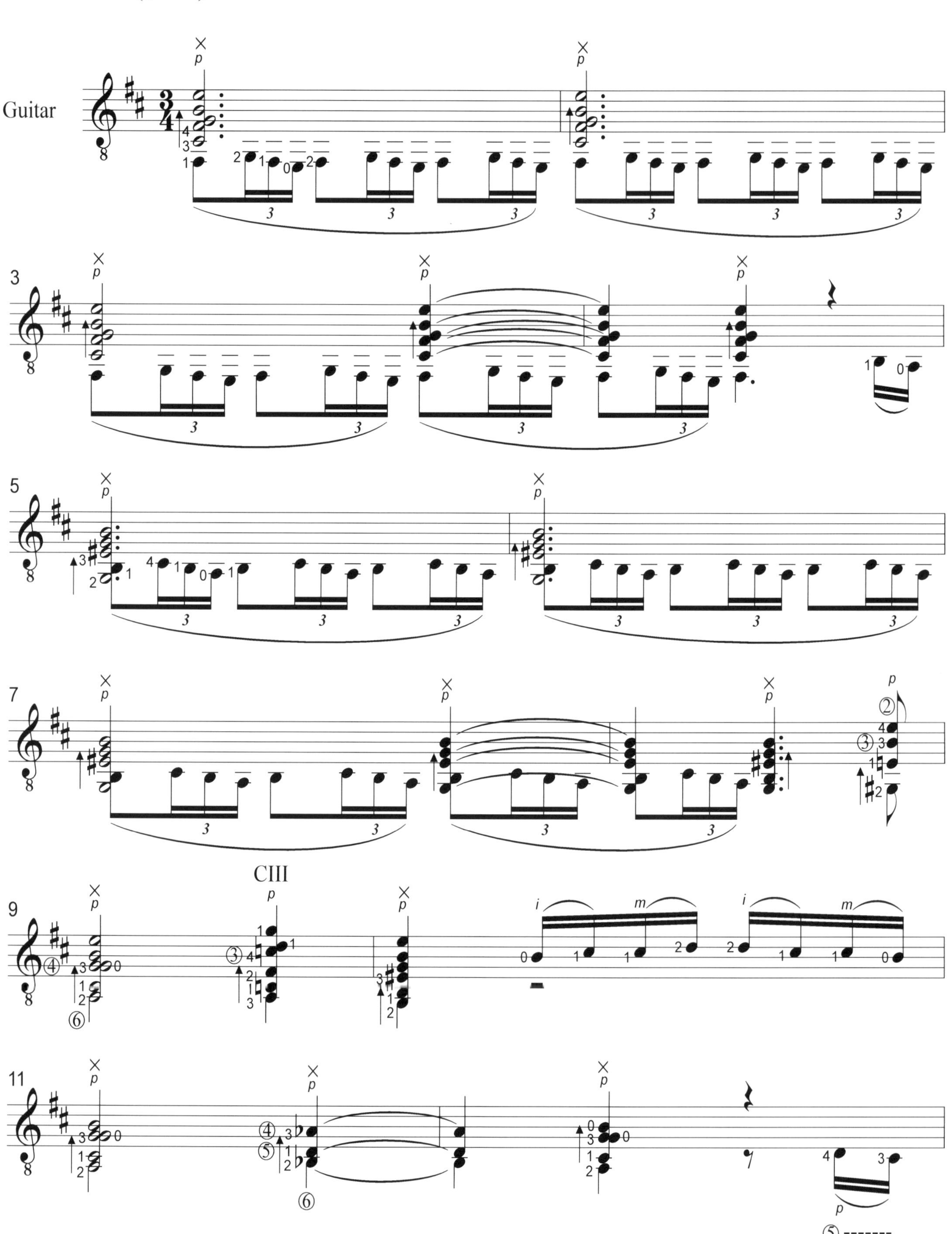

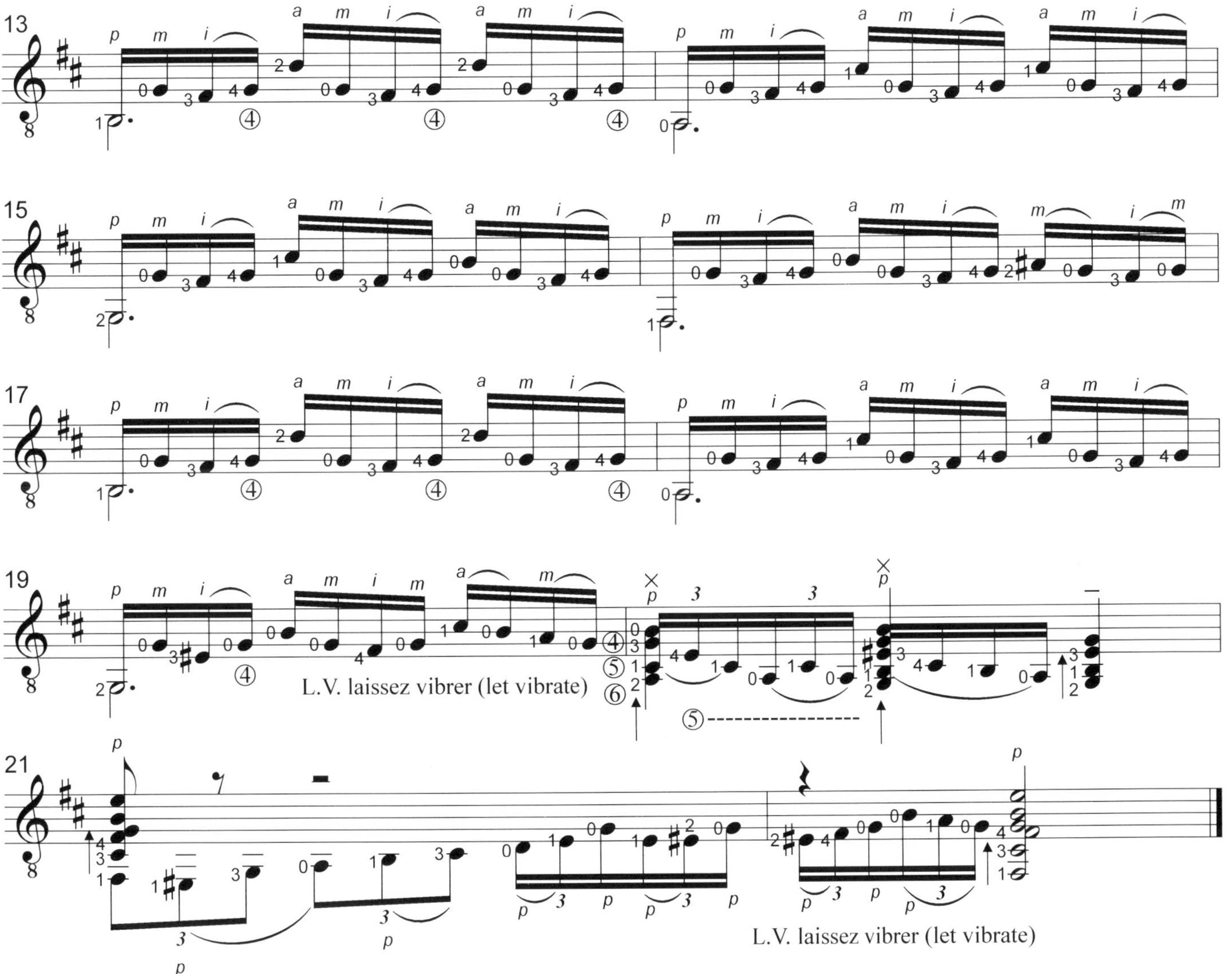

Performance Notes

*1) The term "palo" originally referred to the rhythm created by beating the "stick" of a butter churn as percussion accompaniment to the Verdiales and Fandangos de Huelva.**

2) Fandangos are one of the four primary "palos" of flamenco.

3) The other primary forms are Soleares, Tangos, and Siguiriyas. All other forms are related to these.

4) The beat pattern of Fandangos is 6 or 12 beats.

*5) The 12-beat pattern is: | **1**-2-3 | **1**-2-3 | **1**-2-3 | 1-**2**-3 |*

*6) The 6-beat pattern is: | **1**-2-3 | 1-**2**-3 |*

7) Keep fingers pressed when possible. This will produce temporary dissonances (seconds) which resolve.

8) The first 12 measures are the rhythm, also referred to as the "compás." A clear sense of compás is essential for flamenco dancers to dance to your music.

9) The musical term "compás" actually refers to the meter.

10) One musical phrase, sometimes erroneously referred to as "compás," is an amalgam of measures "una amalgama de compáses."

**This information comes from my teacher Manolo Sanlúcar. He was adamant about communicating this information correctly.*

Flamenco Studies Part 2/Unit 2

R2. Tangos rasgueados

Richard Marlow

Edited by Corey Whitehead

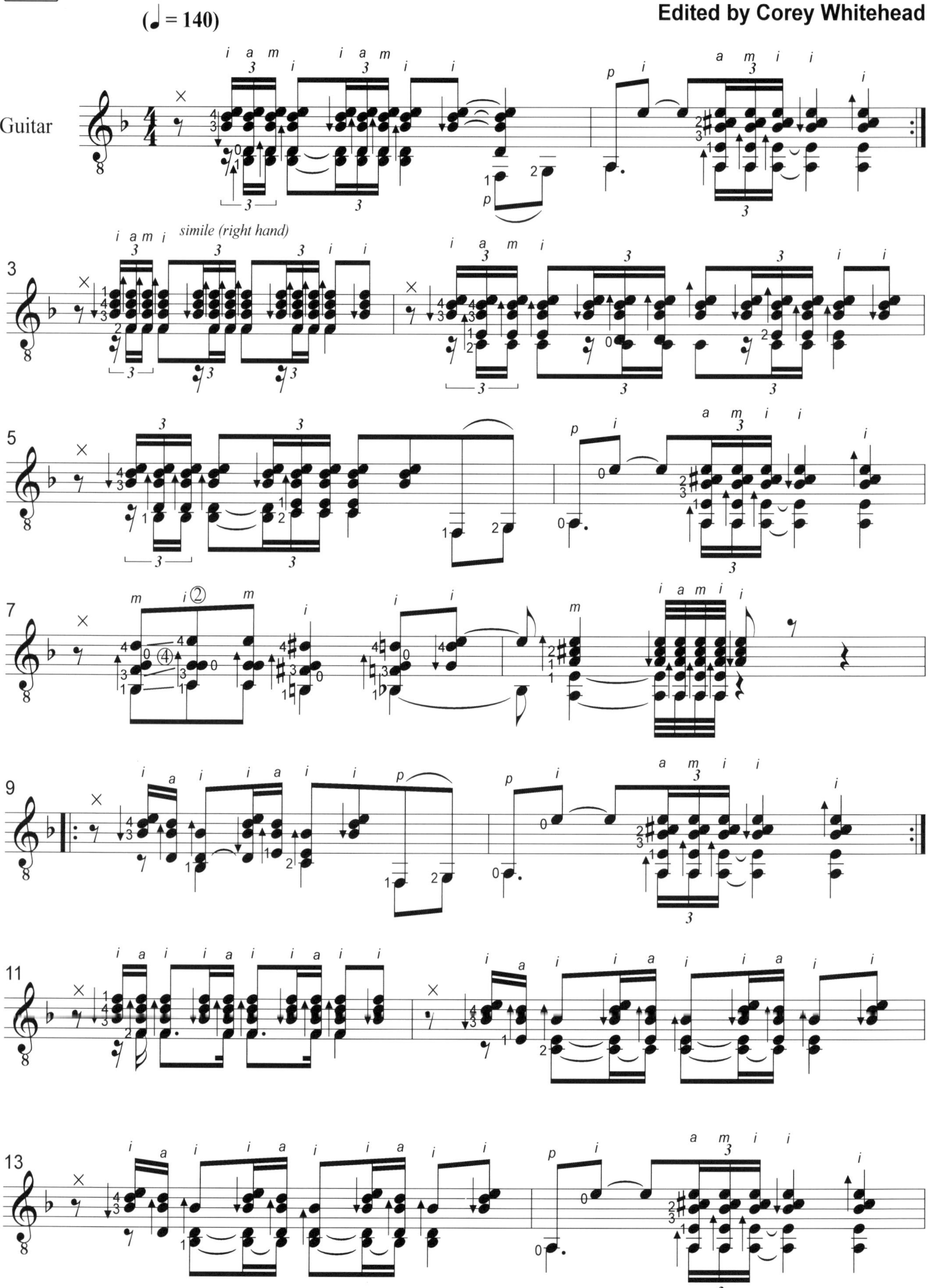

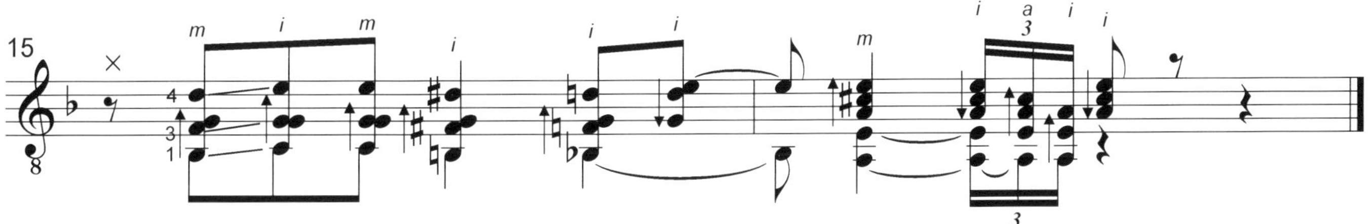

Performance Notes

1) Tangos are one of the four primary palos of flamenco; and the only palo in 8 counts formed by two measures of 4/4 or common time.

2) The pulse accents for the feet are on counts 1 and 3. Beats 2 and 4 are where the palmas and guitar accents reside.

3) All instruments break or close on beat 3 of the second measure of 4/4.

4) The "x" symbol indicates a golpe with "a-m" simultaneously with the downstroke played with the pulgar (thumb).

5) This example serves as an intro to the cante, *or as a solo* falseta, *or accompaniment to the dancer.*

6) Anchor the thumb (pulgar) of the right hand on the 6th string.

7) When the thumb (pulgar) plays a single bass note, use rest stroke.

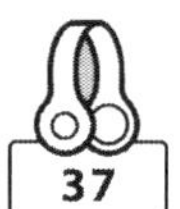

A2. Soleá por medio arpegios

Richard Marlow
Edited by Corey Whitehead

p-i-m-a-m-i, p-am-i, p-a-m-i, p-i-m-a

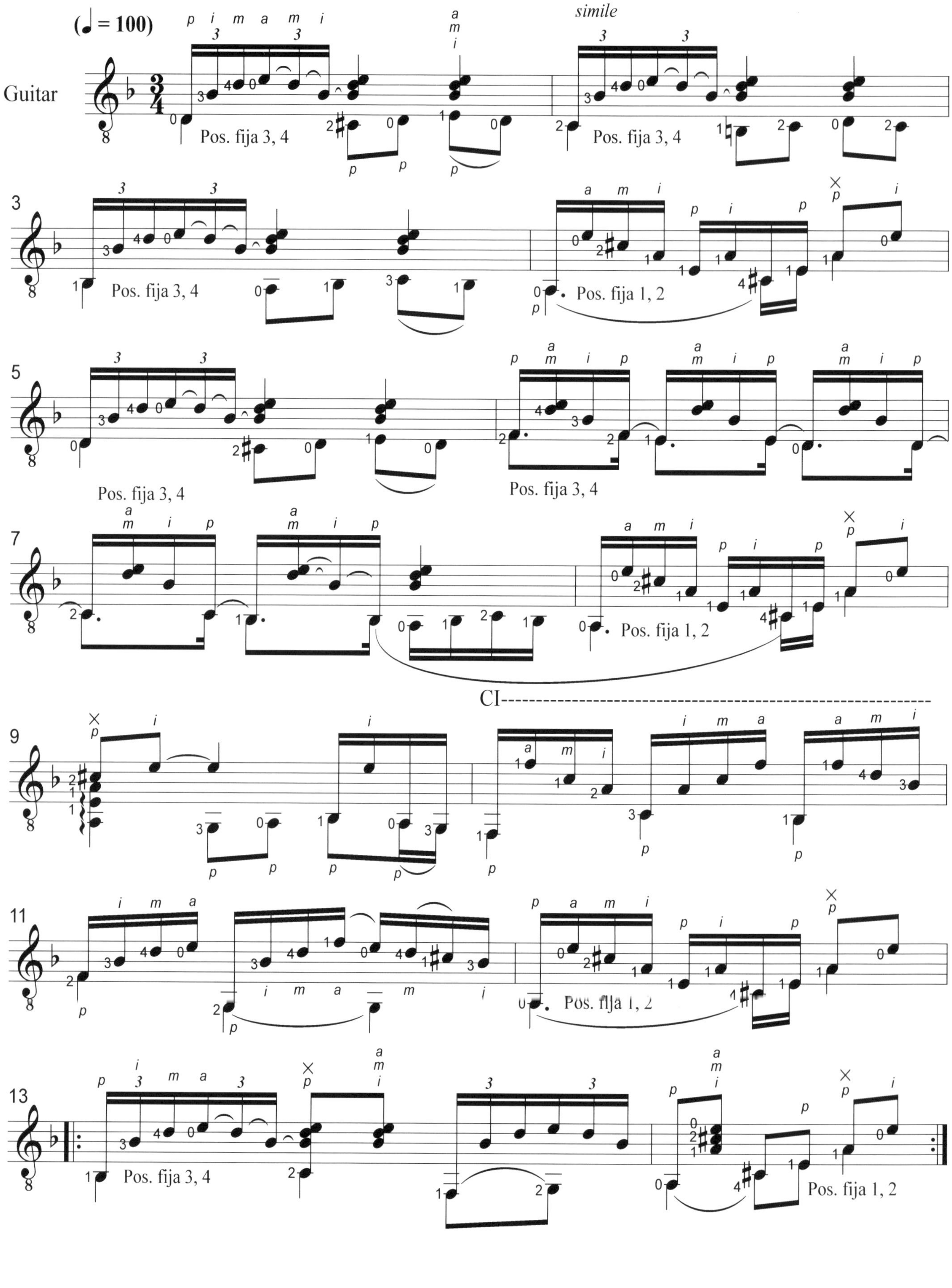

(♩ = 100)

Guitar

simile

Pos. fija 3, 4

Pos. fija 1, 2

CI

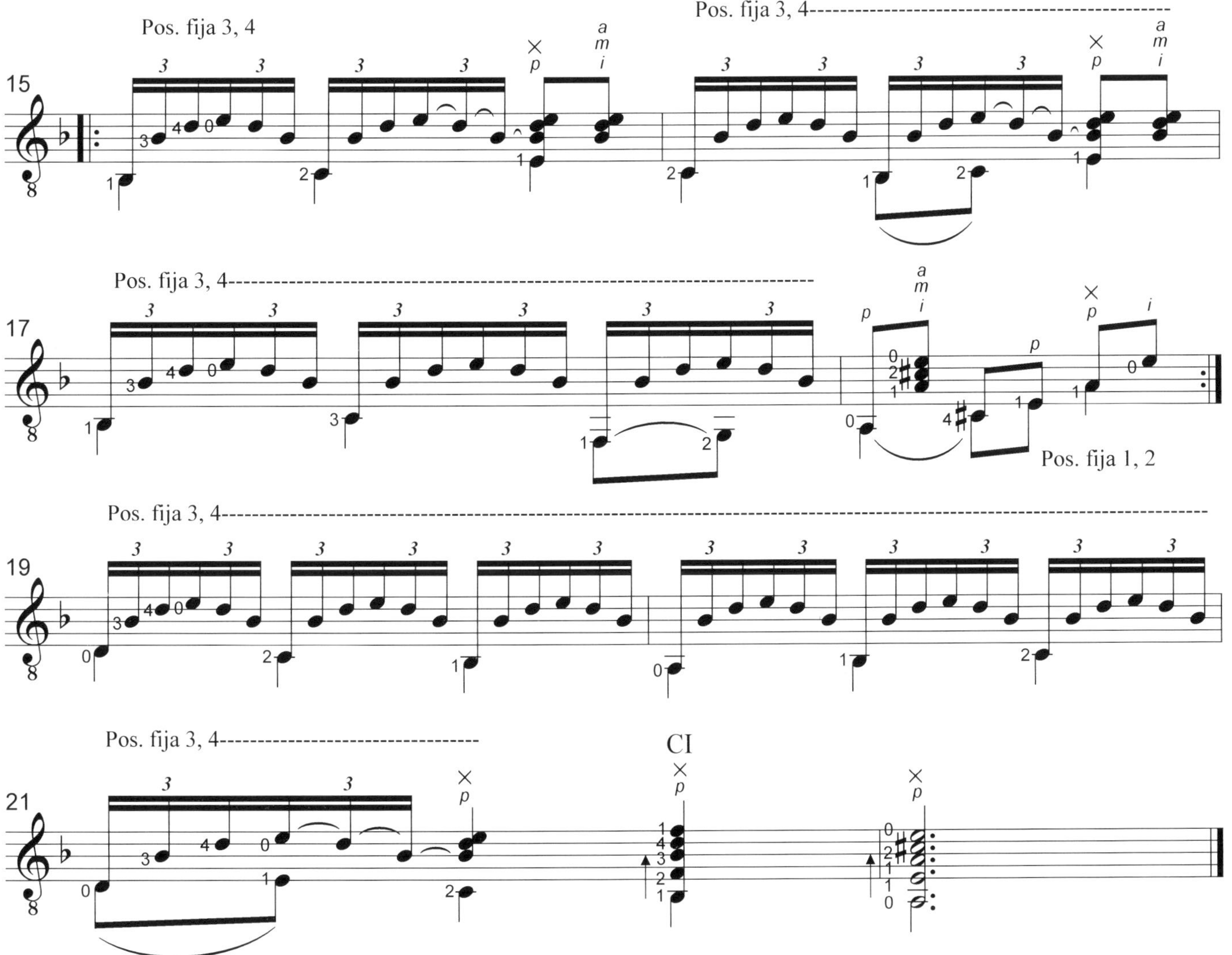

Performance Notes

1) Play apoyando with pulgar (thumb) when possible; sometimes it is not possible when the bass is on an adjacent string or when the bass note is on the same string.

2) "Soleá por medio" (La) has the same beat pattern as "Soleá por arriba" (Mi) but is in the tonality of A (La).

3) "Soleá por arriba" (Mi) typically refers to accompanying a singer in the key of E. A capo (cejilla) *can be used to raise the vocal tessitura.*

E

D7/F# G

C7/G F

Am G F

E

4) "Soleá por medio" refers to playing in the key of A; with or without a capo (cejilla).

A

G7 C

F7 Bb

Dm C Bb

A

5) Playing the thumb (pulgar) rest stroke (apoyando) allows for a stronger and louder trémolo.

6) "Posicion fija" indicates that certain notes are held for the period of time indicated under the dotted lines.

7) The "x" symbol indicates a golpe with "a-m" simultaneously as the pulgar plays.

8) In measure one, the 2nd finger reaches over and beyond fingers 3-4. This is typical in flamenco guitar performance.

P2. Soleá pulgar

Richard Marlow
Edited by Corey Whitehead

(♩ = 100)

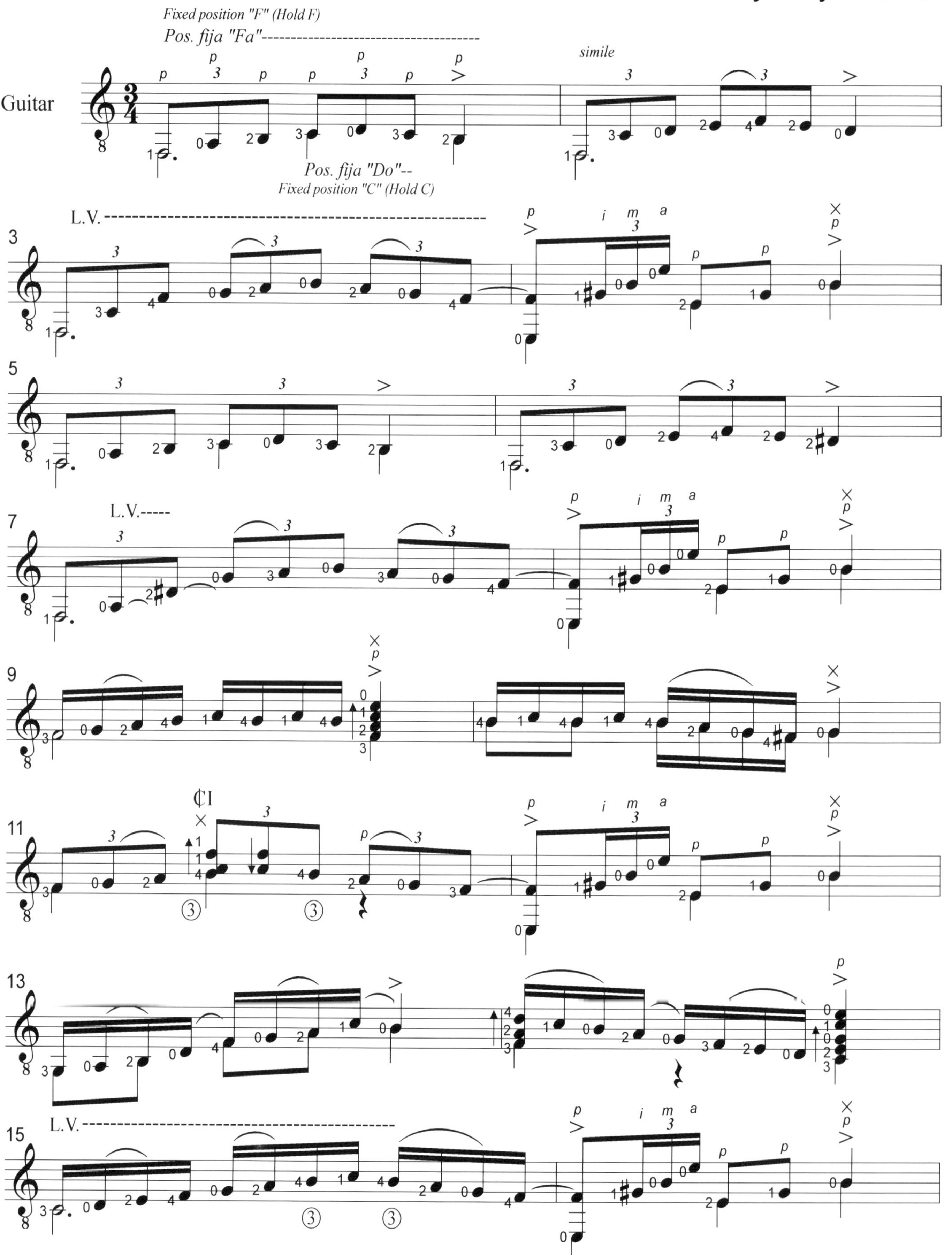

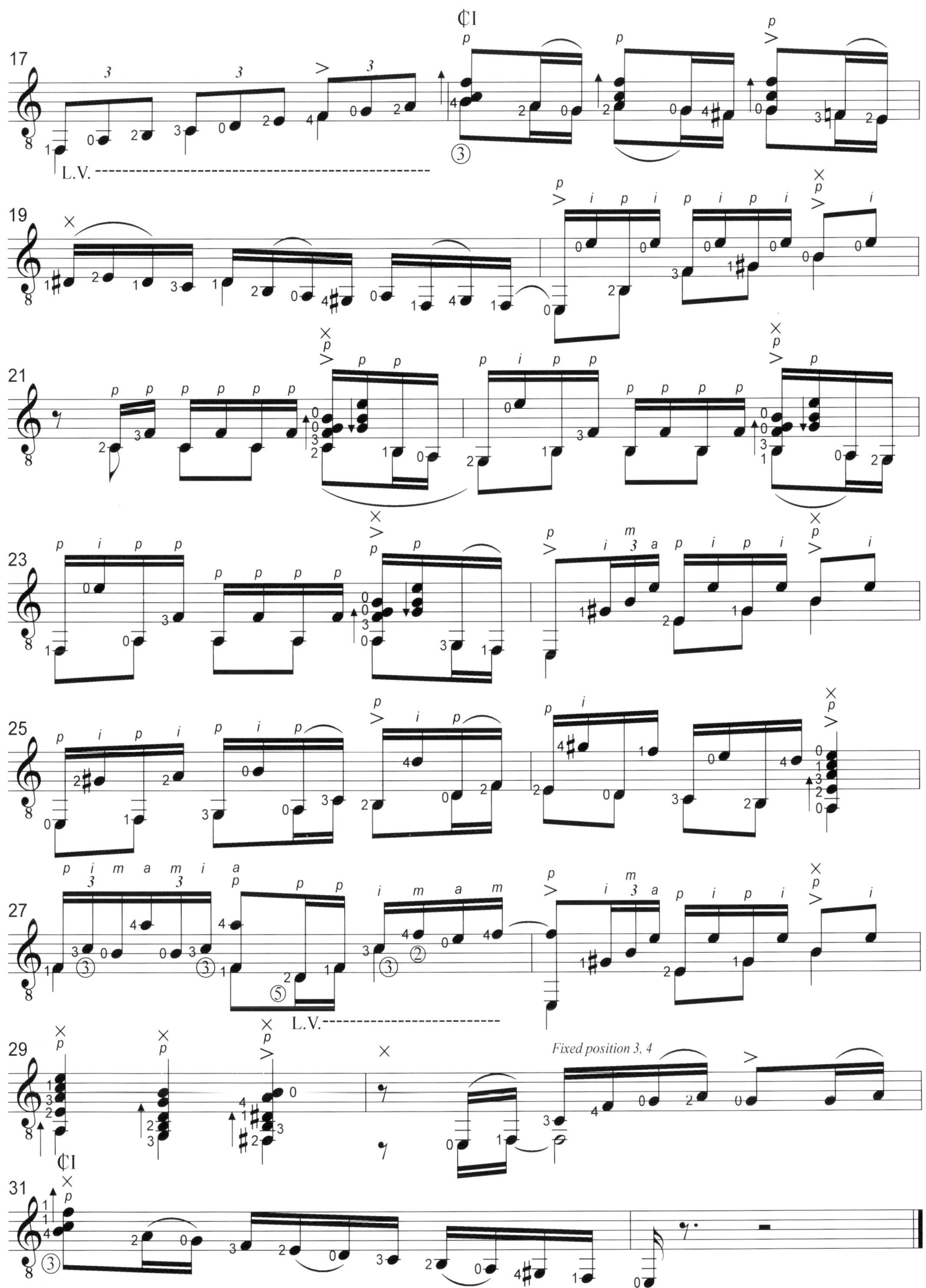

Performance Notes

1) Allow notes to ring together when possible, especially chords, and their neighboring tones.

2) Posición fija "Fa" *means to hold the finger down on the note "F."*

3) Posición fija "Do" *means to hold the finger down on the note "C."*

4) L.V. (laissez vibrer) = "let vibrate."

Pic2. Alegrías picado

Richard Marlow
Edited by Corey Whitehead

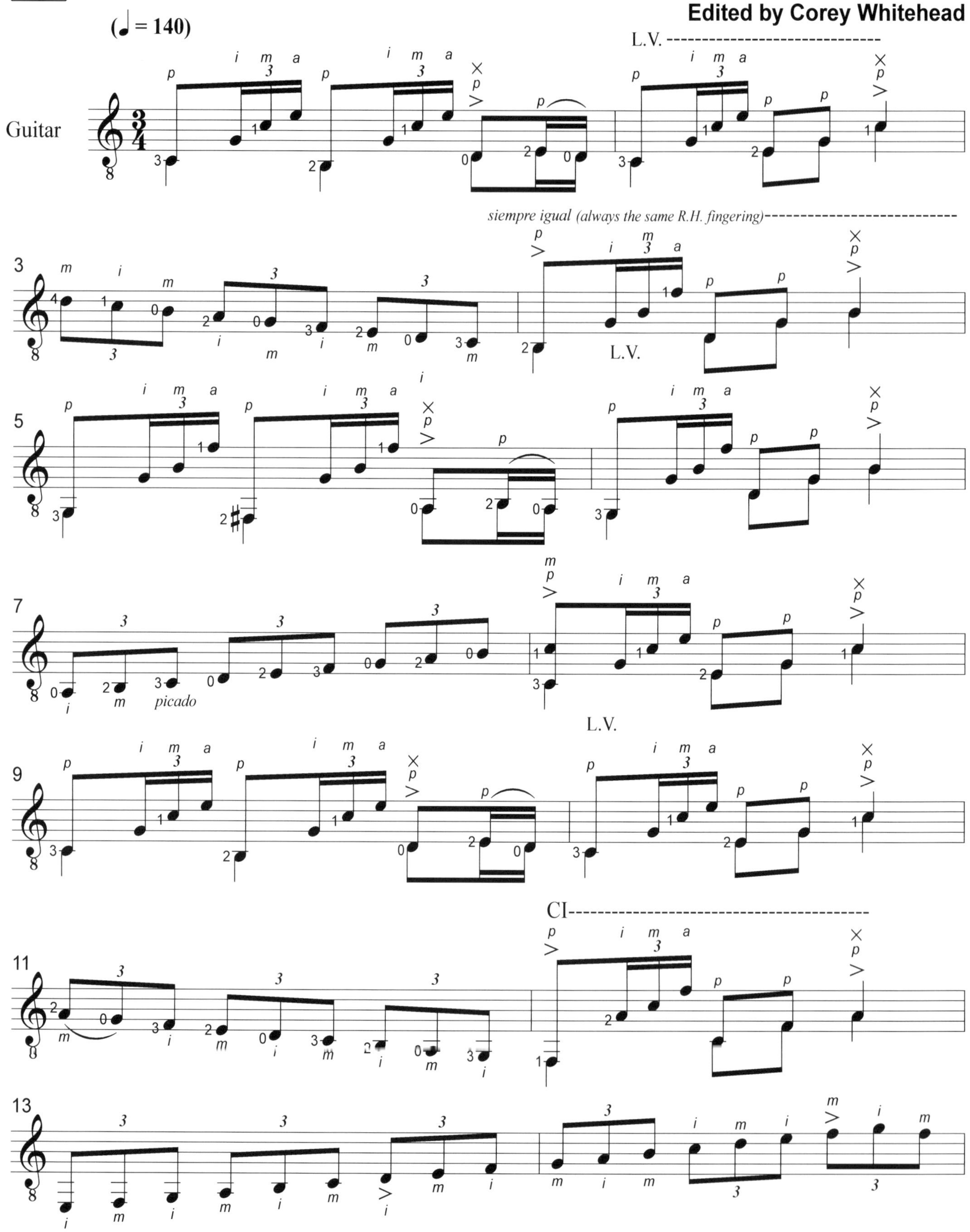

(♩ = 140)

Guitar

L.V.

siempre igual (always the same R.H. fingering)

L.V.

picado

L.V.

CI

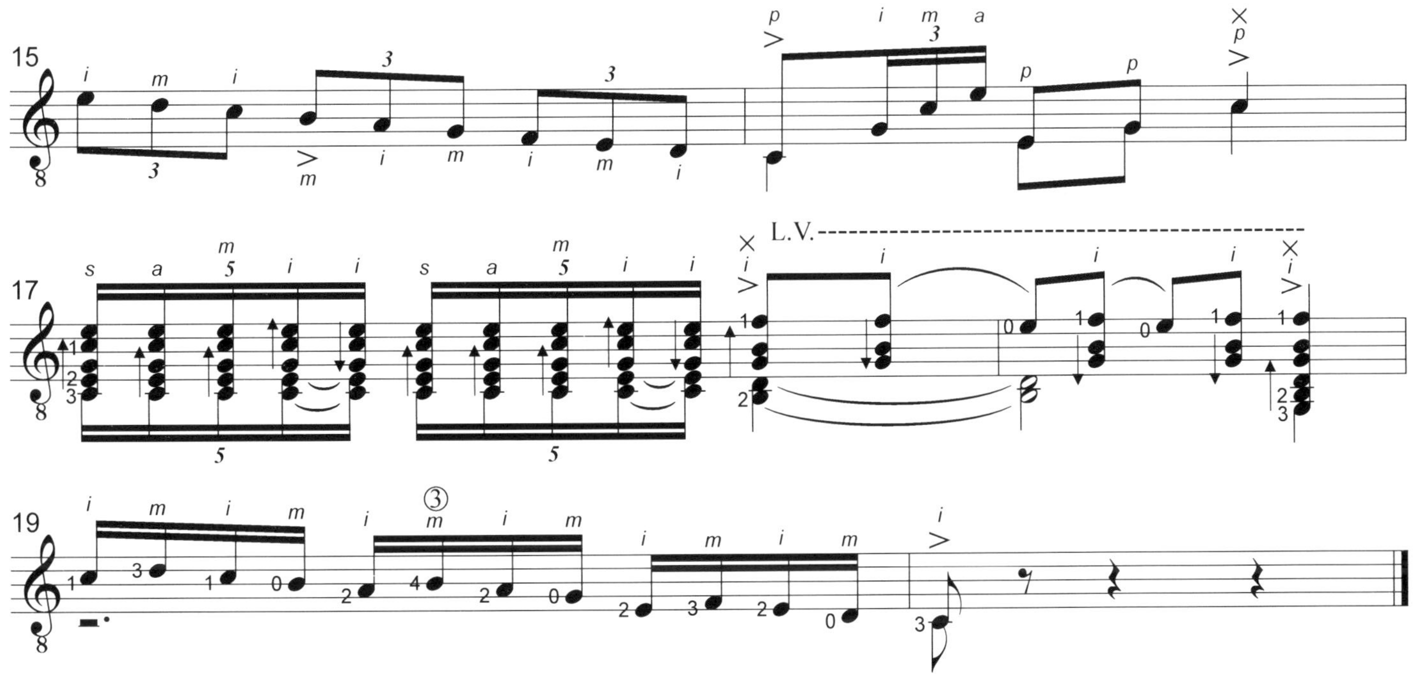

Performance Notes

1) *The palo, Alegrías usually has a tonal center of A (por medio) or E (por arriba); these open chord voicings are often transposed with a* cejilla *or capo.*

2) *The Alegrías is related to the palo, Soleares in form, meter and rhythm, but uses different chords; the lyrics are also lighter or "chico."*

3) *The Alegrías is part a larger sub-family of forms related to Soleares called "Cantiñas" and are from Sanlúcar de Barrameda.*

4) *One of these "cantiñas" is called "Caracoles." Caracoles are essentially Alegrías in Do (C) with specific lyrics about selling snails.*

5) *Alegrías are most common and popular particularly in the region, city of Cádiz. C Major is the most common tonality.*

6) *Camarón de la Isla and Paco de Lucia made many great recordings of Alegrías in C, E, and A.*

7) *Fix the pulgar (thumb) when playing picado.*

8) *When playing the rasgueado in measure 17, try to crescendo through the first two beats.*

9) *The "L.V." in measures 2, 10 and 18 means to "let vibrate" or "laissez vibrer."*

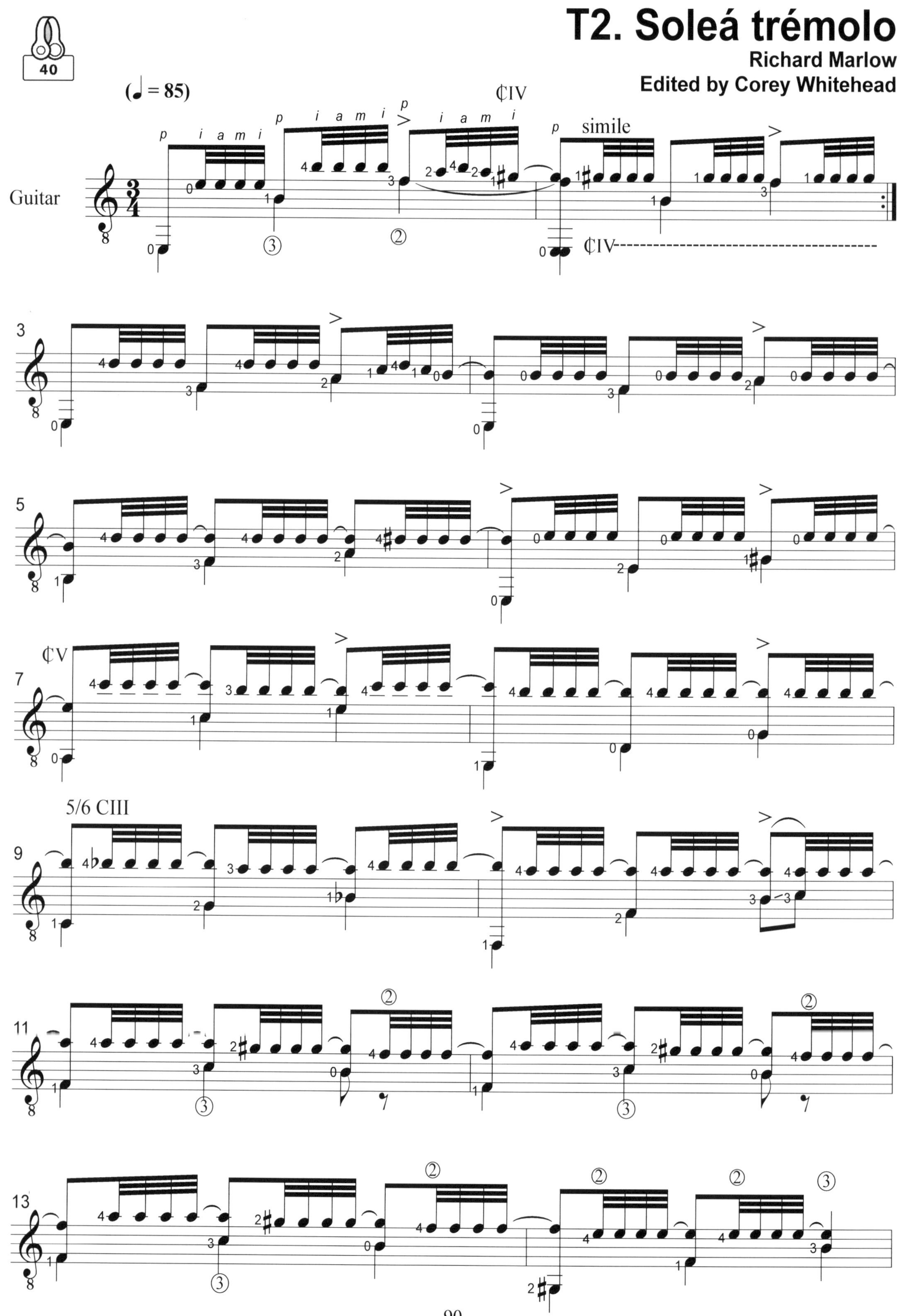
40
T2. Soleá trémolo
Richard Marlow
Edited by Corey Whitehead
(♩ = 85)
Guitar
p i a m i
simile
¢IV
¢V
5/6 CIII
90

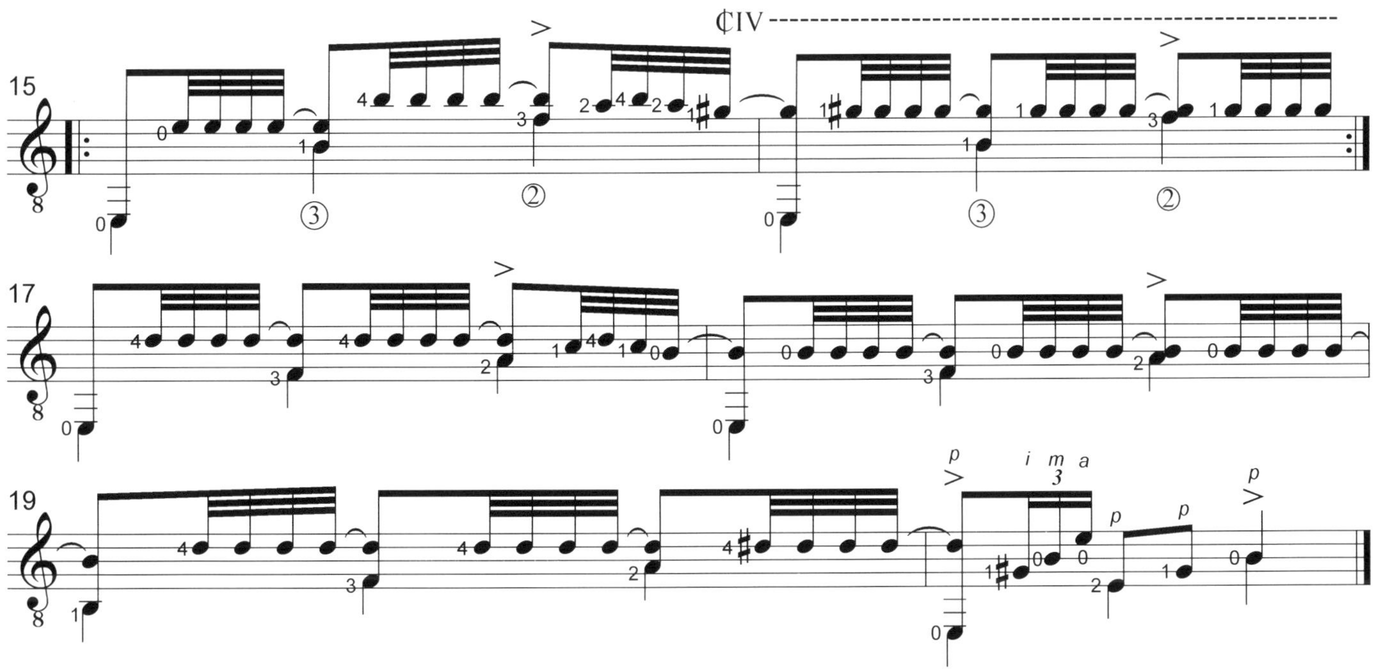

Performance Notes

1) Using a "cejilla" or capo at the 2nd or 3rd fret will make this piece easier to play at first.

2) Hold down the fingers of the left hand as much as possible to allow notes to vibrate together within the measure.

3) The trémolo may be played as an even quintuplet of sixteenth-notes as a variation.

4) The quintuplet may be alternated with the indicated rhythm as desired when composing or improvising falsetas.

Flamenco Studies
Part 2/Unit 3

R3. Soleá por bulerías rasgueados

Richard Marlow
Edited by Corey Whitehead

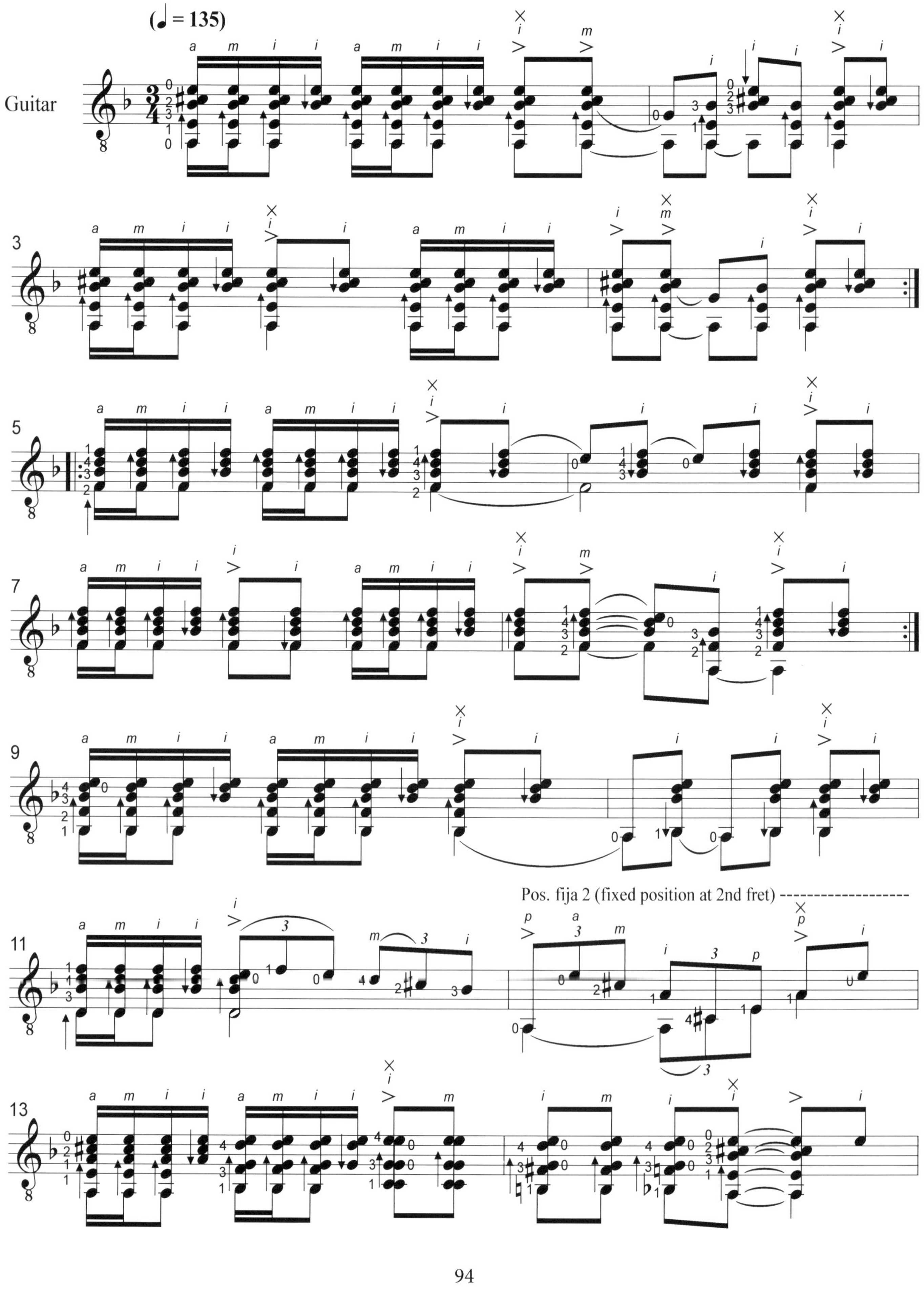

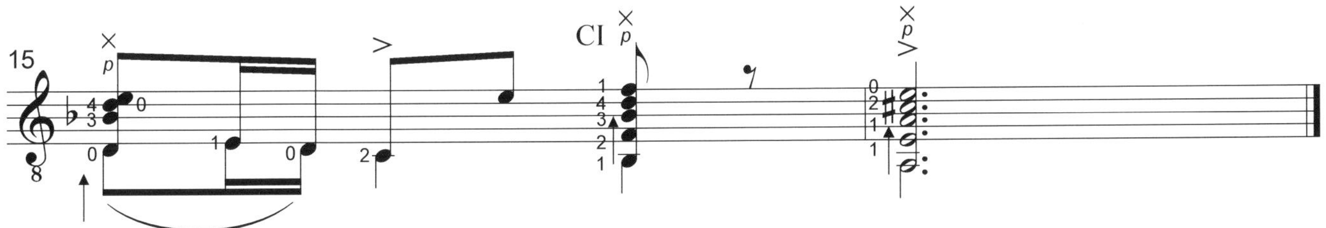

Performance Notes

1) The phrasing of this palo is an amalgam of four measures of 3/4, or twelve beats. The chord progression follows this meter/time signature, which is actually incorrect as it should demonstrate the organization of the accented beats.

2) The actual metric organization of accents is an amalgam of 3/4, 3/4, 4/4, and 2/4. The first measure of 3/4 features an anacrusis/pickup.
Chords: **|:** *1-2-**3** | 4-5-**6** | 7-8-9 | **10**-11-**12*** **:|**
Meter: |: *2-3|**1** - 2-3|**1** -2-3-4 | **1** - 2 | **1*** :|

3) The palo, "Soleá por bulerías" is meant to accompany the lyrics and melody of the Soleá with the rhythm of a Bulerías.

4) Some would argue that the sound of the rhtyhm of the dancers is more closely related to Alegrías, which is, in fact, a faster Soleá.

5) The chord progression follows the melody, which is associated with the Soleares lyrics.

6) Soleares is typically played "por arriba" or in "Mi" (E), except in Jerez de la Frontera where Soleares are played "por medio" in "La" (A).

7) Play apoyando with thumb on the downbeat of measure 12.

8) The right-hand fingering in measure one, beat three is intentional. This is a characteristic technique to create a syncopation by accenting the second half of beat three. In order to execute this fingering with ease, one must quickly relax the index finger after the downstroke on beat three, allowing the index finger to recoil towards the palm of the hand. As the index finger relaxes and comes toward the palm, the middle finger follows in order to be in position to play a downstroke on the second half of beat three.

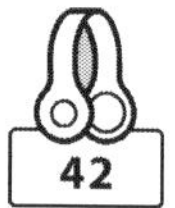

A3. Siguiriyas arpegios

Richard Marlow
Edited by Corey Whitehead

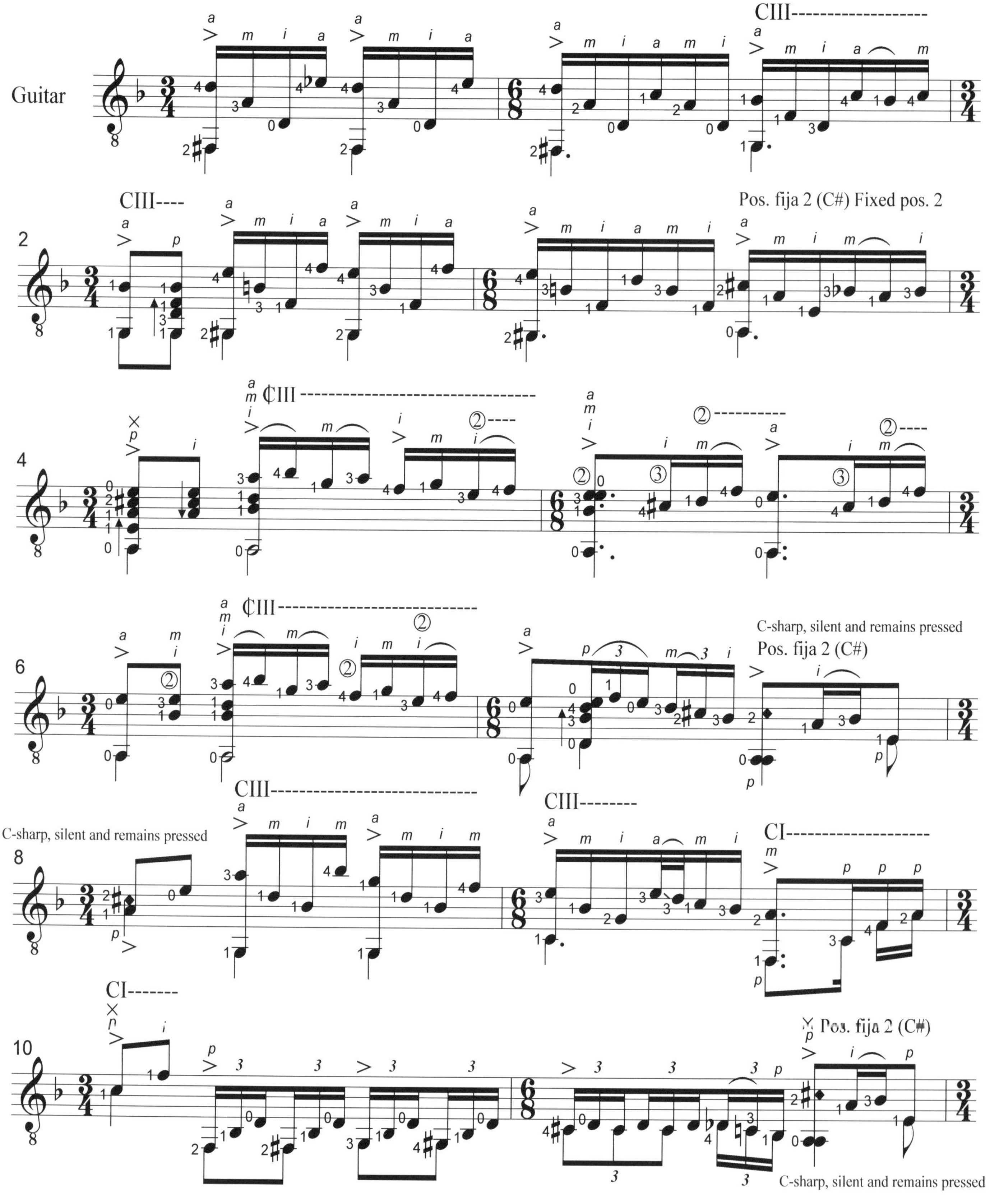

Guitar

CIII

Pos. fija 2 (C#) Fixed pos. 2

C-sharp, silent and remains pressed

Pos. fija 2 (C#)

C-sharp, silent and remains pressed

CI

Pos. fija 2 (C#)

C-sharp, silent and remains pressed

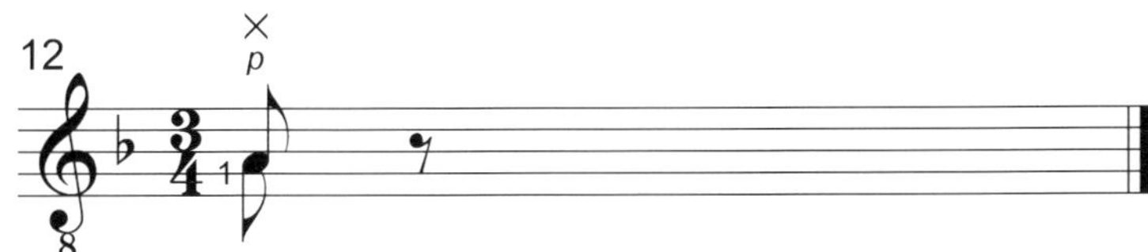

Performance Notes

1) This study focuses on the right-hand rasgueado pattern (a-m-i-a-a-m-i) and (a-m-i).

2) An alternative pattern is (a-m-i-m-a-m-i) and (a-m-i).

3) Siguiriyas is one of the four primary forms of flamenco.

4) The sub-forms of this palo include Serranas, Livianas, and other unaccompanied forms such as Trilla, Tonada, and Martinete.

*5) The beat pattern for dancers is : |**1**-2-**1**-2-**1**-2 | **1**-2-3-**1**-2-3 |*
*or: **1 2 3 1 2***

*6) The guitarist must conceptualize the phrase: **1**-2-**1**-2 | **1**-2-3-**1**-2-3 |**1**-2*

7) Fix (fijar) or anchor (a-m) on the golpeador in measures 10 and 11 when playing rapid notes with the thumb.

8) Keep common left-hand fingers fixed (pressed) when possible.

9) Diamond-shaped noteheads represent "fixed-position" notes that retain left-hand fingering but are not always sounded.

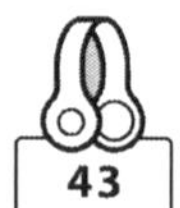

P3. Bulerías pulgar

Richard Marlow
Edited by Corey Whitehead

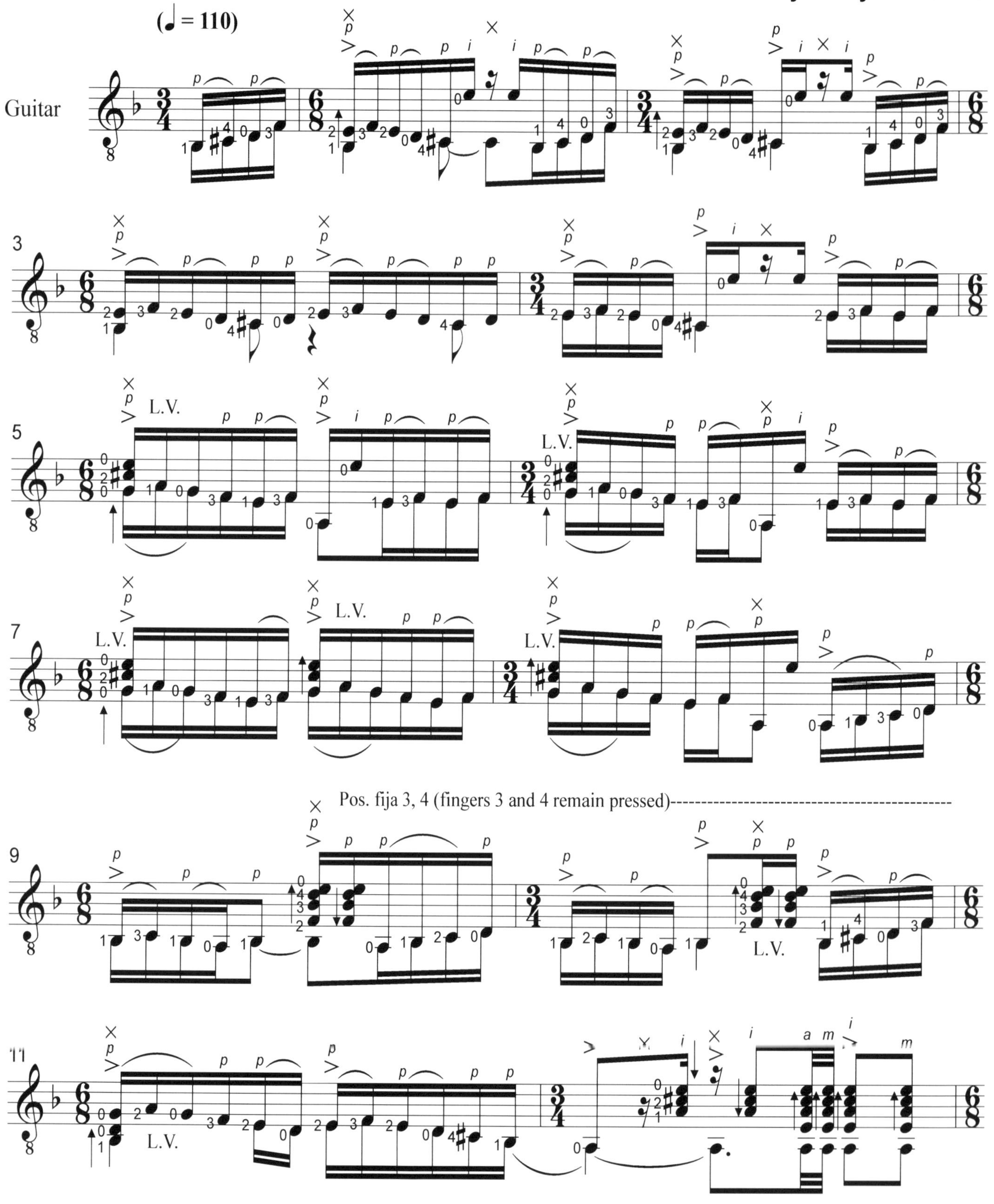

(♩ = 110)

Guitar

Pos. fija 3, 4 (fingers 3 and 4 remain pressed)

L.V.

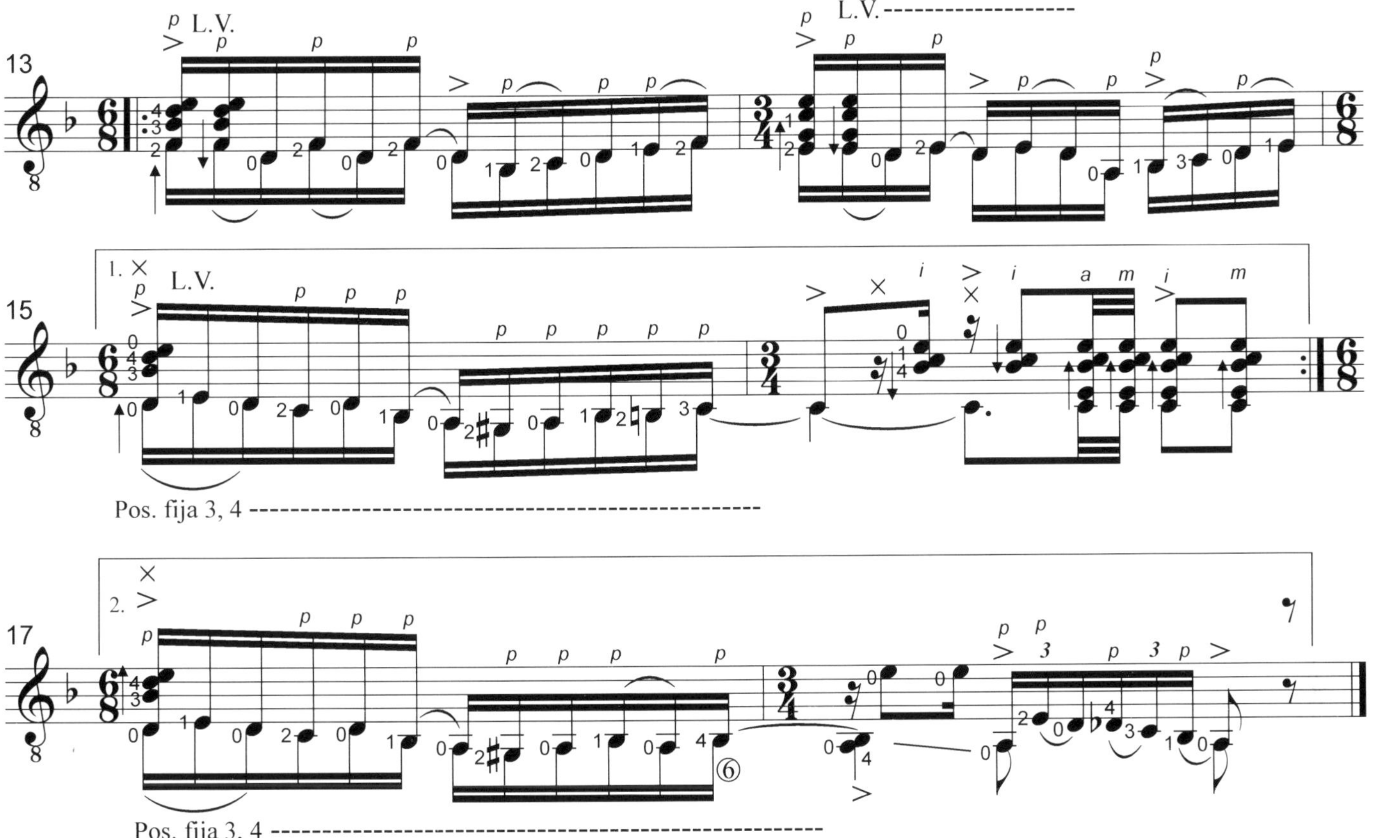

Performance Notes

1) The palo Bulerías has been described as being in the form of the "Alegrías para baile" and is similarly a part of the Soleares form.

2) When playing with the R.H. thumb, anchor fingers "m-a" on the golpeador on the soundboard (tapa) 1cm from the bridge (puente).

3) Beat 12 of the 12-beat pattern begins on the first eighth note of the measures in 6/8.

4) The rhythmic pulse is represented by eighth notes. The beat is divided by using two sixteenth notes.

5) The "x" symbol means to tap on the "golpeador" on the soundboard with "a-m."

6) The anacrusis or "pickup" measure represents beats 10 and 11 of the 12-beat pattern.

7) L.V. means "let vibrate."

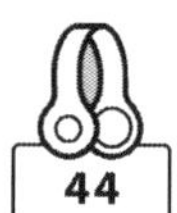

Pic3. Soleá por bulerías picados

Richard Marlow
Edited by Corey Whitehead

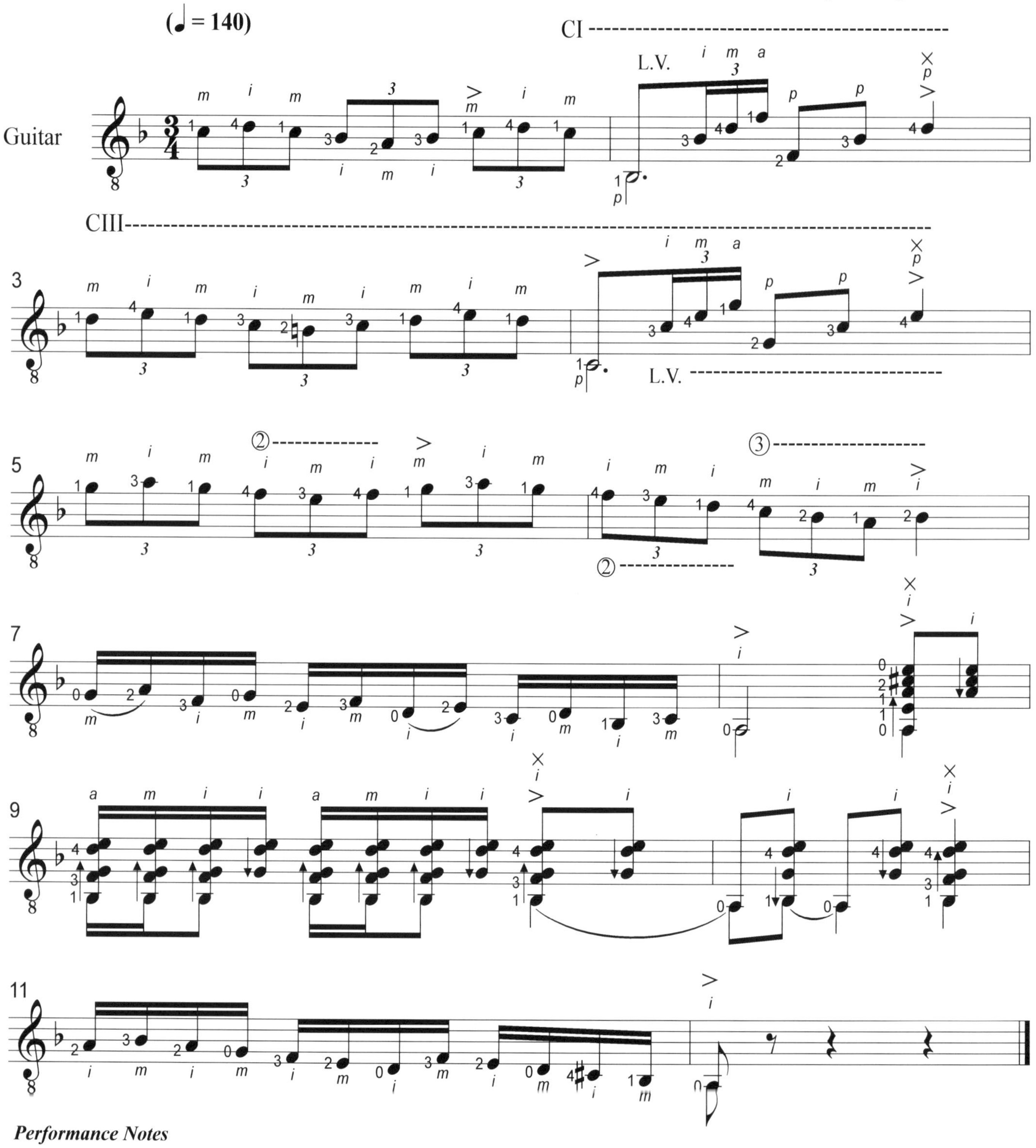

(♩ = 140)

Guitar

Performance Notes

1) The "x" symbol indicates a simultaneous golpe by "a-m" when the thumb plays.

2) The phrase of this palo is an amalgam of four measures of 3/4, or twelve beats. The chord progression follows this meter/time signature, which is actually ***incorrect,*** *as the meter/time signature should demonstrate the organization of the accented beats.*

3) The actual metric organization of accents is an amalgam of 3/4, 3/4, 4/4, and 2/4. The first measure of 3/4 features an anacrusis/pickup:

Chords: **|:** *1-2-**3** | 4-5-**6** | 7-8-9 |* ***10****-11-**12** **:|***

Meter: **|:** *2-3|**1** - 2-3|**1** -2-3-4 | **1** - 2 | **1*** **:|**

4) The palo "Soleá por bulerías" accompanies the lyrics and melody of the Soleá with the rhythm of a Bulerías.

5) Anchor the thumb on the 6th string when playing picado or rasgueado.

This page has been left blank to avoid an awkward page turn.

Flamenco Studies Part 2/Unit 4

T4. Soleá por medio trémolo

Richard Marlow
Edited by Corey Whitehead

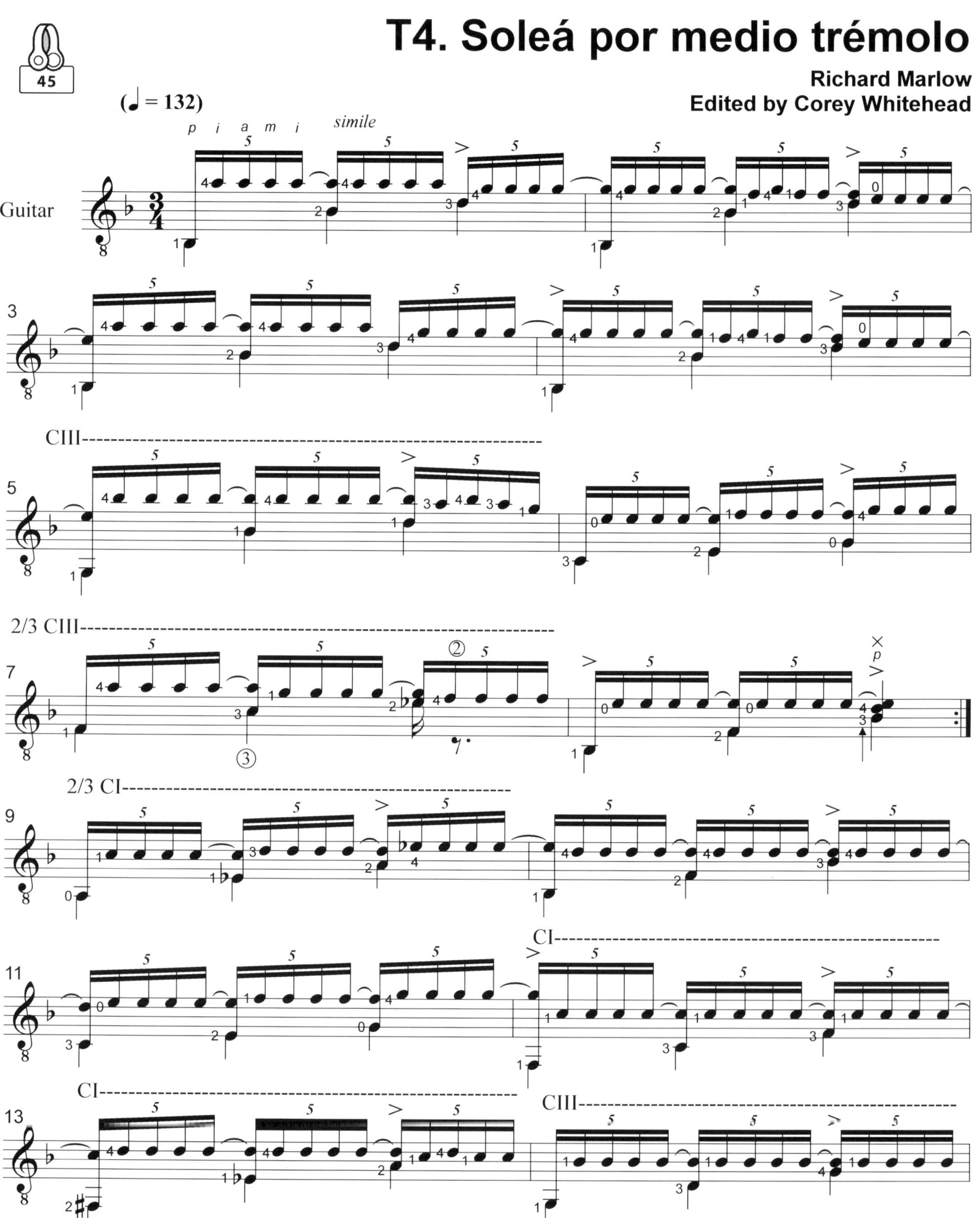

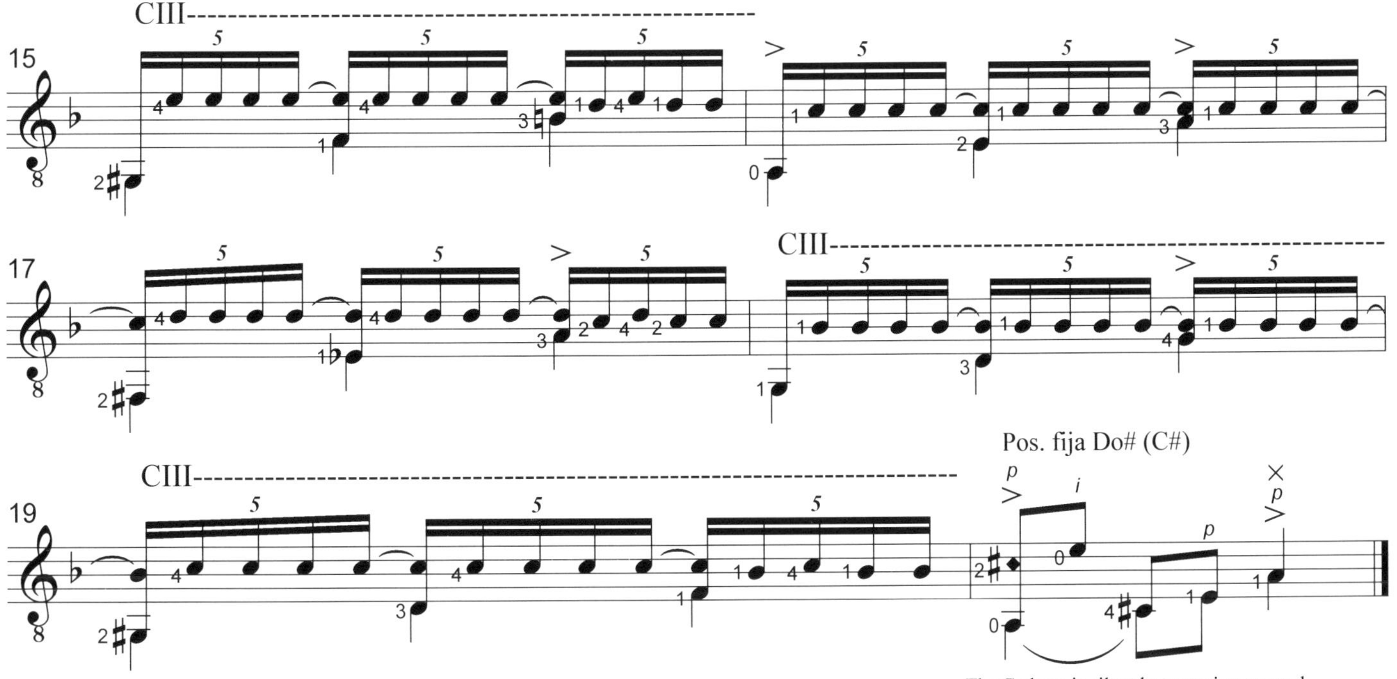

Performance Notes

1) Play apoyando with the thumb when possible; sometimes it is not possible, for example when the bass note is on an adjacent string or on the same string as the trémolo.

2) "Soleá por medio" in A (La) has the same beat pattern as "Soleá por arriba" in E (Mi).

3) "Soleá por arriba" (Mi) accompaniment chords for the song lyrics are typically:
E
D7/F# G
C7/G F
Am G F
E

4) "Soleá por medio" (La) accompaniment chords for the song lyrics are typically:
A
G7 C
F7 B♭
Dm C B♭
A

5) Playing the thumb rest-stroke allows for a stronger and louder trémolo.

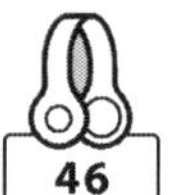

R4. Siguiriyas rasgueados

Richard Marlow
Edited by Corey Whitehead

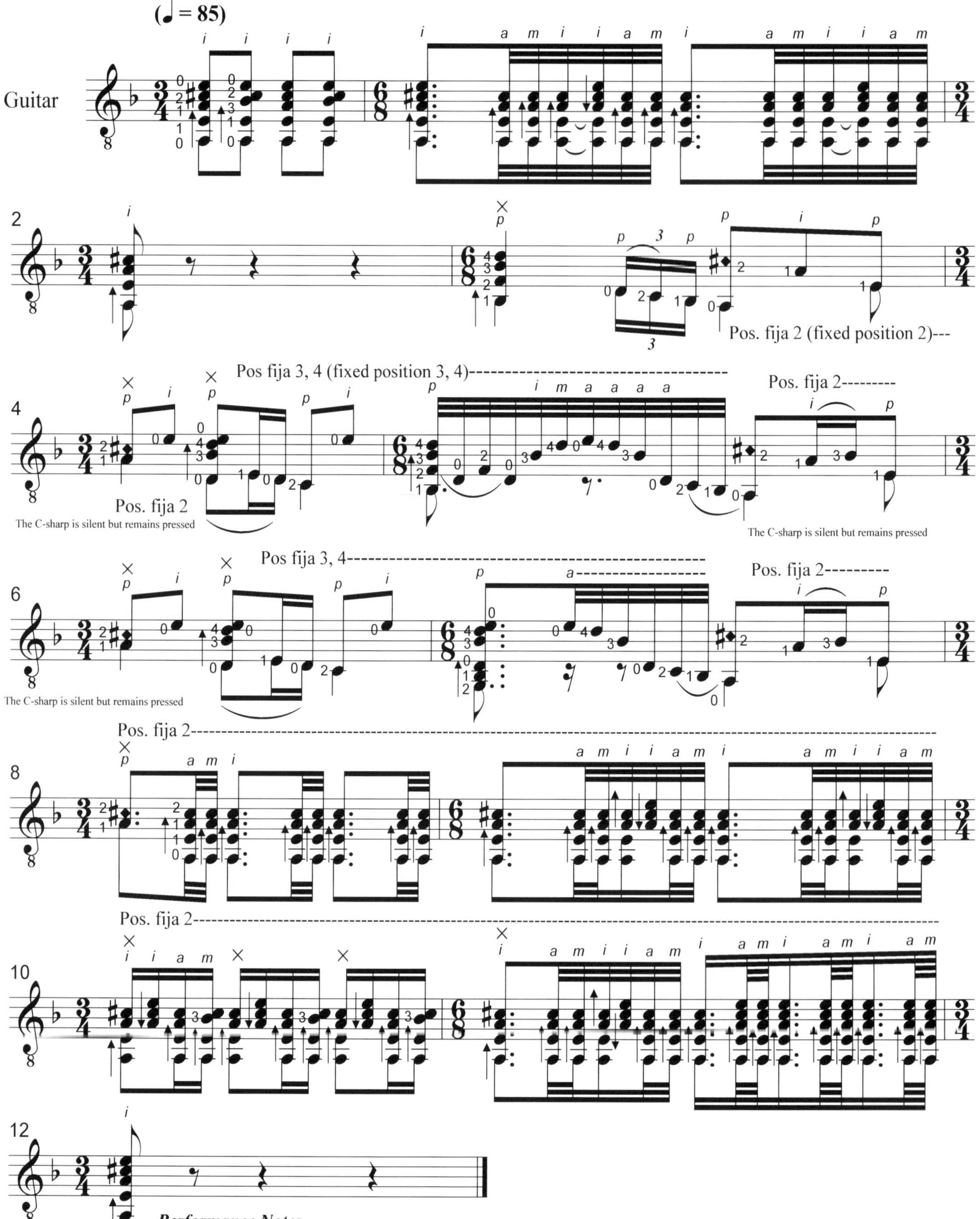

Performance Notes

1) Keep the R.H. thumb anchored on the 6th string while playing rasgueado.
2) When playing with the thumb, keep (a-m) anchored on the golpeador on the soundboard.

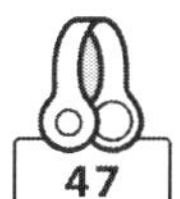

A4. Bulerías arpegios

Richard Marlow
Edited by Corey Whitehead

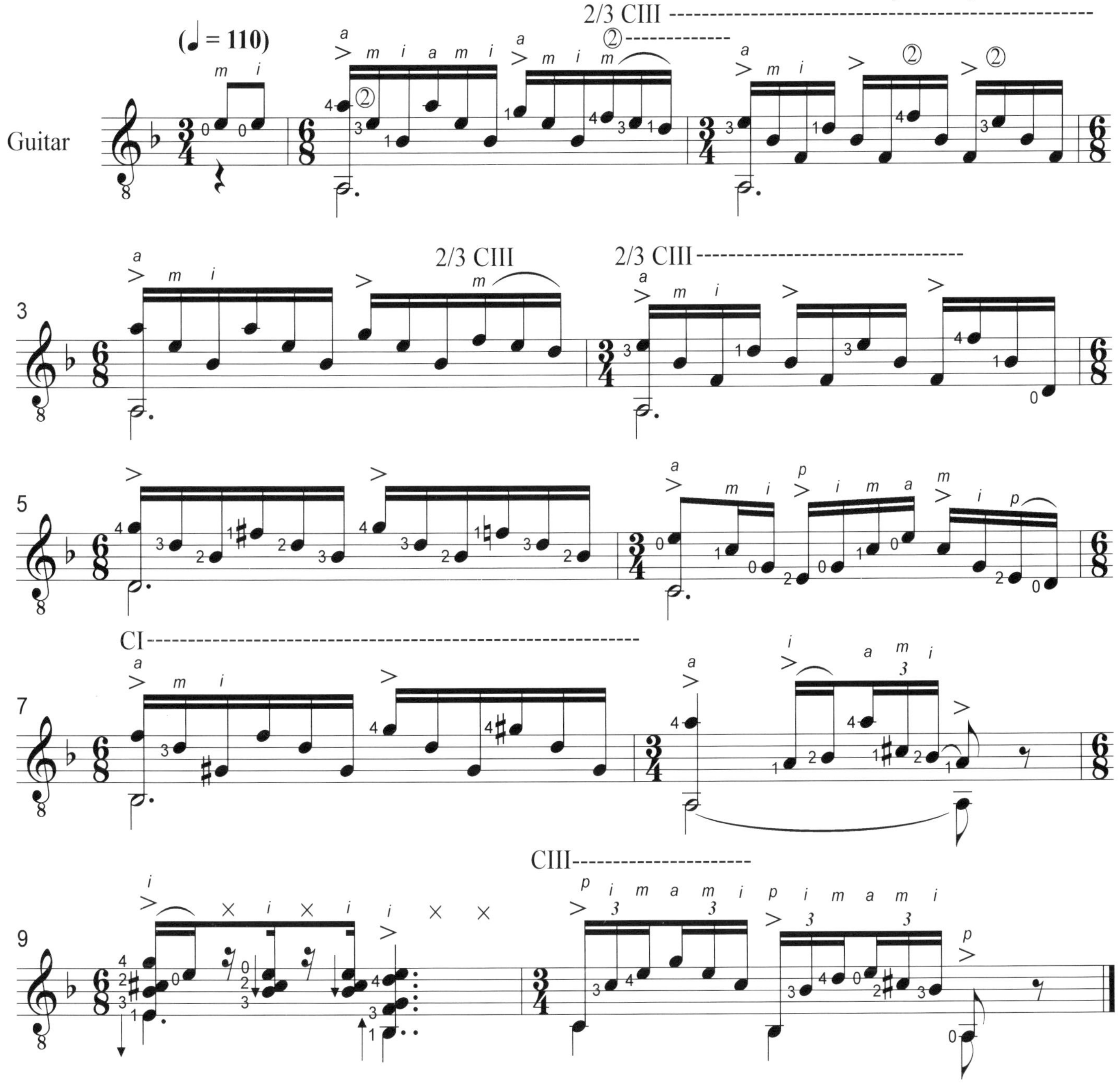

Performance Notes

1) The Bulerías is a 12-count phrase with an 8th note representing the pulse in one measure of 6/8 and one of 3/4.

2) Beat 12 of the cycle is the first accented beat of the phrase. Phrases often start on beat one or the second 8th note of the 6/8 measure.

3) This example starts on "Beat 10," or the last quarter note of the 3/4 measure.

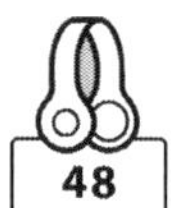

P4. Soleá alzapúa

Audio track voice introduction by Ricardo Marlow

(♩ = 100)

Richard Marlow
Edited by Corey Whitehead

Pulgar

Guitar

Pos. fija 4 "FA" (Keep the F pressed on the 4th string)

sim.

Pos. fija 3 "FA" (Keep the 3rd finger pressed on F on the 4th string)

Fingers 2 and 3 remain pressed

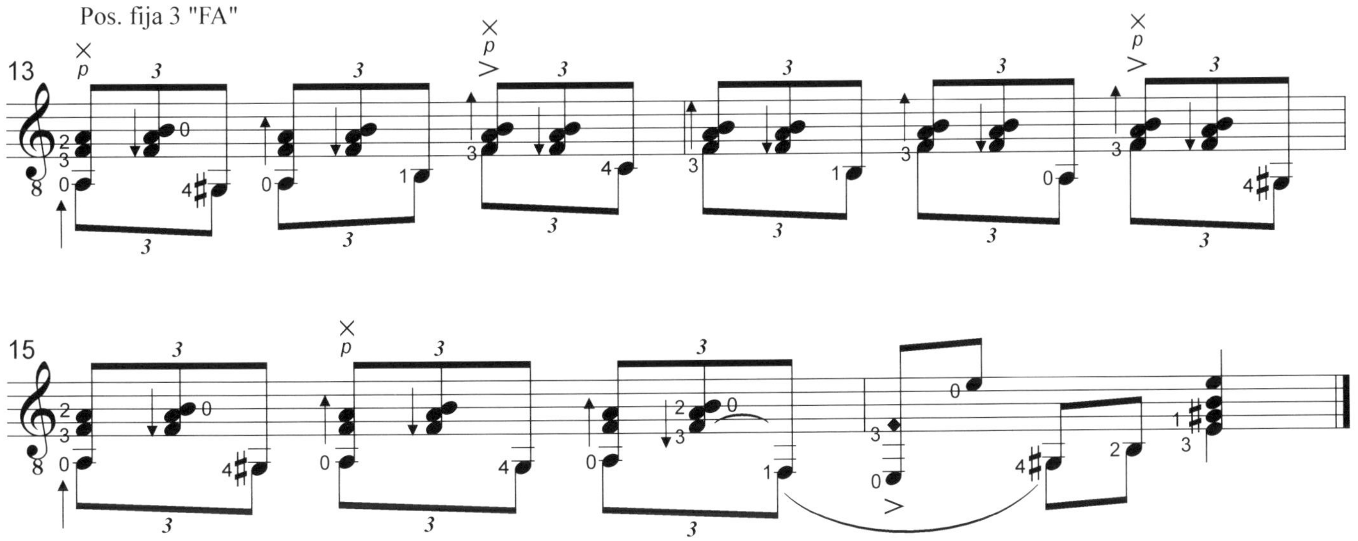

Performance Notes

1) "Soleá por arriba" in E (Mi) accompaniment chords for the lyrics are typically:
E
D7/F#   G
C7/G   F
Am   G   F
E

2) The phrase for this palo is an amalgam of four measures of 3/4, or twelve beats. The chord progression follows this meter/time signature, which is actually incorrect, as the meter/time signature should demonstrate the organization of the accented beats.

3) The correct metric organization of accents is an amalgam of 3/4, 3/4, 4/4, and 2/4. The first measure of 3/4 is an anacrusis/pickup.
Chords: **|:** *1-2-**3** | 4-5-**6** | 7-8-9 | **10**-11-**12*** **:|**
Meter: **|:** *2-3|**1** - 2-3|**1** -2-3-4 | **1** - 2 | **1*** **:|**

4) "Posición fija" refers to the position of a finger on a certain note, most commonly on F (Fa) when playing "por arriba" in E (Mi).

5) Fix (a-m) of the right hand lightly on the soundboard on the golpeador when playing alzapúa.

6) "Alzar" means to come forth, raise or come forward with the "púa" or pick, otherwise known as the thumb (pulgar).

7) When playing alzapúa, "...the flesh should hit on the downstroke and the fingernail on the upstroke." (Gerardo Núñez).

49

Pic4. Farruca picados

Richard Marlow
Edited by Corey Whitehead

(♩ = 100)

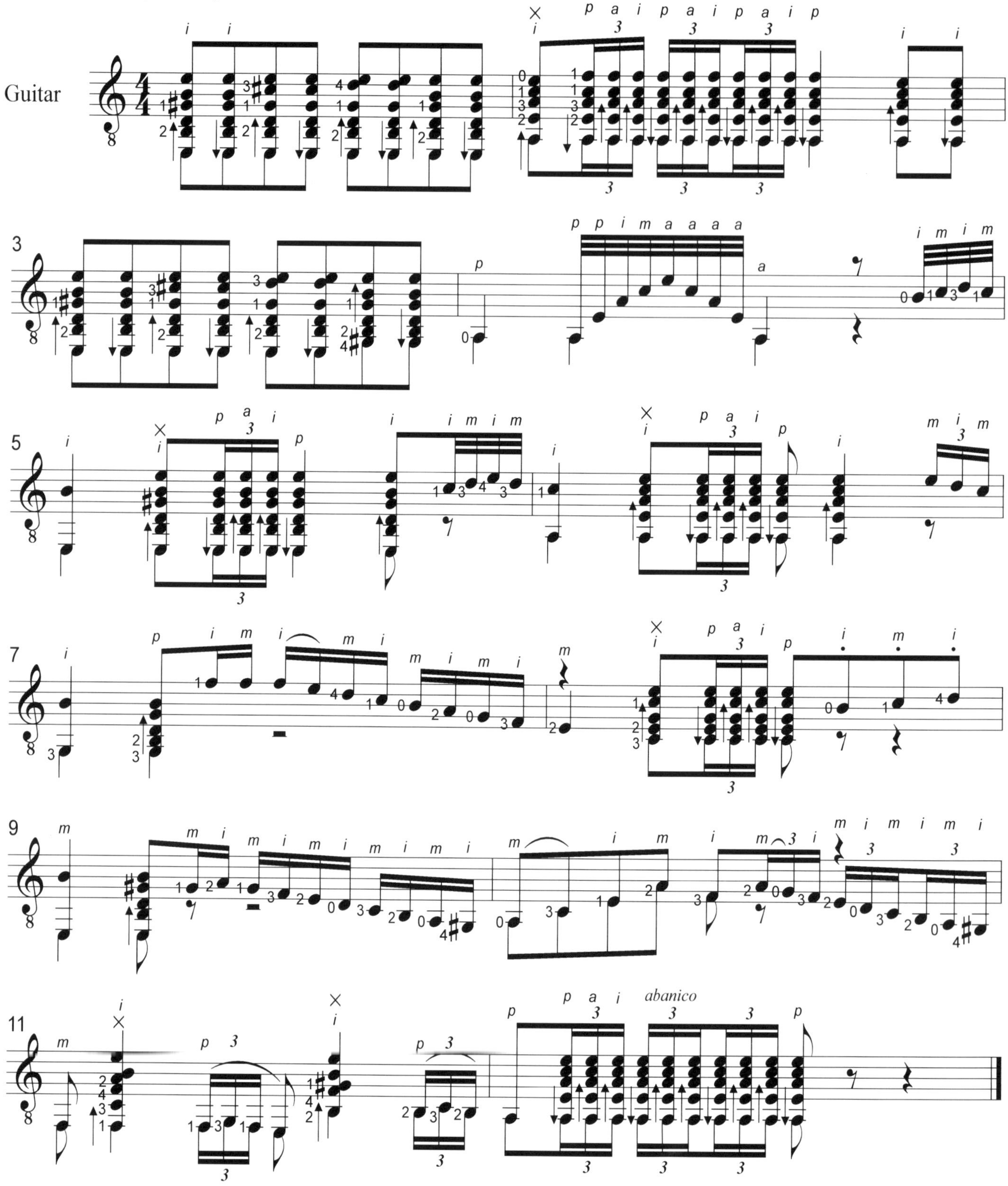

Guitar

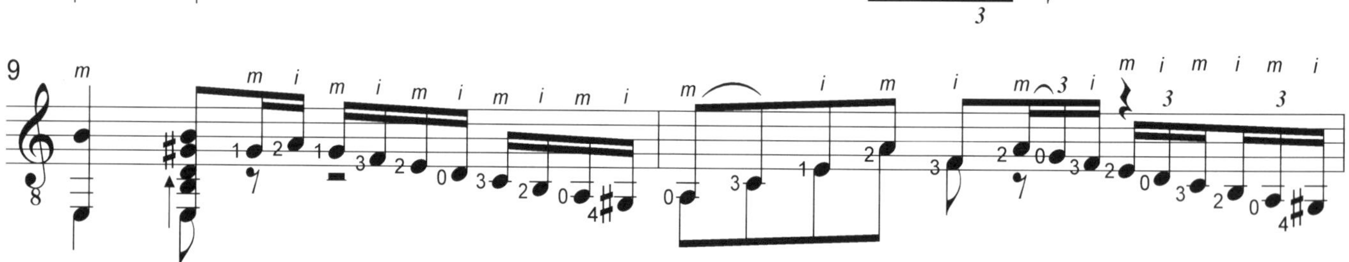

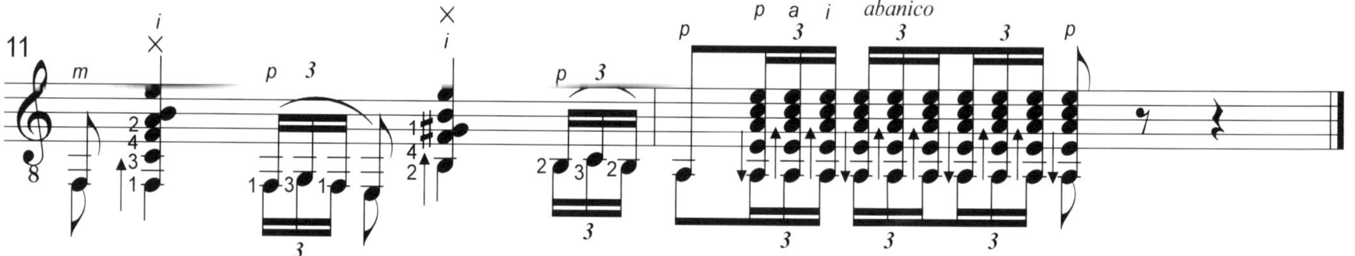

Performance Notes

1) Always play picado (i-m) with rest-stroke.

Flamenco Studies
Part 2/Unit 5

R5. Alegrías rasgueados

Richard Marlow
Edited by Corey Whitehead

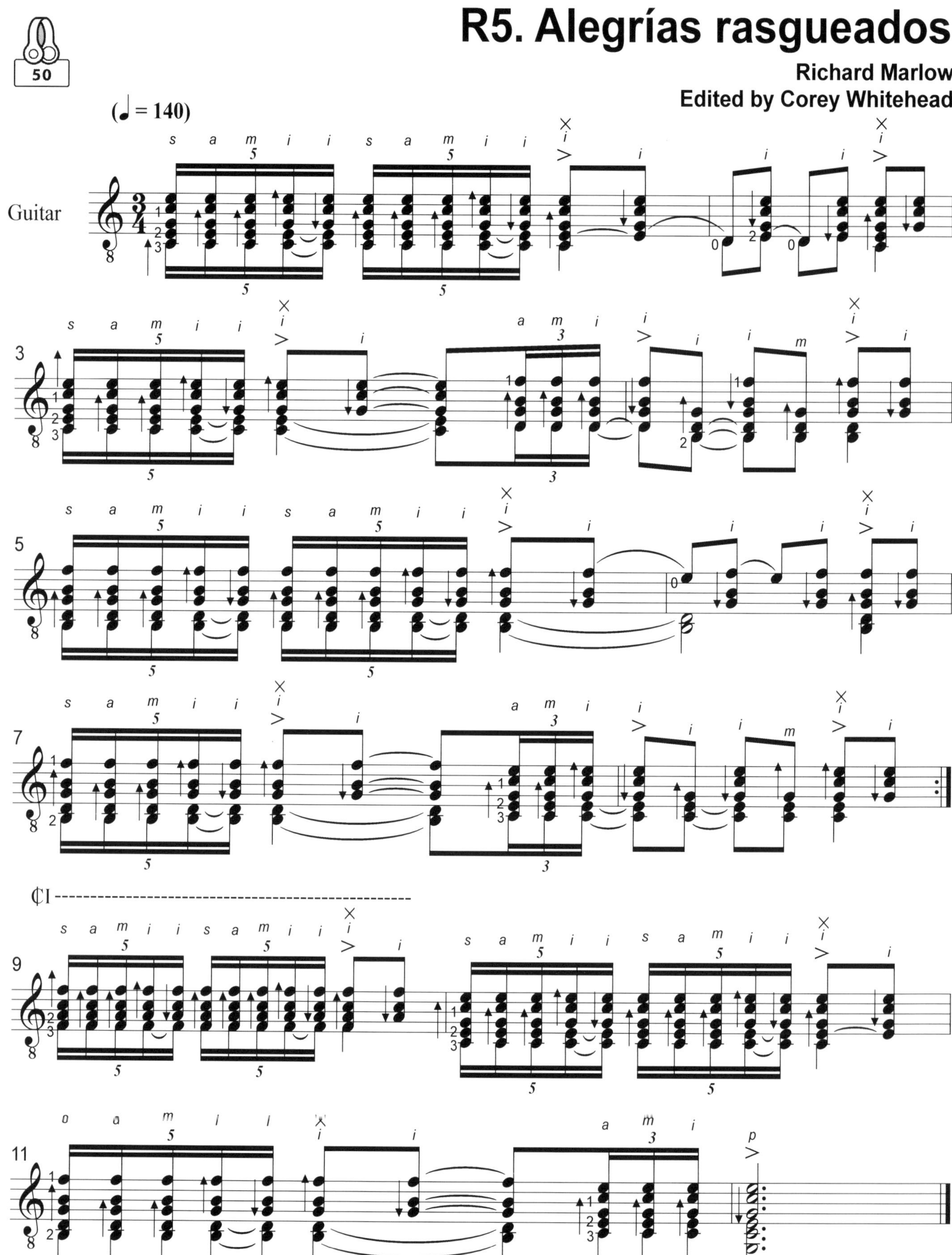

Performance Notes

1) Previous examples of Alegrías address the form, meter, rhythm and key centers of this palo. This example adds the (s-a-m-i-i) rasgueado pattern.

2) Keep the pulgar anchored on the 6th string or on the soundboard next to it, muting the 6th string effectively.

3) As before, the "x" symbol indicates a "golpe" on the golpeador with the "a" finger simultaneously with the downstroke of "i."

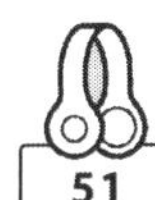

A5. Alegrías (Mi Menor) arpegios

Richard Marlow
Edited by Corey Whitehead

Performance Notes
1) "Alegrías de Córdoba" is in E minor or Mi menor.
2) The R.H. pattern in mm. 5-11 is by design and is an intentional excercise.

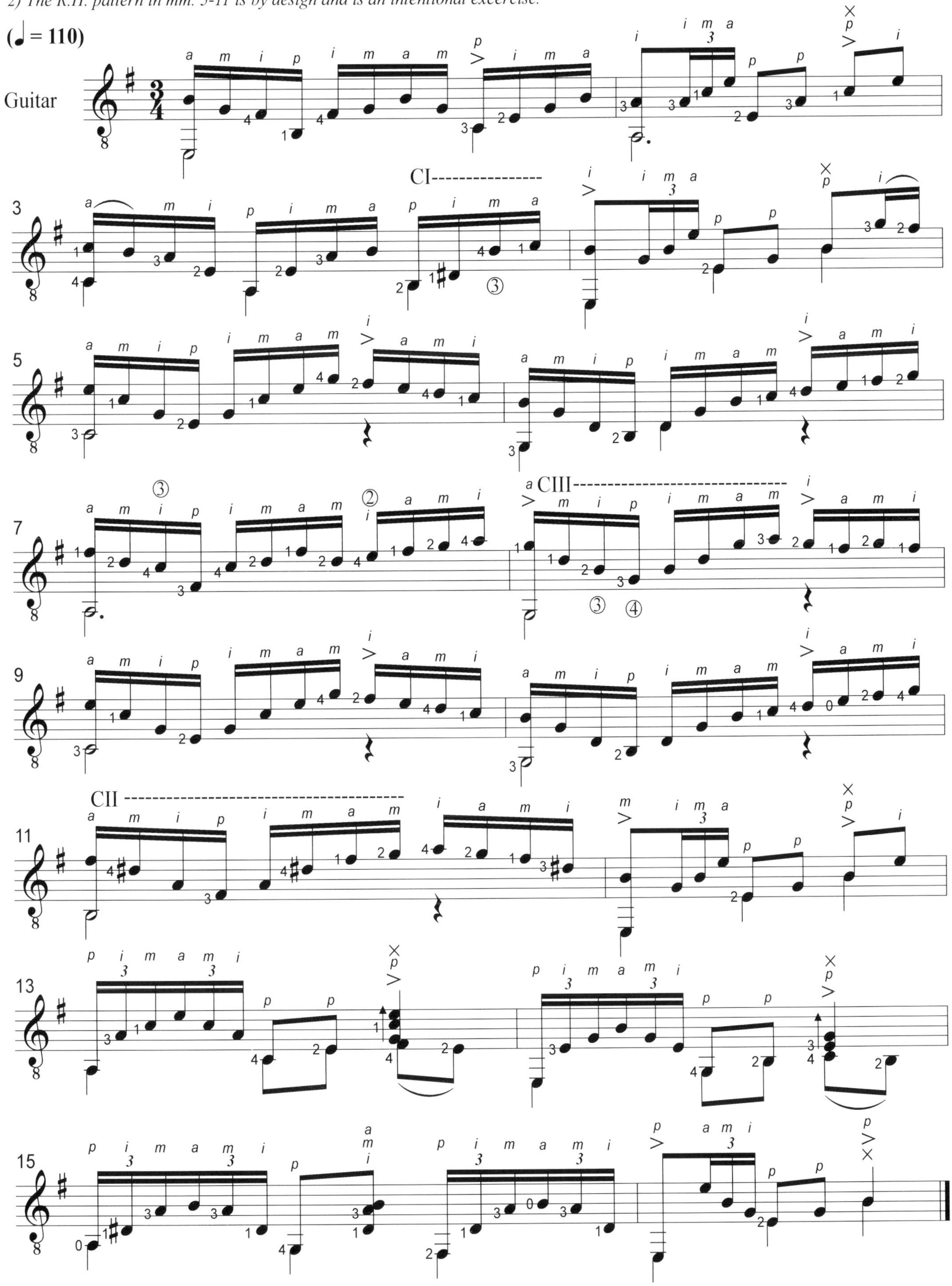

(♩ = 110)

Guitar

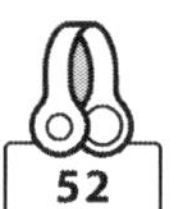

P5. Fandango alzapúa

Richard Marlow
Edited by Corey Whitehead

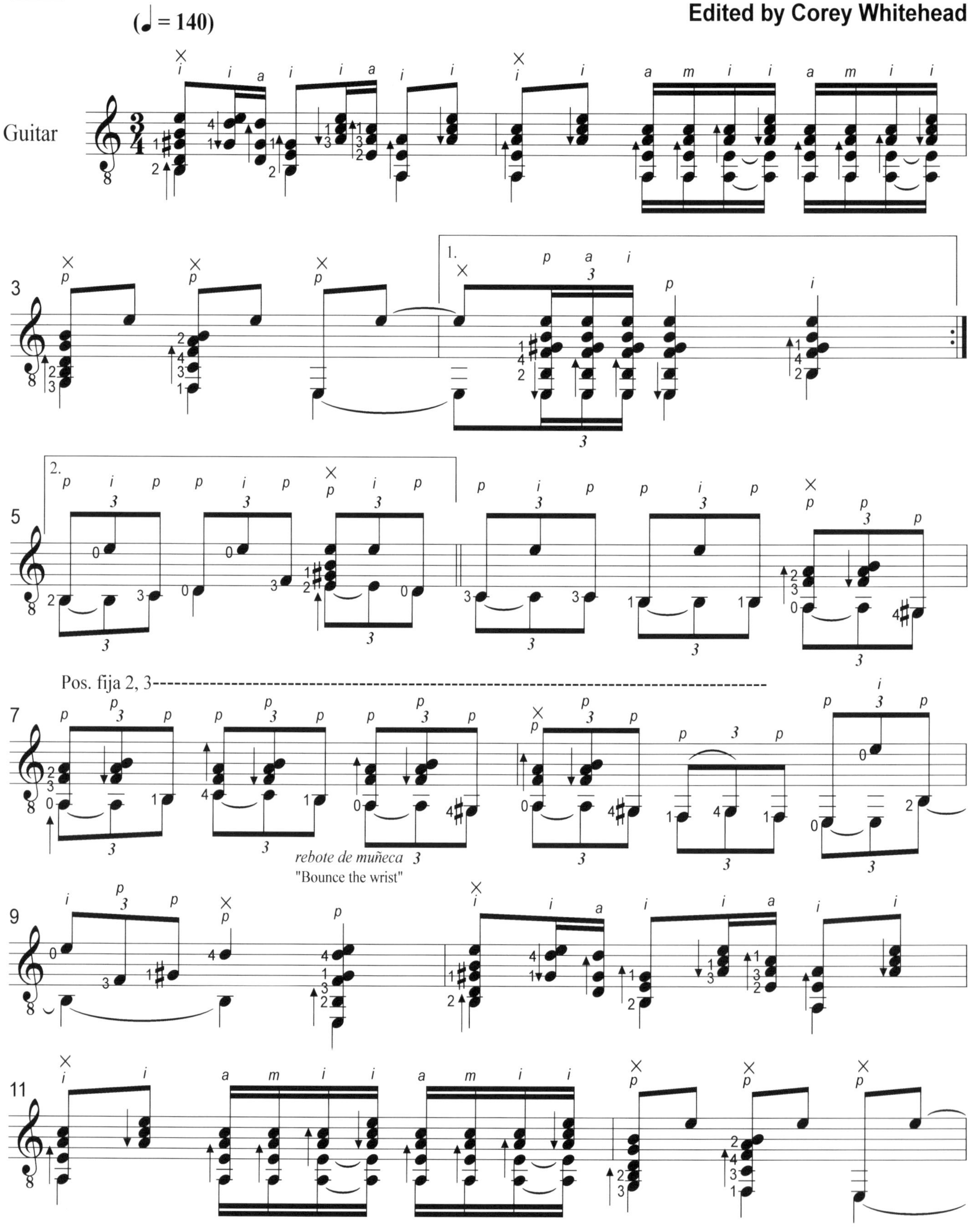

(♩ = 140)

Guitar

Pos. fija 2, 3

rebote de muñeca
"Bounce the wrist"

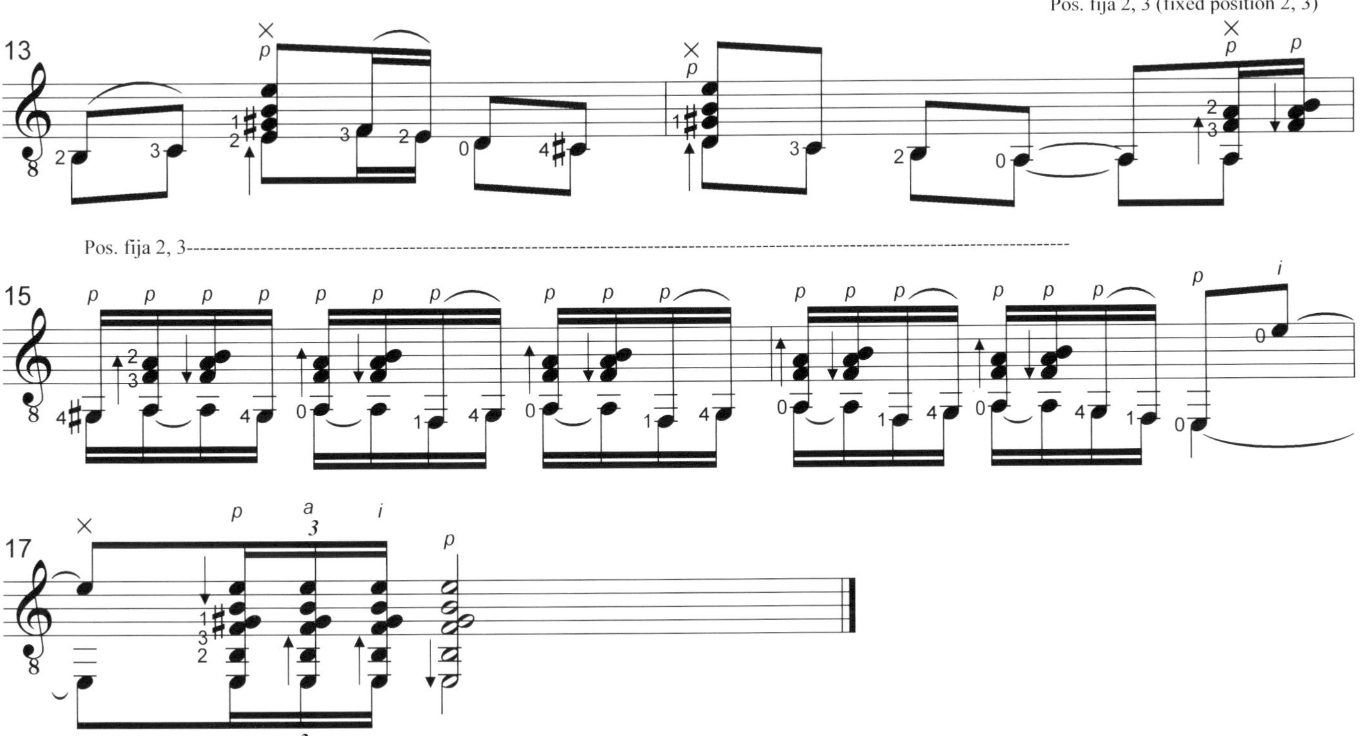

Performance Notes

1) "Posicion fija 2, 3" or "Fixed position 2, 3" indicates fixed fingers on the notes held by fingers 2 and 3.

2) "Rebote de muñeca" or "bounce the wrist" indicates a bouncing motion to play subsequent strokes in the same direction.

3) "p-p-i" is an old type of alzapúa (to come forth or raise up with the thumb) which creates a melody with "p" and accompaniment with "i." The composite sound of the three notes (two melodic notes in the bass, and an upper pedal tone) makes a harmony (mm. 5-6). The resulting melodic rhythm is an uneven division of the beat into three parts. The first note is a quarter-note and the second is an eighth. This is known as "swing" or "notes inégales" in French-Baroque performance practice.

4) "p-p-p" (down-up-down) begins at the end of measure 6, and creates a melody in the bass voice with the same "swing" rhythm. Simultaneously with the first melodic bass note, are two strokes of eighth-note duration (down-up) on 2-3 notes, creating a chord.

5) When playing the rasgueado in measures 2 and 11, anchor the thumb on the sixth string.

6) The chords for the introduction to the "copla" of the Fandango is shown below:

Intro: above

Copla: (G7) | C - C - C7/G - F |

(G7) | C - C - D/F# - G |

| G - G - G7 - C |

| C - C - C7/G - F |

| F - F - F(aug.6)- E |

Llamada/cierre:

(Bm7♭5) | Am - Am - (G7) - F - E |

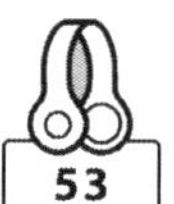

Pic5. Bulerías picados

Richard Marlow
Edited by Corey Whitehead

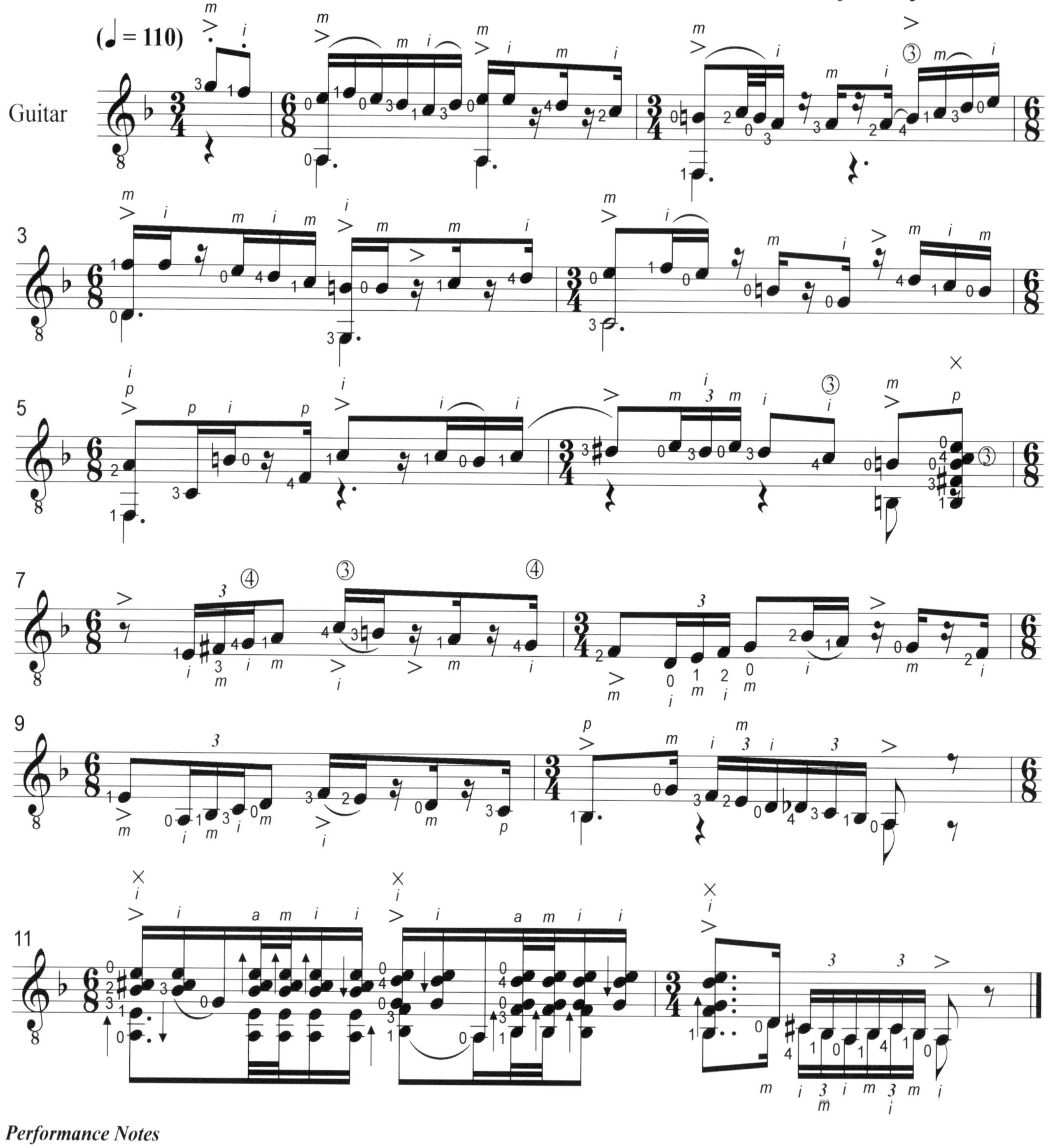

(♩ = 110)

Guitar

Performance Notes

1) The Bulerías is a 12-count phrase with the 8th note representing the pulse, organized into a measure of 6/8 and one of 3/4.

2) "Beat 12" of the cycle is the first accented note of the phrase. Often, phrases start on "beat one" or the second 8th note of the 6/8 measure.

3) This example starts on "Beat 10" or the last quarter note of the 3/4 measure.

4) When rests occur in the bass voice, prepare by placing the thumb on the string that will be played next.

5) Play picado with rest strokes. When bass notes coincide with the melody, play the bass with free strokes.

Flamenco Studies Part 2/Unit 6

R6. Fandango rasgueados

Richard Marlow
Edited by Corey Whitehead

(♩ = 140)

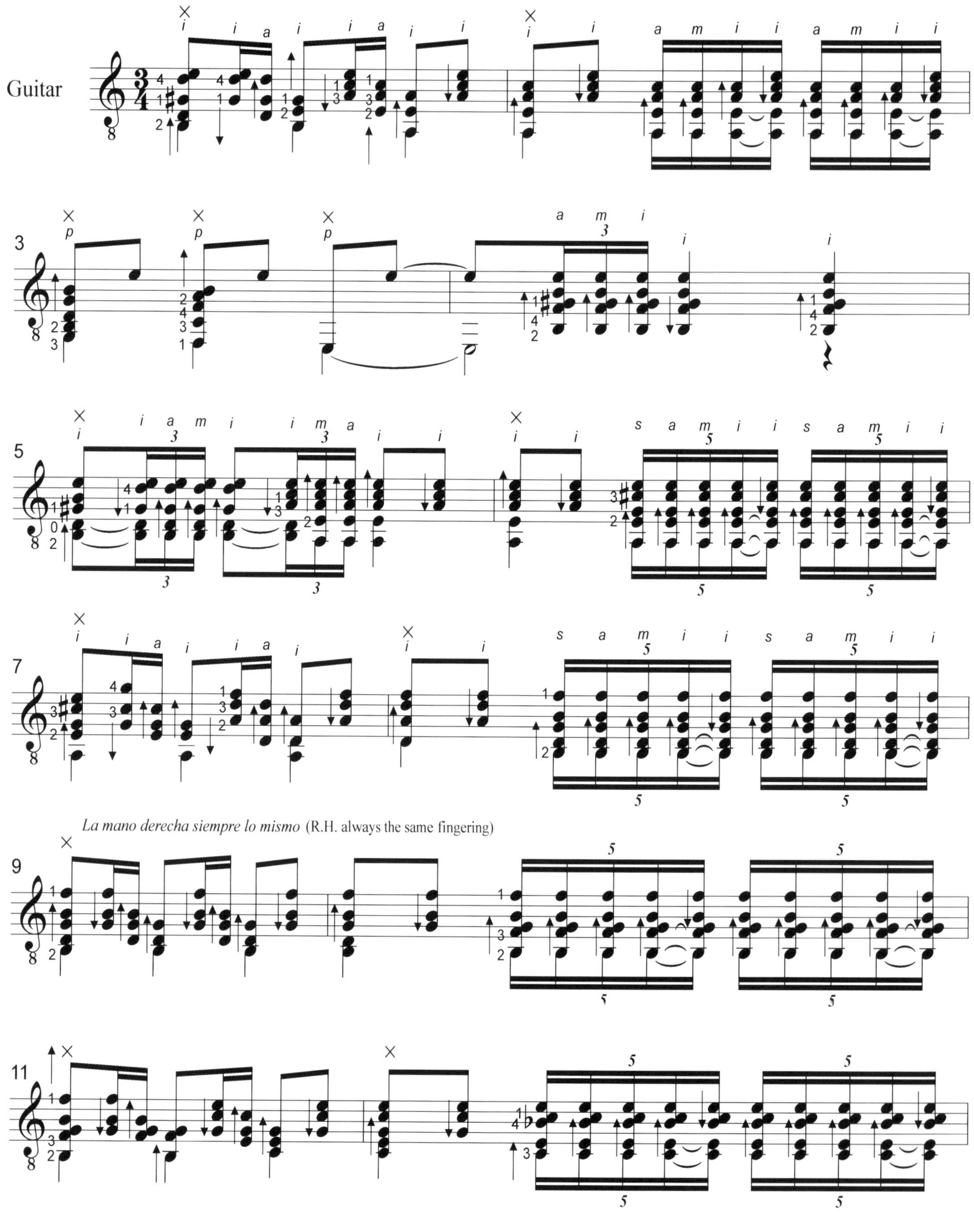

Guitar

La mano derecha siempre lo mismo (R.H. always the same fingering)

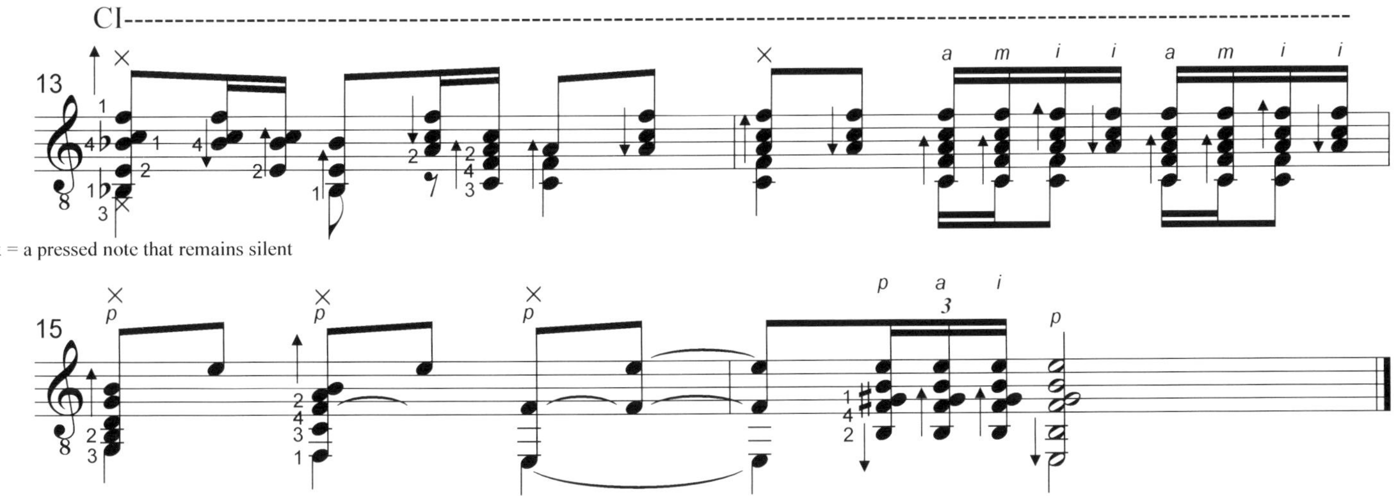

Performance Notes

1) This is a passage that serves as the introduction to the "copla" or verse of the Fandango. The term "copla" is used when referring to popular song lyrics. There are 37 regional and personal types of Fandango, each named for a person, or a place. Many of these lyrics are popular song lyrics interpreted by flamenco singers with great affectation and anguish. The most common accompaniment is shown below:

Intro: above, mm. 1-16

Copla: (G7) | C - C - C7/G - F |

(G7) | C - C - D/F# - G |

| G - G - G7 - C |

| C - C - C7/G - F |

| F - F - F(aug.6)- E |

Llamada/cierre (call/closing):

(Bm7♭5) Am - Am - (G7) - F - E |

2) This example can serve as accompaniment to a dancer or as a "llamada" or call to the singer.

3) This example presents a study in mixed rasgueados patterns.

4) Keep the thumb anchored as much as possible when playing rasgueado.

5) In measure 13, beat one, the "G" bass note with the special "x" notehead is pressed by the L.H. but does not sound. The index finger of the right hand plays an upstroke here and does not contact the 6th string. However, in measure 15 the note does sound as the 6th string is played by the thumb of the right hand and the G does sound.

Pic6. Fandango picados

Richard Marlow
Edited by Corey Whitehead

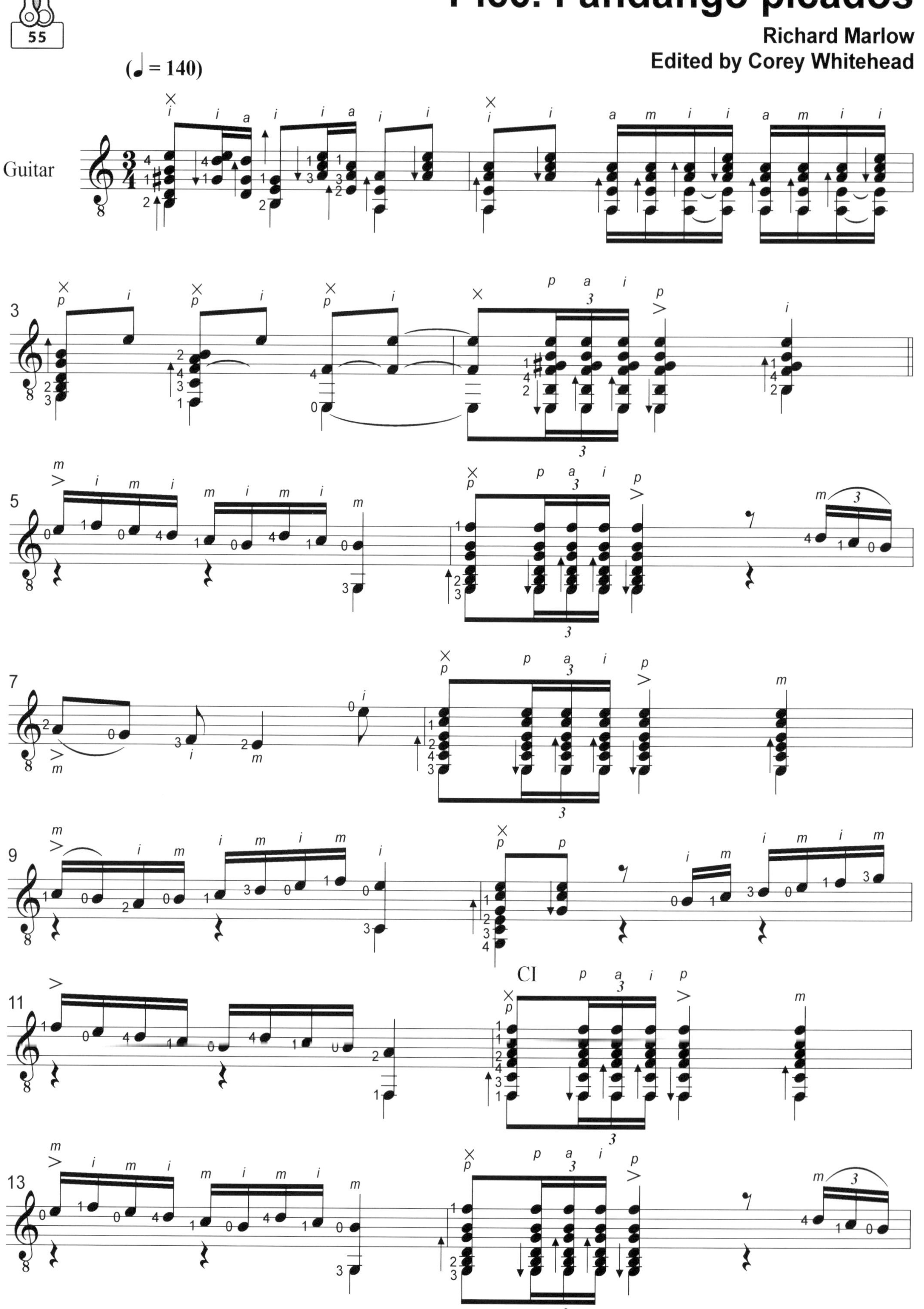

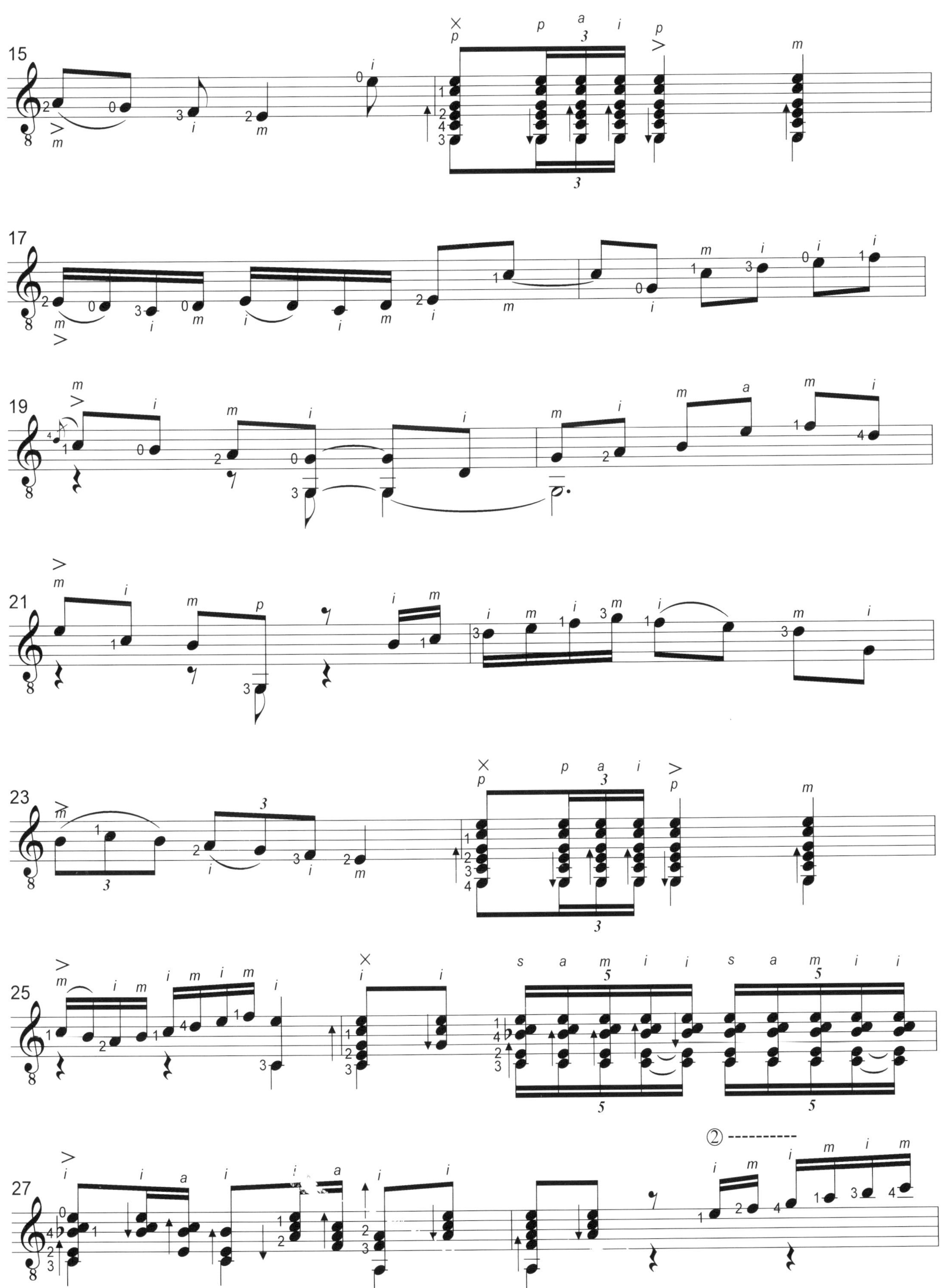

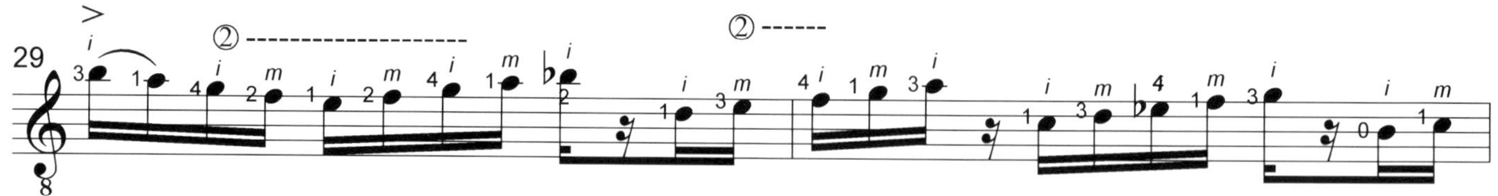

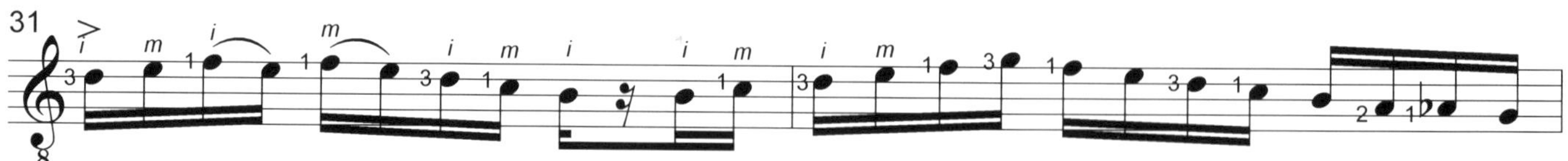

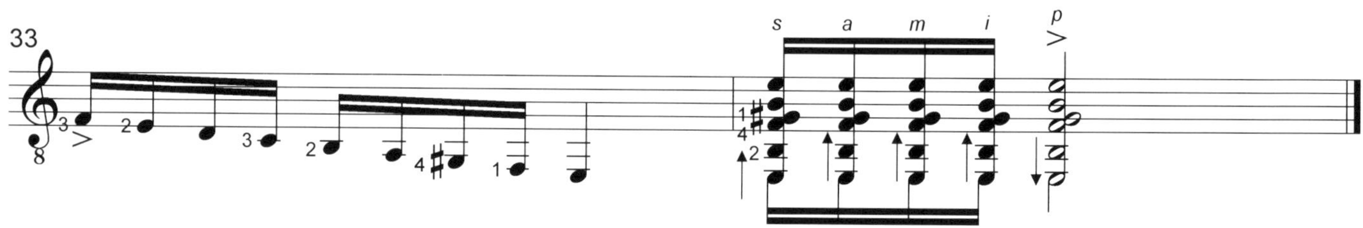

Performance Notes

1) This passage can serve as the introduction to the "falseta" or guitar solo variations of the Fandango. The most common accompaniment is shown below:

Intro: above

Copla: (G7) | C - C - C7/G - F |

(G7) | C - C - D/F# - G |

| G - G - G7 - C |

| C - C - C7/G - F |

| F - F - F(aug.6)- E |

Llamada/cierre:

(Bm7♭5) | Am - Am - (G7) - F - E |

2) Anchor the thumb on a bass string when playing picado (i-m).

3) The "x" symbol indicates a golpe with "a" simultaneously as "i" or "p" plays. Each golpe is played with the "a" finger.

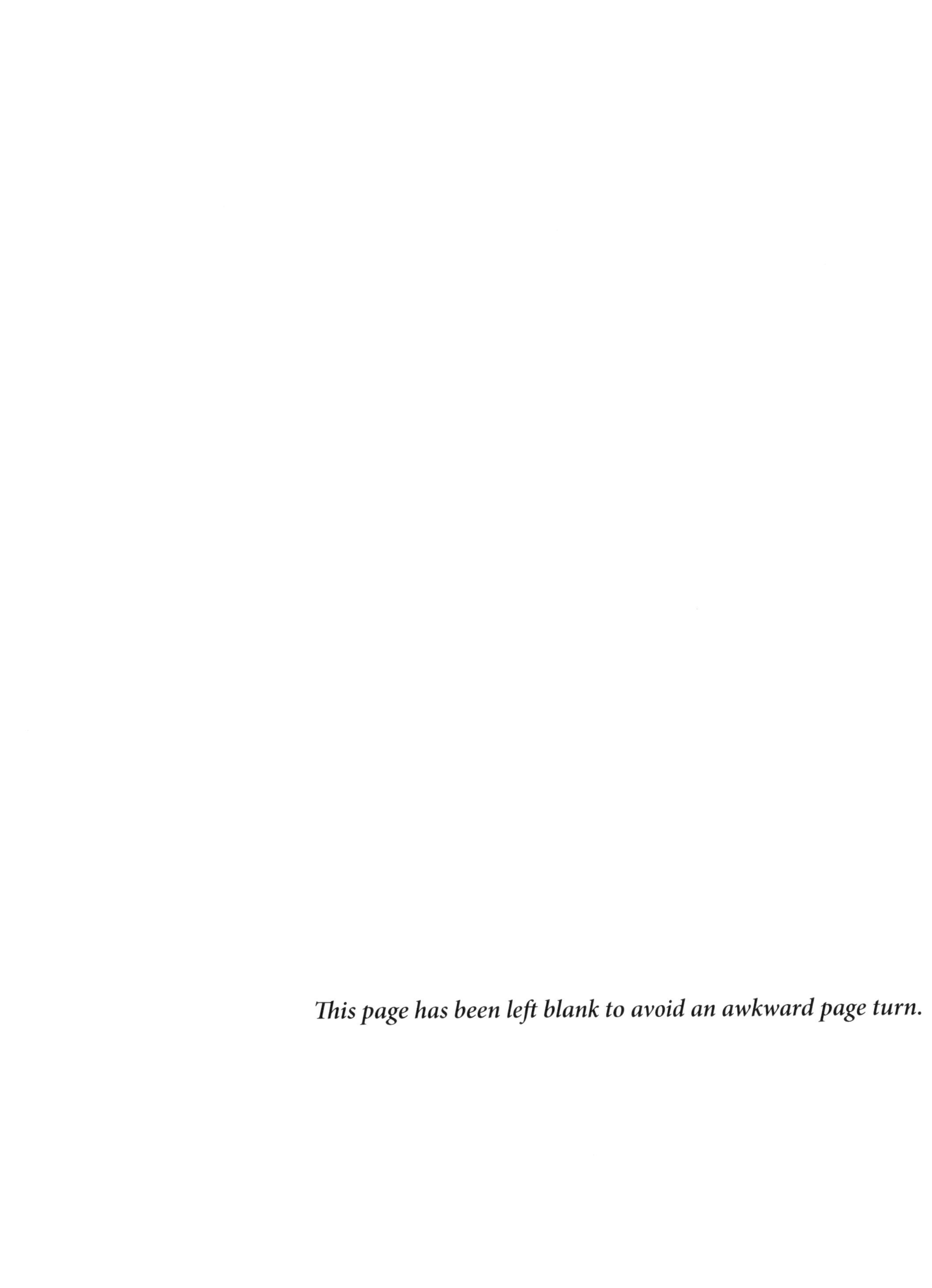

This page has been left blank to avoid an awkward page turn.

P6. Tangos alzapùa

Richard Marlow
Edited by Corey Whitehead

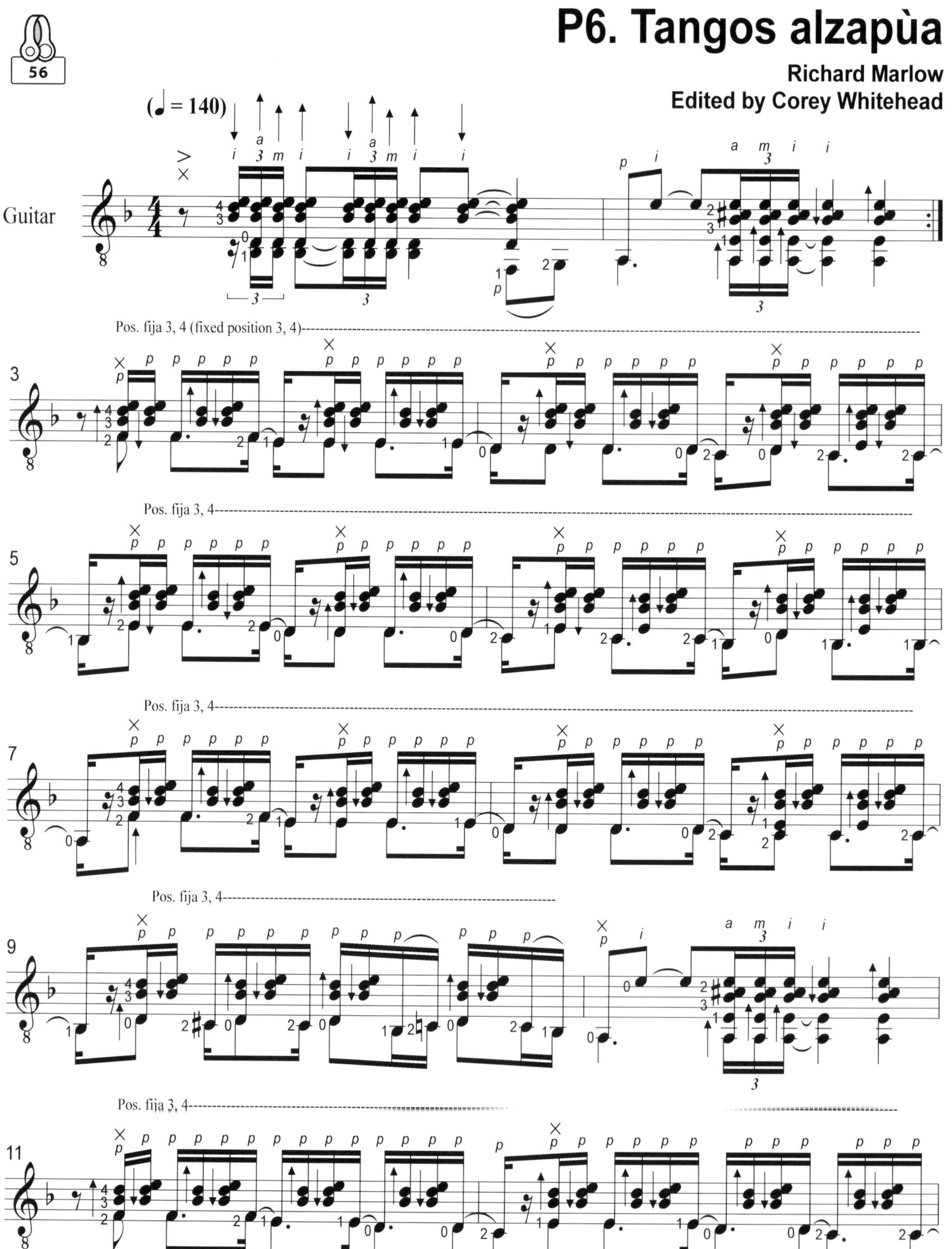

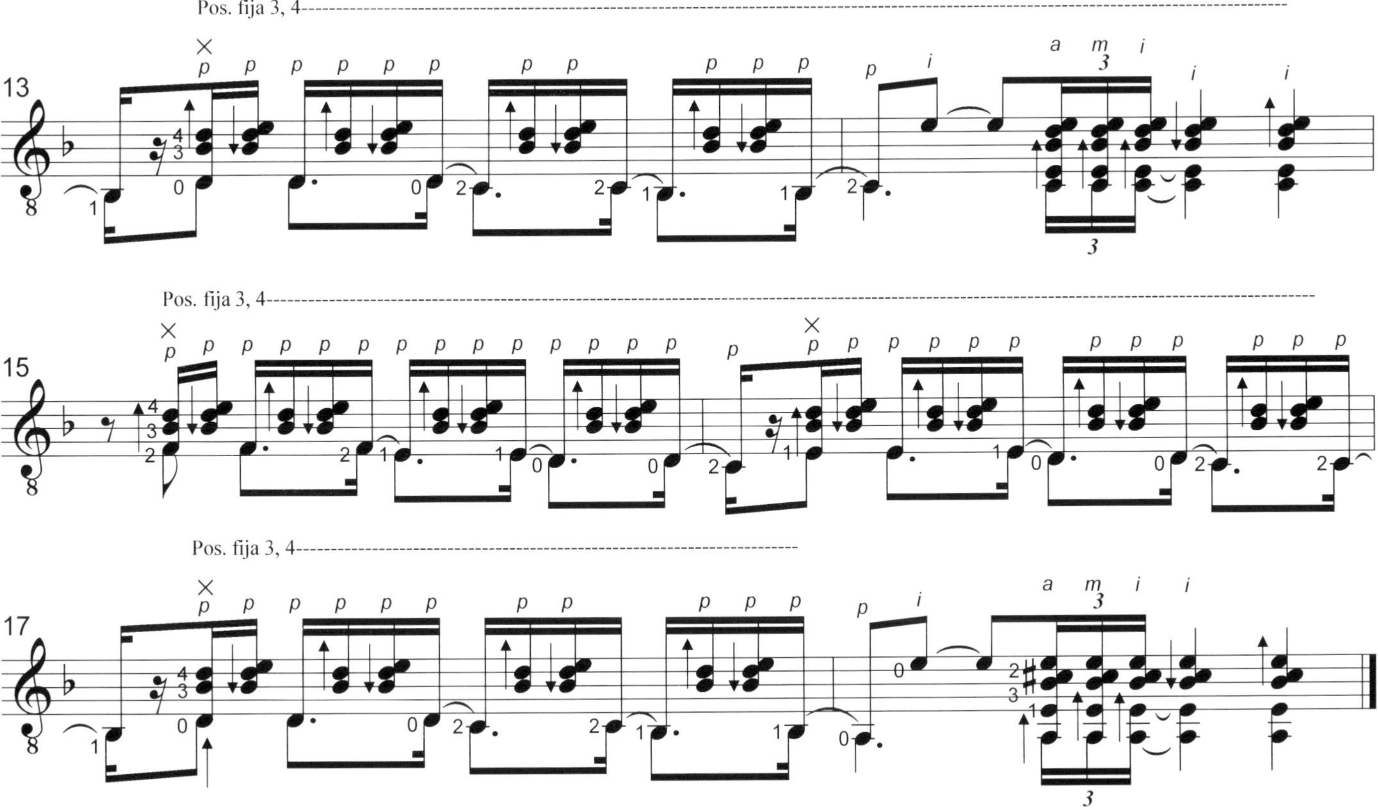

Performance Notes

1) Tangos are one of the four primary palos of flamenco, and the only palo with 8 counts or two measures of 4/4 or common time.

2) The pulse accents for the feet are on counts 1 and 3. Beats 2 and 4 are where the palmas (clapping) and guitar accents reside.

3) All instruments "break" or close on beat 3 of the second measure of 4/4.

4) The "x" symbol indicates a golpe with "a-m," either alone or simultaneously with the downstroke of the thumb.

5) R.H fingers "a-m" may rest gently on the golpeador as the alzapúa is played.

6) This kind of alzapúa "jumps" the beat or anticipates the arrival of the chord with two 16th notes.

7) This example can serve as an intro to the cante (song), or as a solo variation (falseta), or as accompaniment to a dancer.

Flamenco Studies
Part 2/Unit 7

P7. Soleá por bulerías alzapúa

Richard Marlow
Edited by Corey Whitehead

(♩ = 135)

16ths, p-i-p "antiguo" (old rasgueado pattern)

Guitar

Pos. fija 3, 4 (fixed position 3, 4)

Pos. fija 3, 4

L.V.

Pos. fija 3, 4

Pos. fija 3, 4

C-sharp is pressed but remains silent
Pos. fija 2 en Do# (C#)

Pos. fija 3, 4

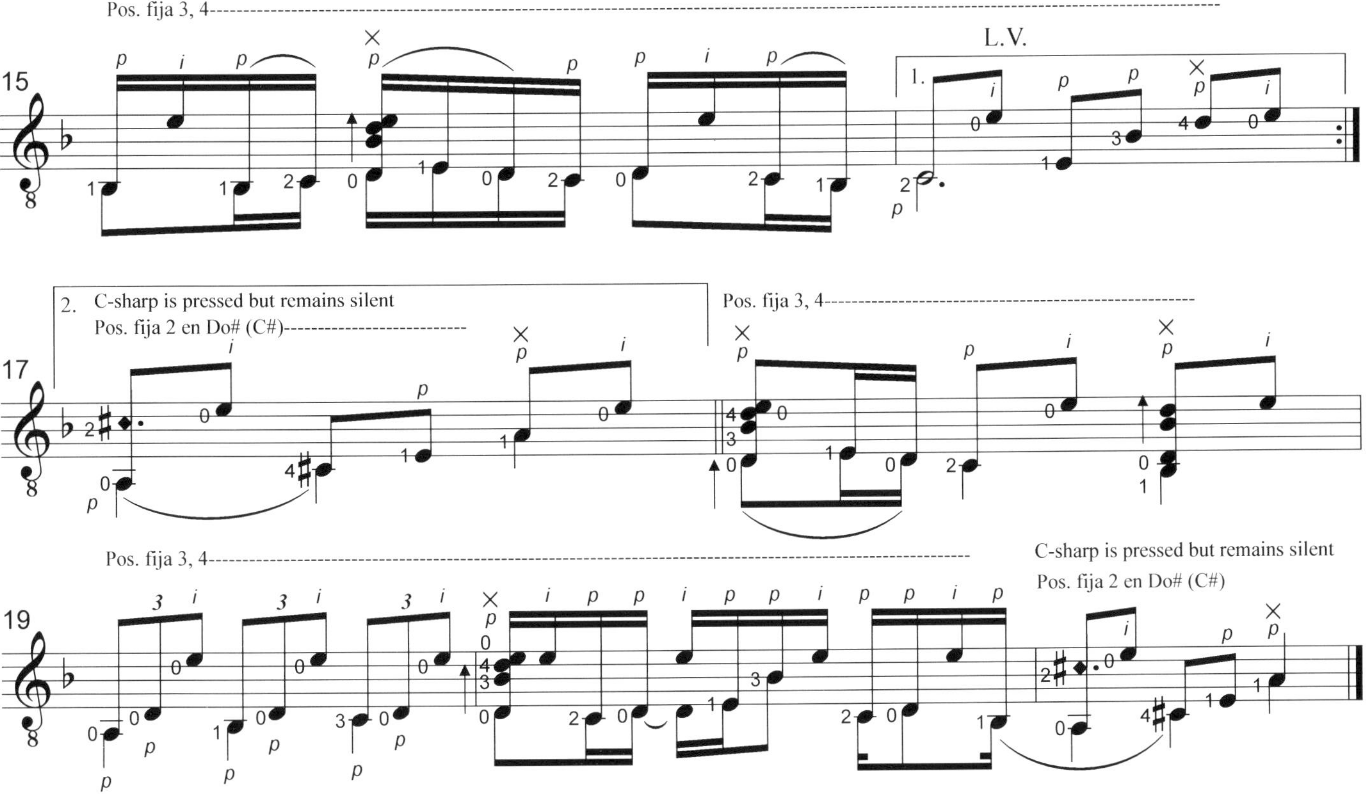

Performance Notes

1) The "C#" (Do sostenido) in "Posicion fija 2 en Do#" does not sound. This applies to all diamond-shaped noteheads in this book. The second finger is prepared or anchored on "C#" for subsequent measures playing the A chord to follow.

2) The "x" symbol indicates a simultaneous golpe by "a-m" when the thumb plays.

3) Play rest stroke with the thumb in measures 4, 12, and 17.

4) The phrasing of this palo is an amalgam of four measures of 3/4, or twelve beats. The chord progression follows this meter/time signature, but is actually incorrect as the meter/time signature should demonstrate the organization of the **accented** *beats.*

5) The actual metric organization of accents in this piece is an amalgam of 3/4, 3/4, 4/4, and 2/4. The first measure of 3/4 features an anacrusis/pickup.
Chords: **|:** *1-2-**3*** | *4-5-**6*** | *7-8-9* | ***10**-11-**12*** **:|**
Meter: **|:** *2-3*|***1*** *- 2-3*|***1*** *-2-3-4* | ***1*** *- 2* | ***1*** **:|**

6) The palo, "Soleá por bulerías" is meant to accompany the lyrics (letras) and melody of the Soleá with the rhythm of a Bulerías.

7) Some would argue that the sound of the rhythm of the dancers is more closely related to Alegrías, which is, in fact, a faster Soleá.

8) The chord progression follows the melody, which is associated with the Soleares letras (lyrics).

9) Soleares is typically played "por arriba" or in "Mi" (E), except in Jerez de la Frontera where Soleares are played "por medio" in "La" (A).

R7. Bulerías rasgueados

Richard Marlow
Edited by Corey Whitehead

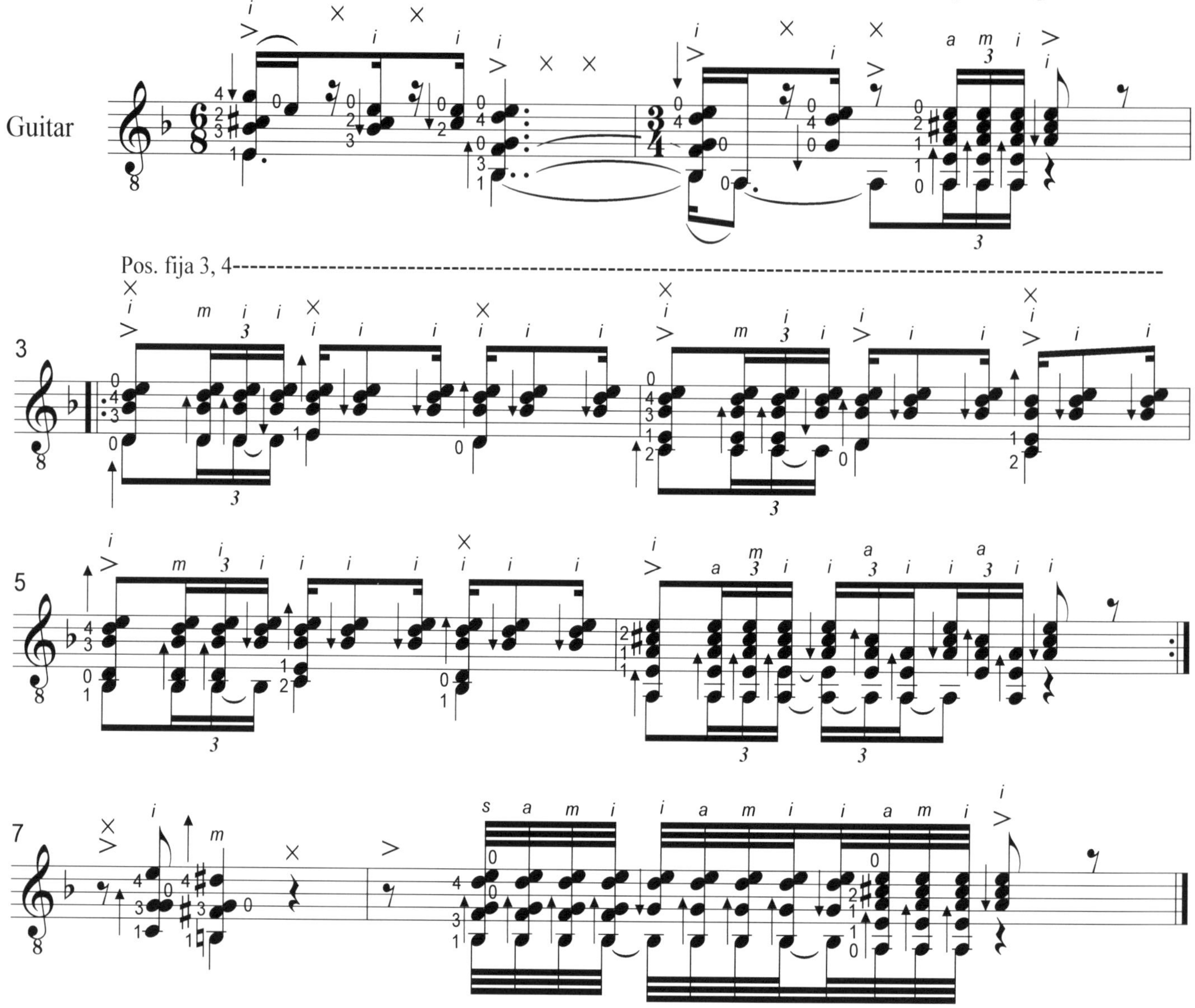

Guitar

Pos. fija 3, 4

Performance Notes

1) The Bulerías is a 12-count phrase with the 8th note representing the pulse, and organized into a measure of 6/8 and one of 3/4.

2) "Beat 12" of the cycle is the first accented beat of the phrase. Phrases often start on "beat one" or the second 8th note of the 6/8 measure.

3) Measure 7 is felt in 6/8 or two groups of three eighth notes.

4) Measures 3-7 are written in 3/4 meter as this typical rasgueado progression uses a repeating pattern of two eighth notes.

5) The two-note pattern described above fills one beat of 3/4 time.

6) Anchor the thumb on the 6th string in measures 1 and 2.

7) The thumb may shift its anchor point to the golpeador and the 6th string together in measures 4-8.

8) The "x" symbol placed over the "i" finger indicates a golpe with "a-m" simultaneously with the stroke of "i."

Flamenco Studies
Part 2/Unit 8

R8. Verdiales rasgueados

Richard Marlow
Edited by Corey Whitehead

59

p-a-i "abanico"

(♩ = 110)

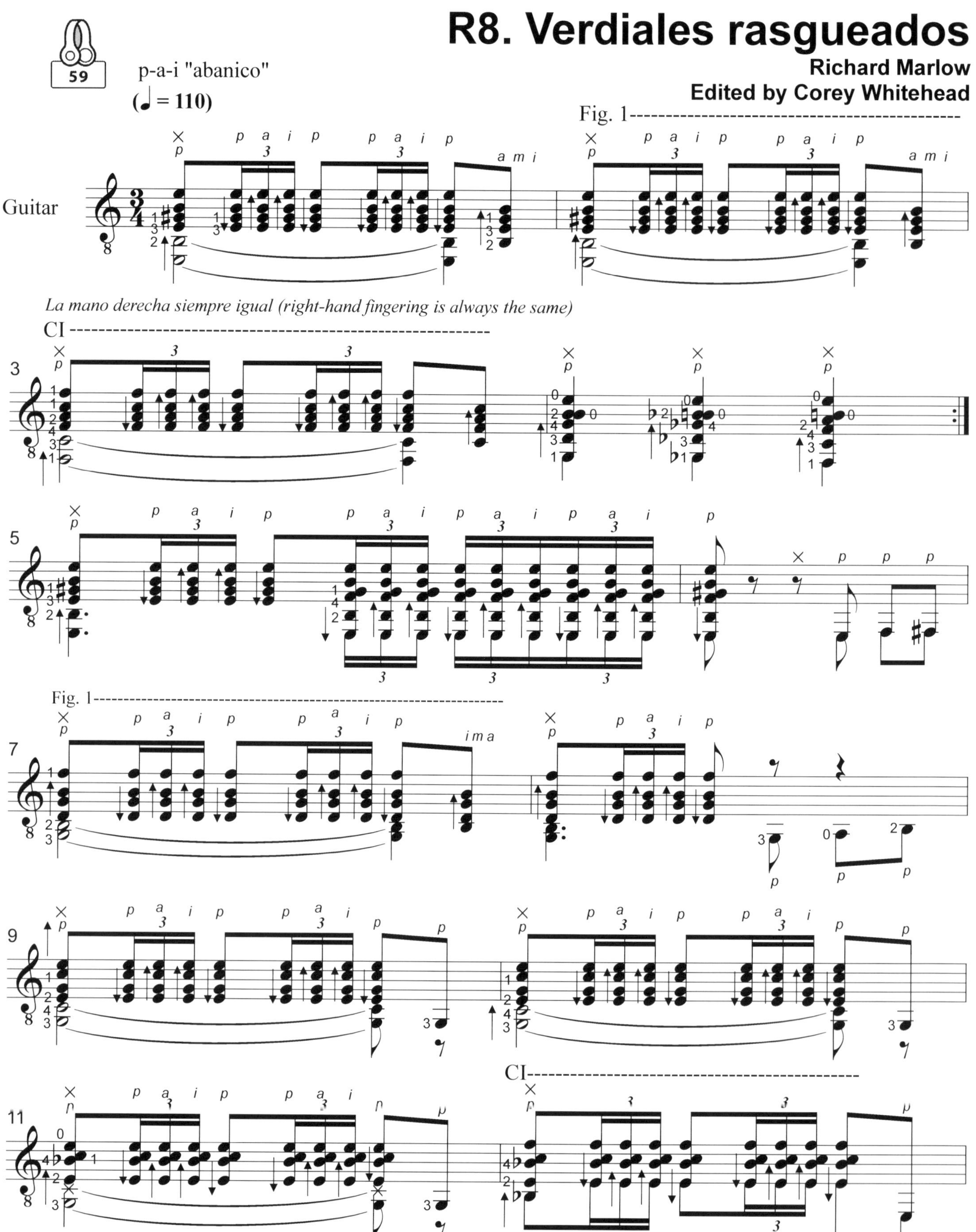

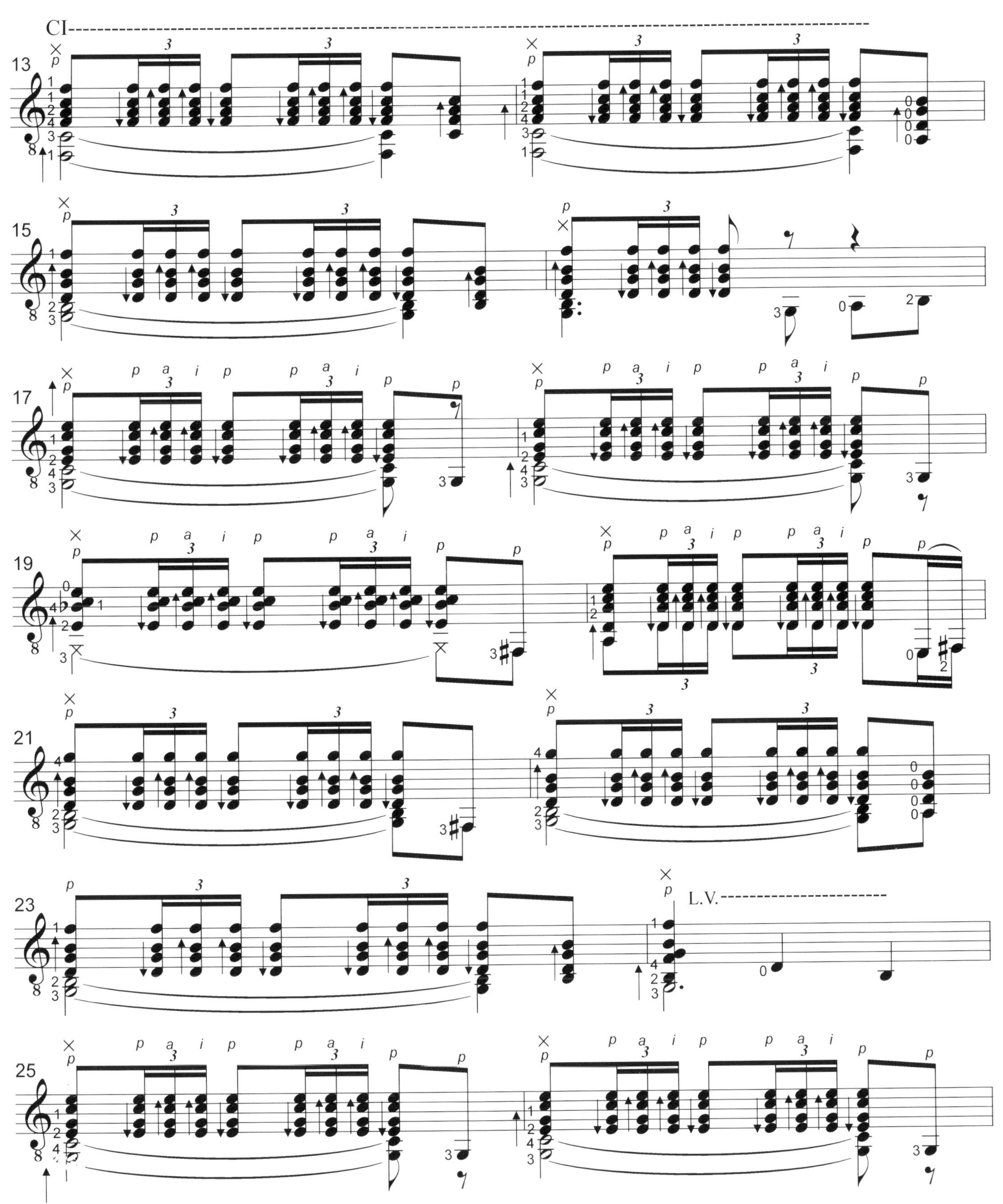
CI
L.V.

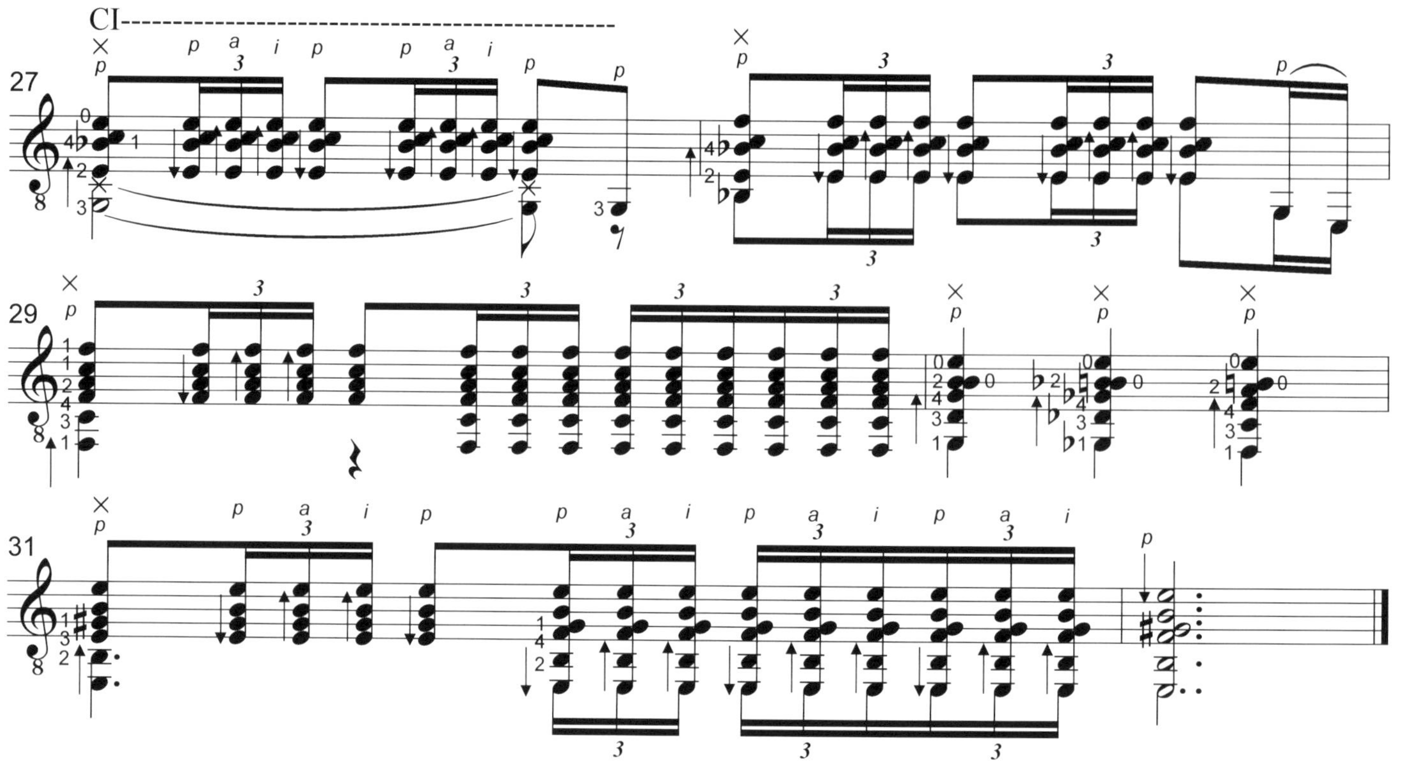

Performance Notes

1) Verdiales were cultivated in the first part of the 19th century and have their roots in the folkloric music of Málaga.

2) The lyrics and accompaniment follow the progression of the Fandango.

3) It is common for Verdiales to be accompanied by violin, oud, lute, pandero, and castanets.

4) Large choral call-and-response arrangements are common.

5) Verdiales are also arranged as virtuoso solo works.

6) The "x" symbol indicates a golpe by "a-m" simultaneously with the pulgar.

7) Noteheads in mm. 11 and 27 with the "x" symbol are pressed but do not sound.

60

P8. Siguiriyas pulgar

Richard Marlow
Edited by Corey Whitehead

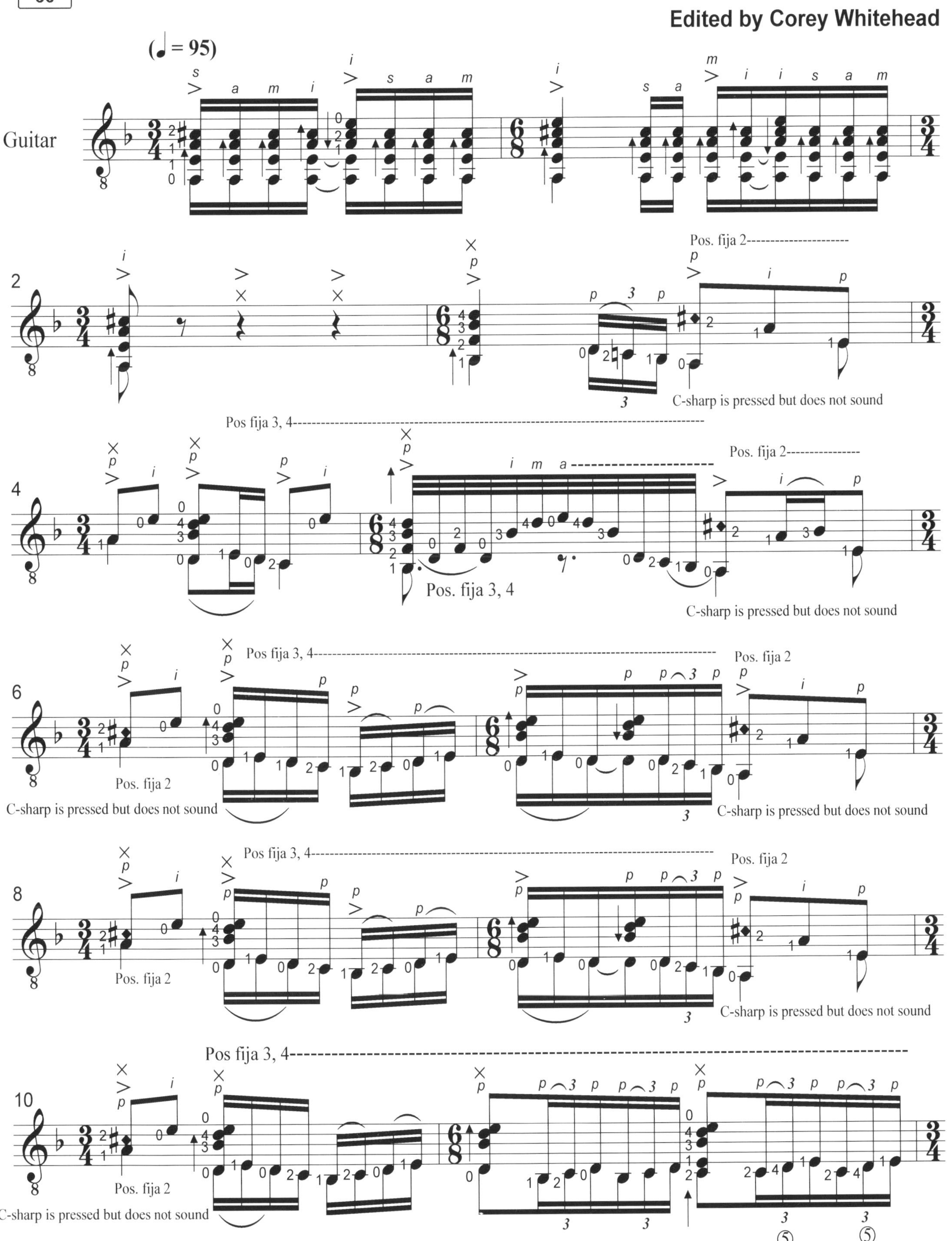

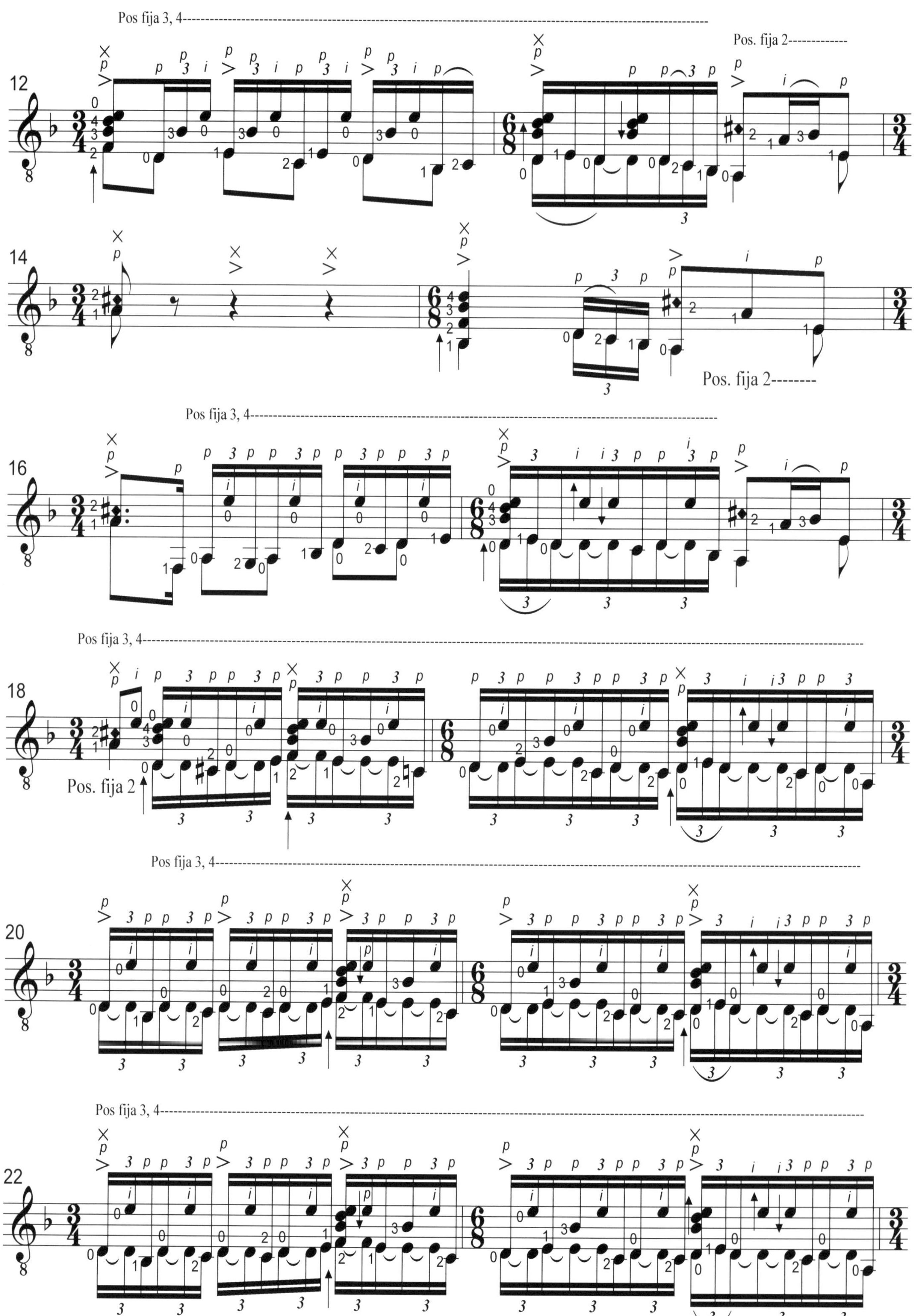

Pos fija 3, 4
Pos. fija 2
Pos. fija 2
Pos fija 3, 4
Pos fija 3, 4
Pos. fija 2
Pos fija 3, 4
Pos fija 3, 4

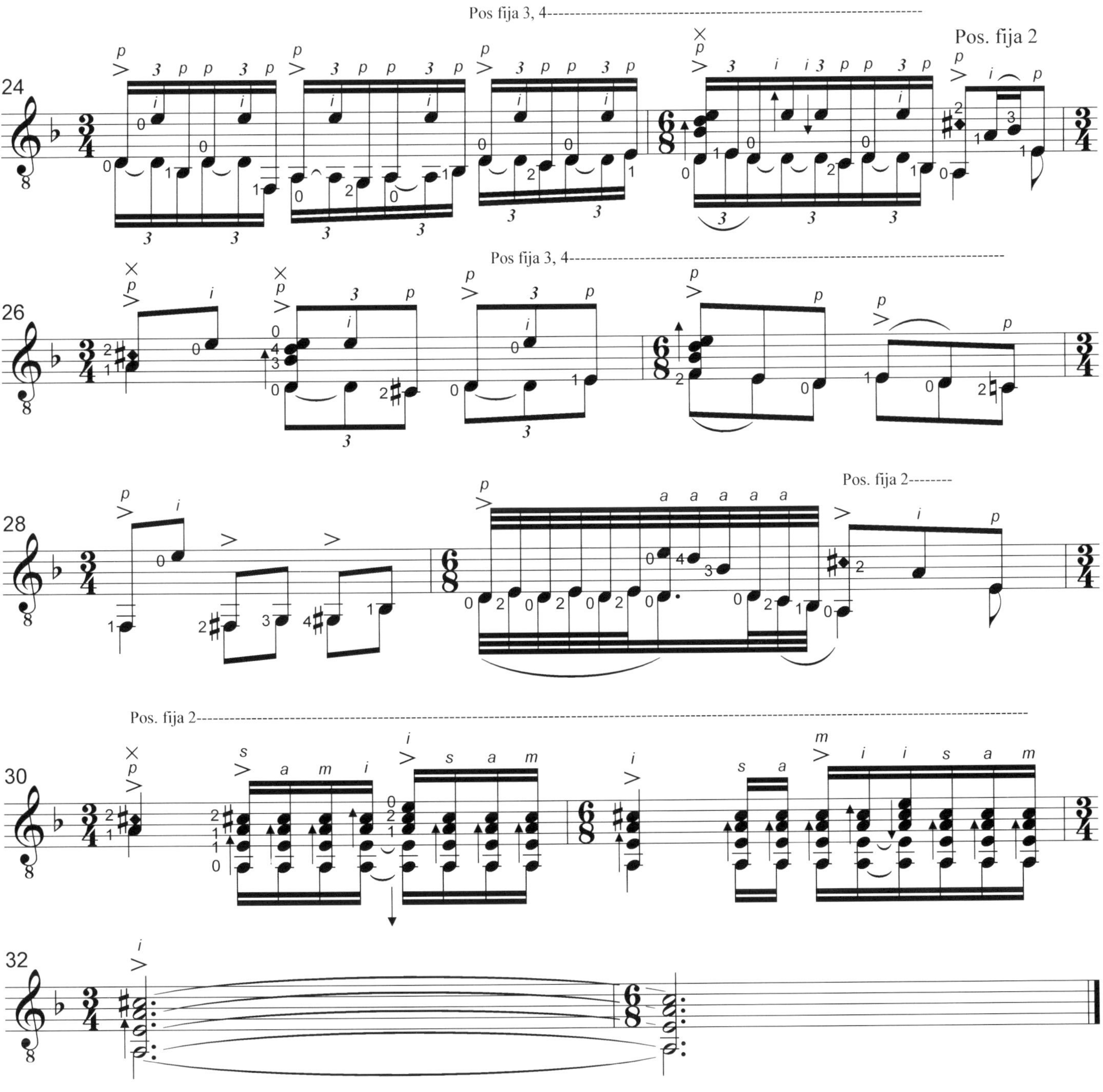

Performance Notes

1) Siguiriyas is one of the four primary palos or forms of flamenco.

2) The sub-forms of this palo include Serranas, Livianas, and other unaccompanied forms such as Trilla, Tonada, and Martinete.

*3) The beat pattern for dancers is: |**1**-2-**1**-2-**1**-2 | **1**-2-3-**1**-2-3 |*

*or: **1 2 3 1 2***

*4) The guitarists conceptualize the phrase: **1**-2-**1**-2 | **1**-2-3-**1**-2-3 |**1**-2*

5) "Posicion fija 2 Do-#" indicates a note that is pressed and held, but not played. The note is held in order to facilitate the left-hand fingering that precedes and/or follows the measure where the diamond-head note is indicated. These notes are not to be confused with harmonics which generally are not used in flamenco music.

6) Fix the thumb on the 6th string when playing rasgueado when possible.

7) Lightly rest fingers "a-m" on the golpeador when playing alzapúa.

Appendix

The Fusion of Classical and Flamenco Guitar in Ensemble Music

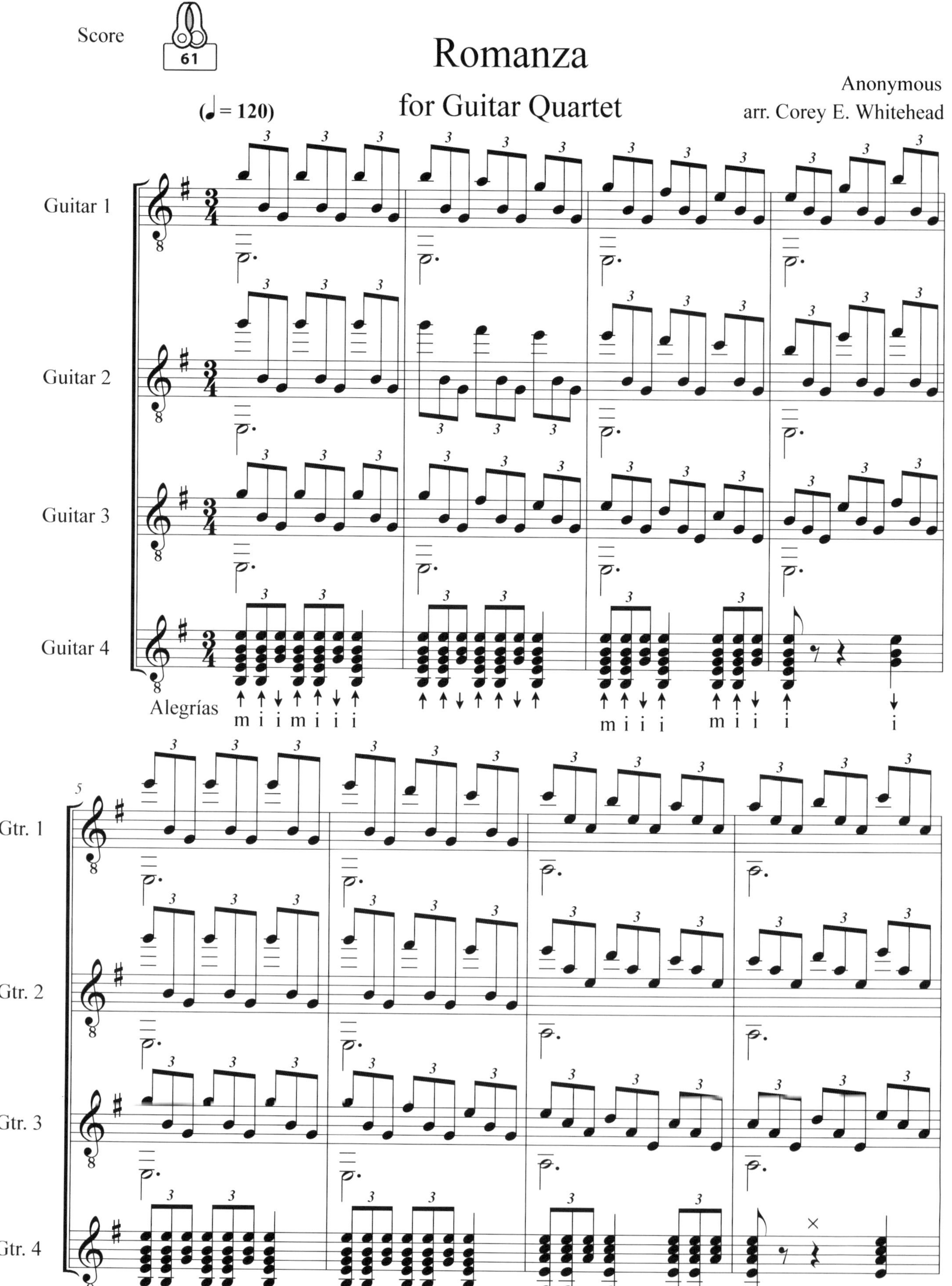
Score
61
Romanza
for Guitar Quartet
Anonymous
arr. Corey E. Whitehead
(♩ = 120)
Guitar 1
Guitar 2
Guitar 3
Guitar 4
Alegrías
m i i m i i i
m i i i
m i i
i
i
Gtr. 1
Gtr. 2
Gtr. 3
Gtr. 4

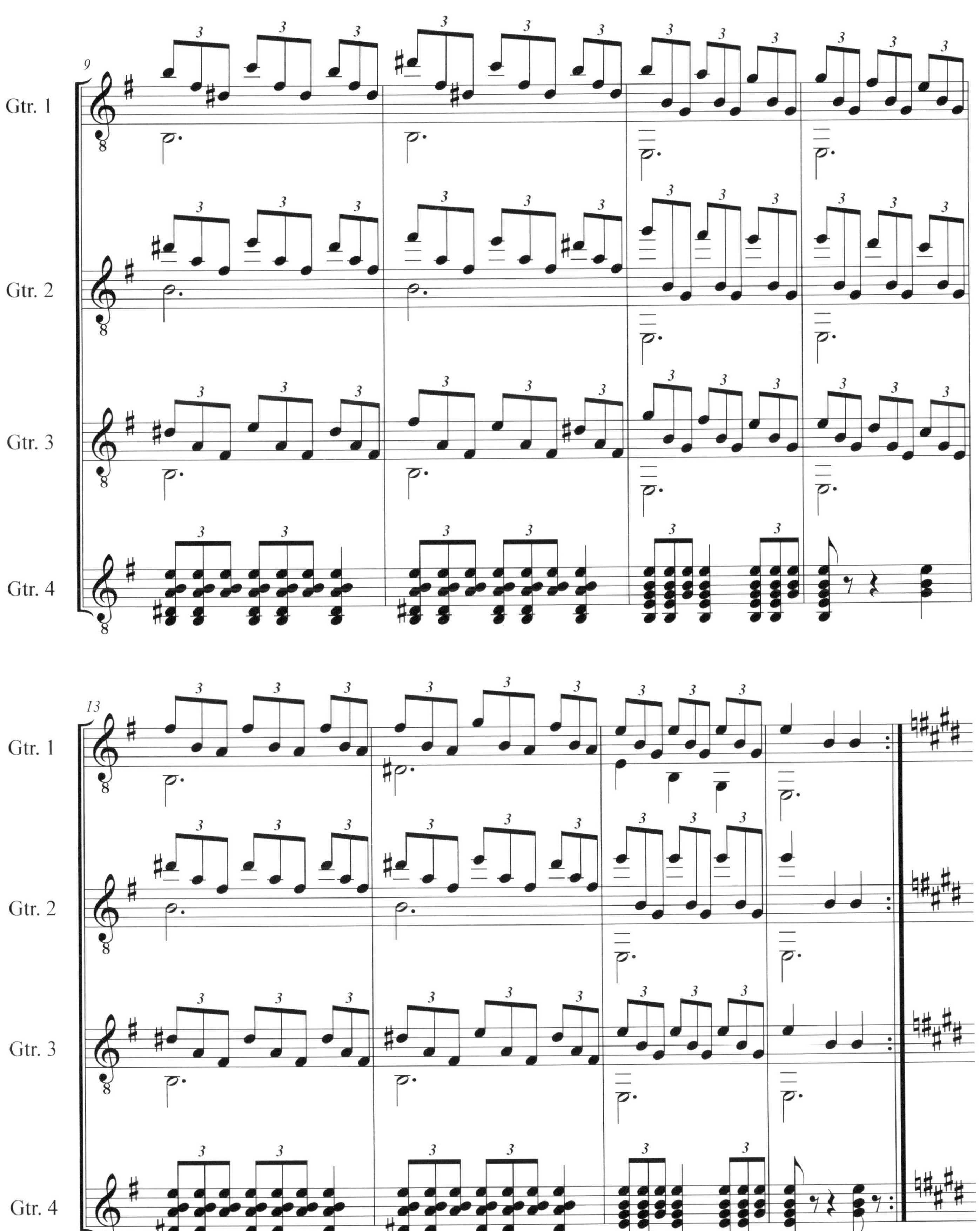

Gtr. 1
Gtr. 2
Gtr. 3
Gtr. 4

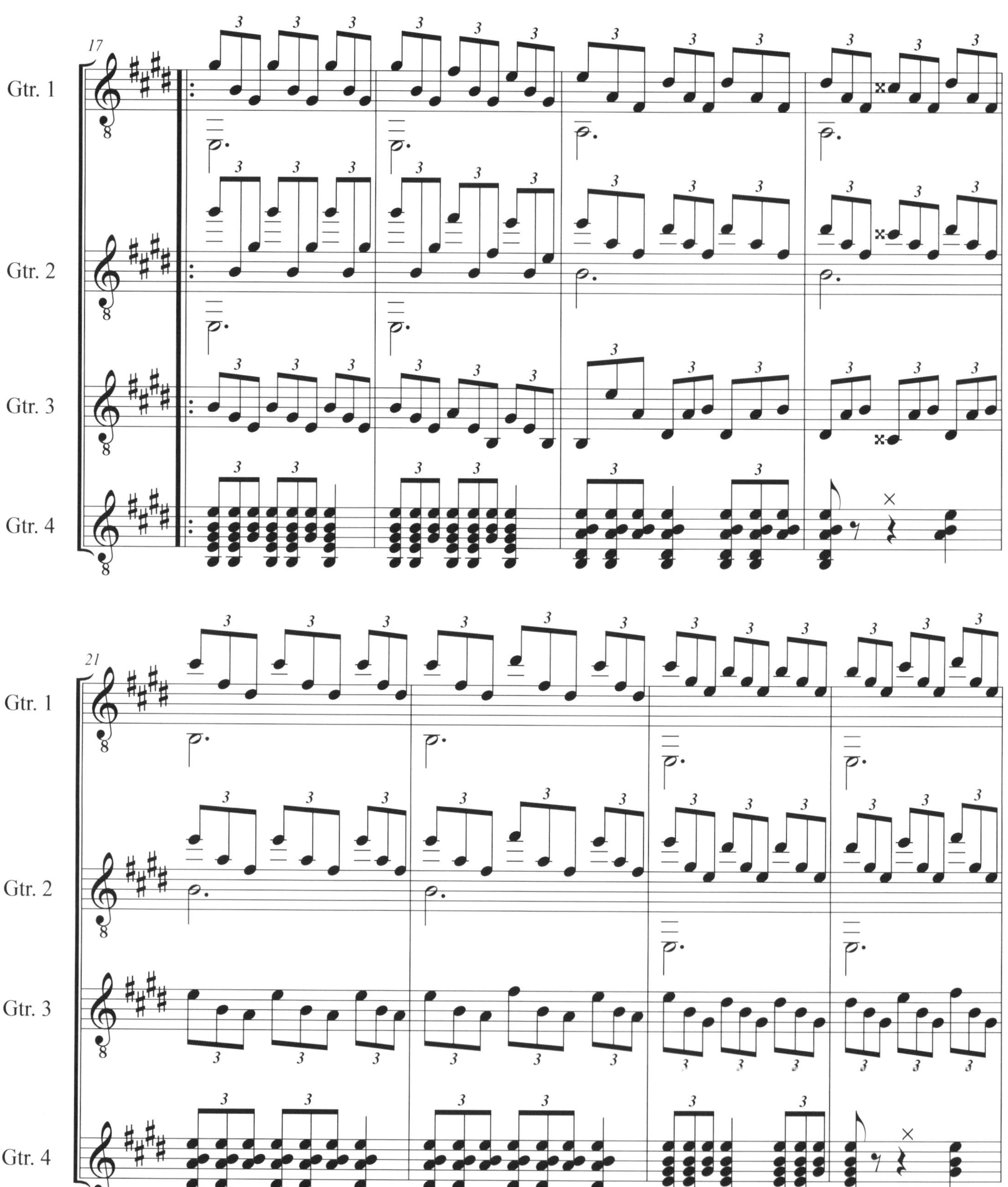

17
Gtr. 1
Gtr. 2
Gtr. 3
Gtr. 4
21
Gtr. 1
Gtr. 2
Gtr. 3
Gtr. 4

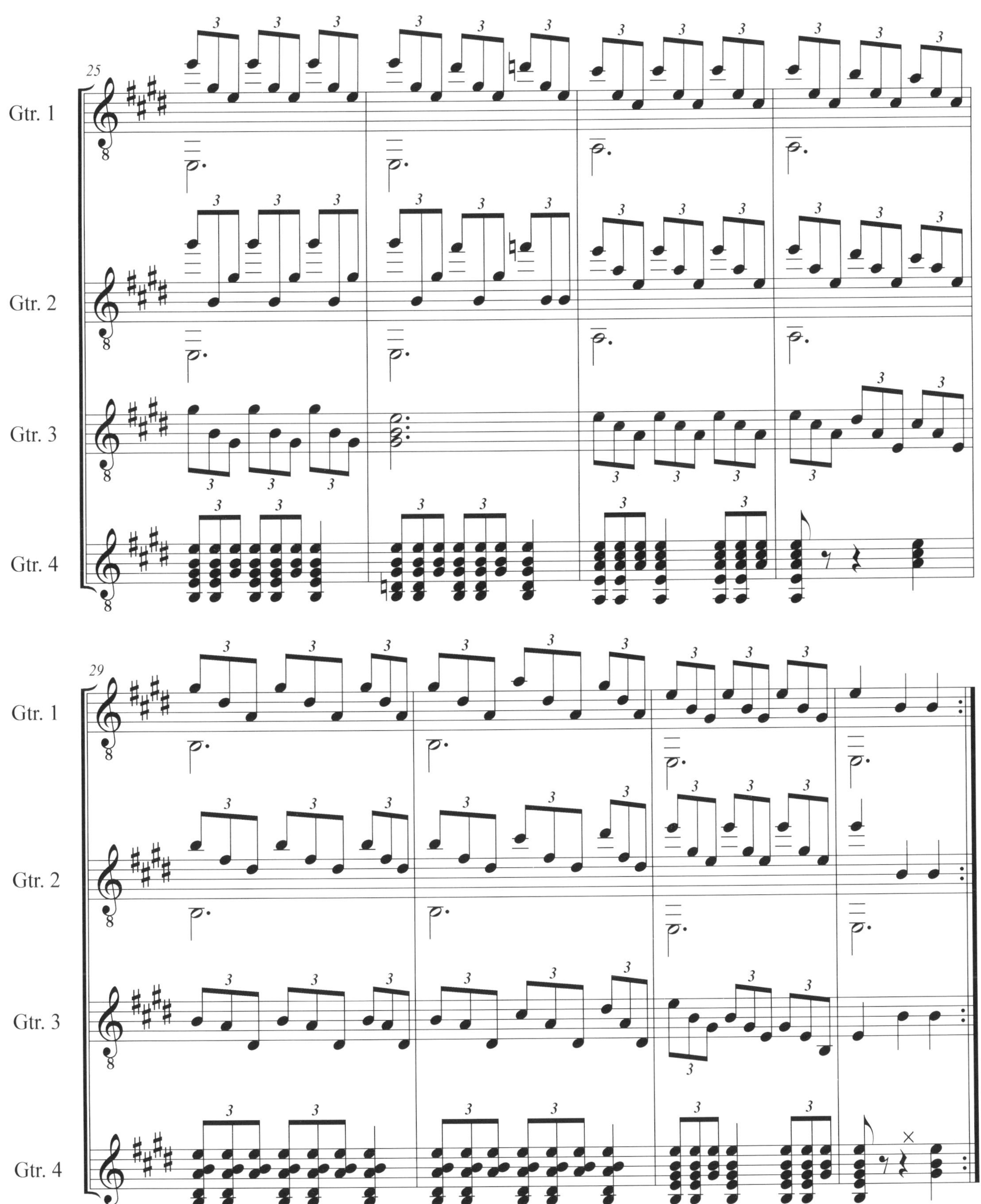
25
Gtr. 1
Gtr. 2
Gtr. 3
Gtr. 4
29
Gtr. 1
Gtr. 2
Gtr. 3
Gtr. 4

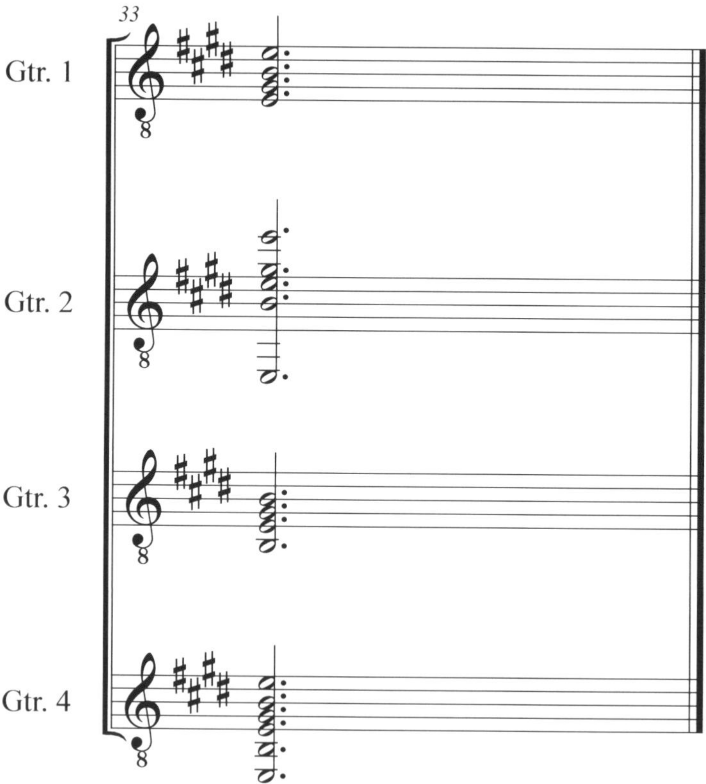

Performance Notes

1) *This arrangement of "Romanza" for guitar quartet differs from the quartet arrangement published by Juan Serrano in his book "Flamenco Guitar: Solo Selections" in several ways. This arrangement is in 12/8 rather than 4/4. Juan Serrano's arrangement in 4/4 creates a rumba pattern by subtracting one 8th note from each measure. This arrangement creates the feeling of "Alegrías de Córdoba" or "Alegrías in E Minor."*

2) *The accompaniment may be strummed with an "abanico" or other rasgueado pattern for a different "aire." For example: one may strum "up-down-down" with various finger combinations such as "p-a-i" or "p-m-p." Each pattern will create emphasis on particular strings while avoiding other strings by virtue of motion.*

3) *As a study, attempt to use all of the above strum patterns in the accompaniment (guitar 4) and use the pattern that best fits your taste.*

4) *One particular rasgueado pattern that is used in Fandango and Sevillanas may be used here as an alternative: Up-down-down with "i-a-i." This pattern produces a very light and articulate feeling. The downbeat being an upstroke creates a different sound as the high-E string is hit before the bass strings. In this case, pay close attention to the volume of the upstroke. A string upstroke works best when using this strumming pattern as an alternative.*

Romanza

for Guitar Quartet

Guitar 1

Anonymous
arr. Corey E. Whitehead

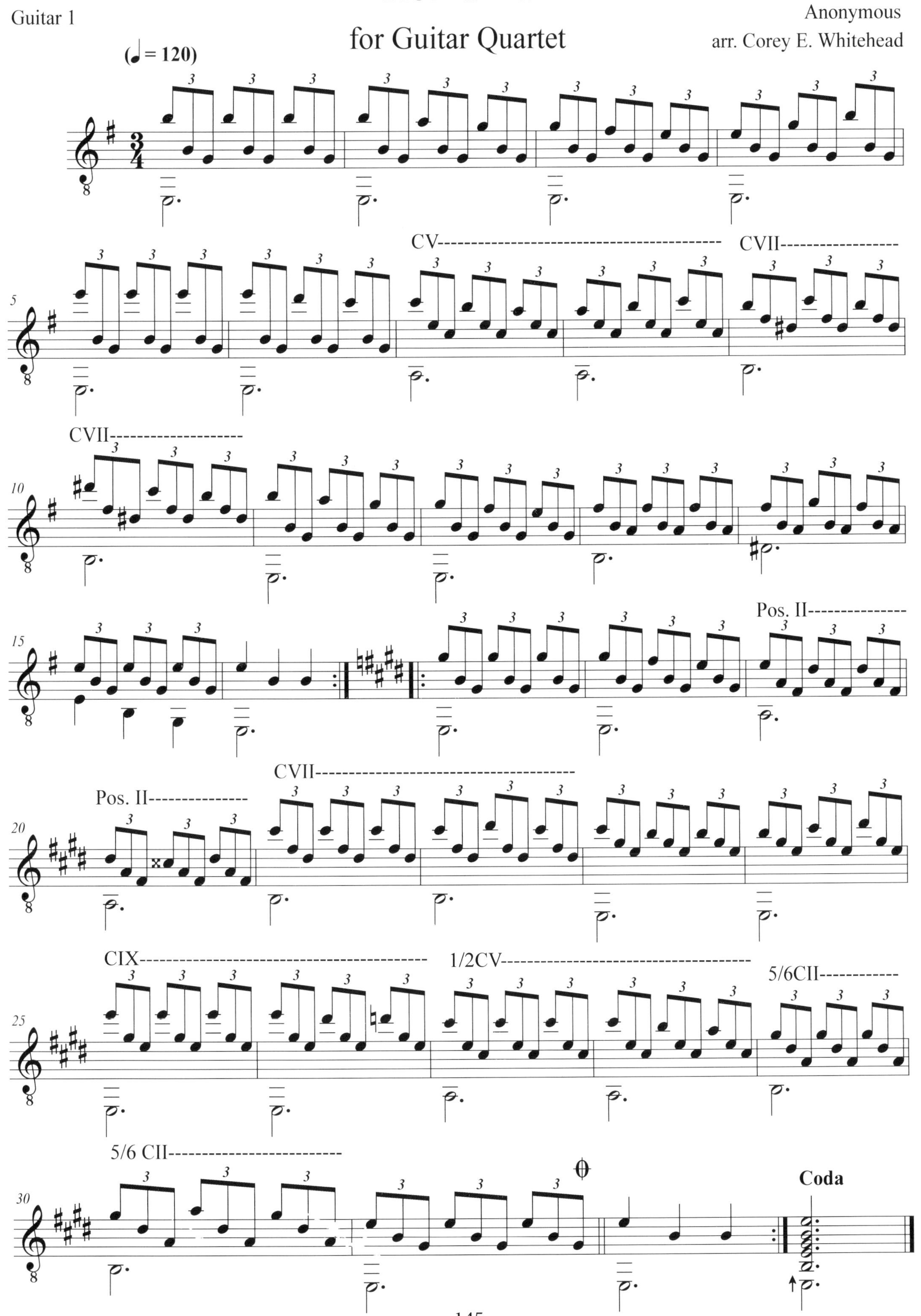

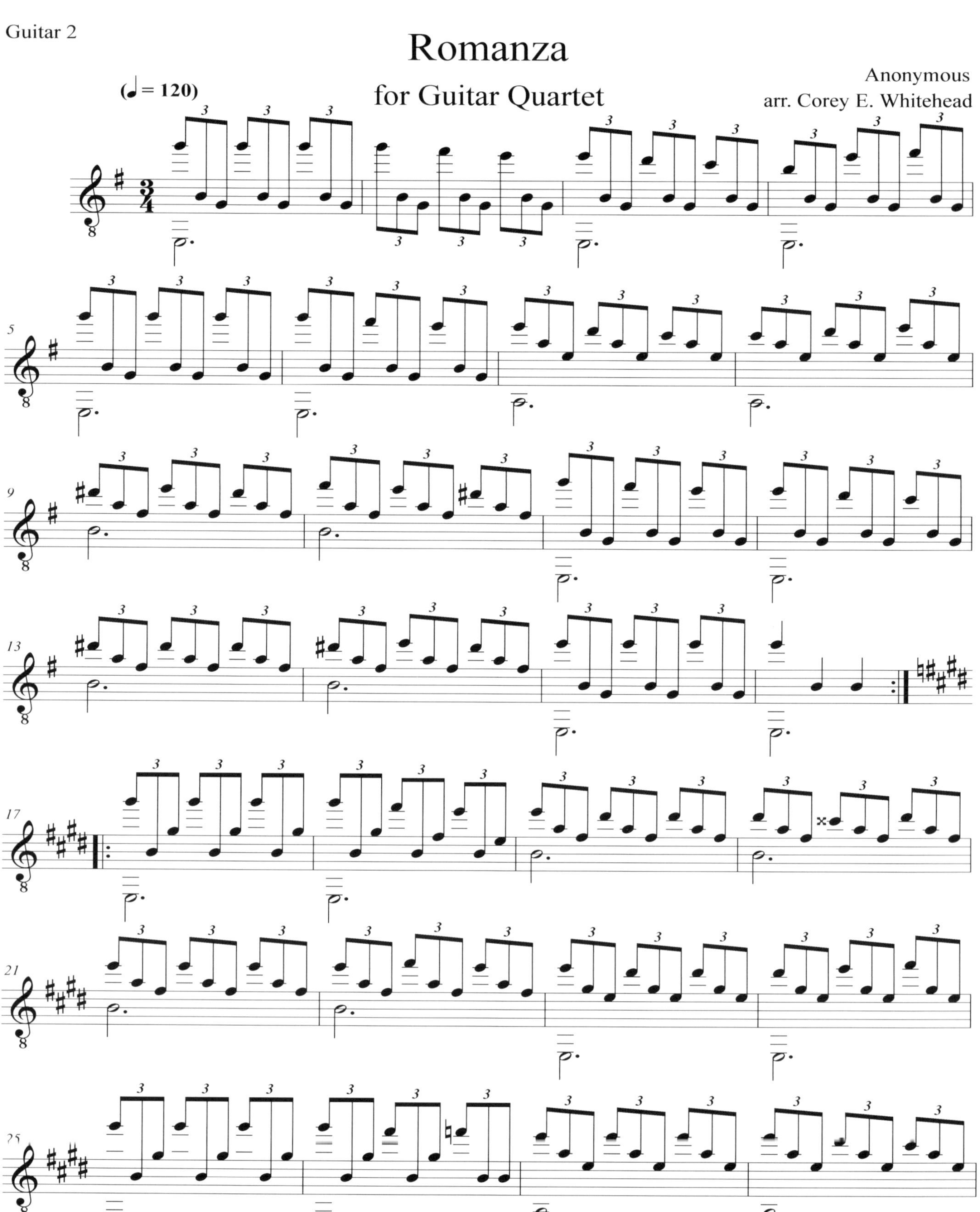
Guitar 2
Romanza
for Guitar Quartet
Anonymous
arr. Corey E. Whitehead
(♩ = 120)
Coda

Guitar 3

Romanza

for Guitar Quartet

Anonymous
arr. Corey E. Whitehead

(♩ = 120)

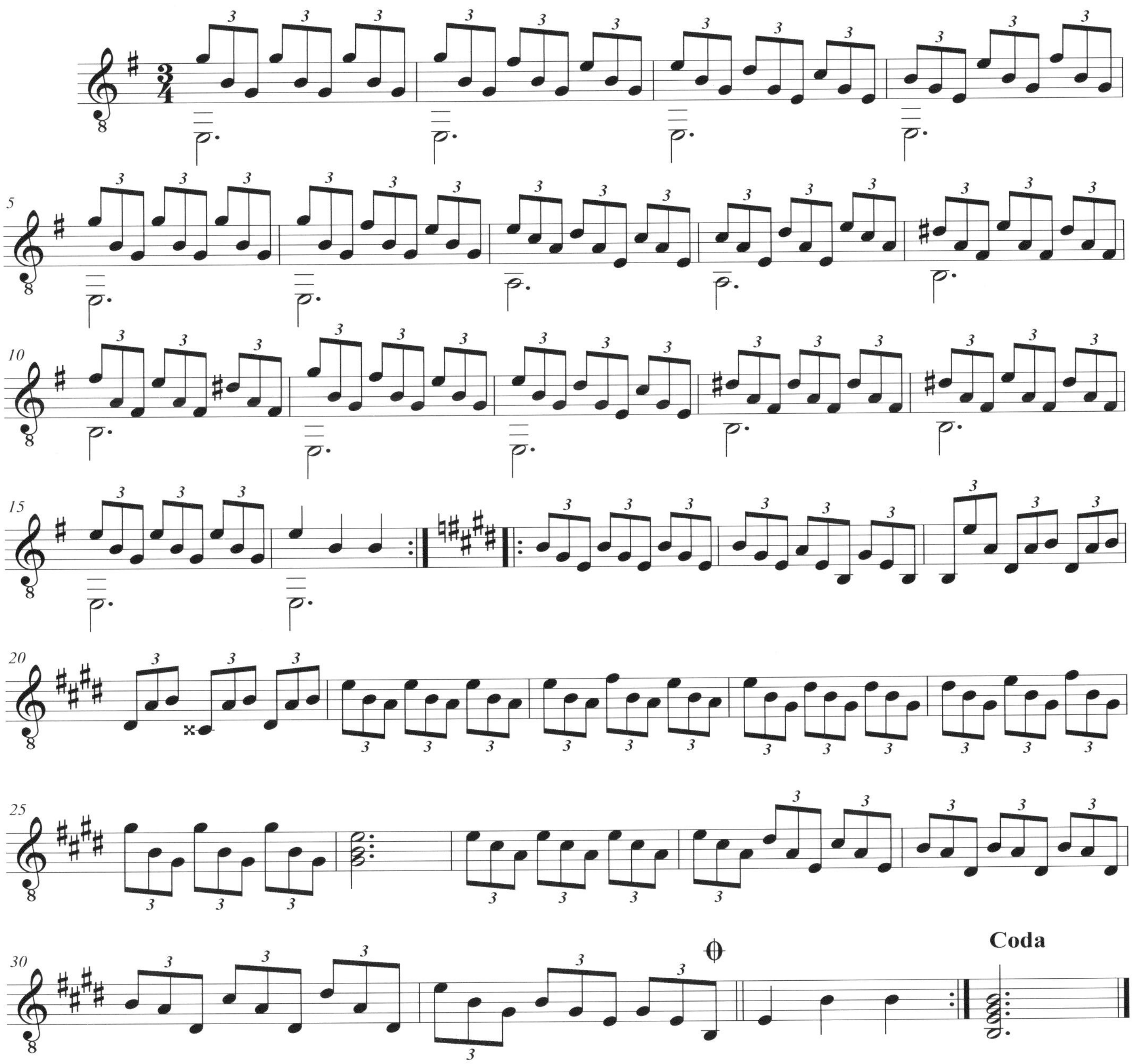

Coda

Guitar 4

Romanza

for Guitar Quartet

Anonymous
arr. Corey E. Whitehead

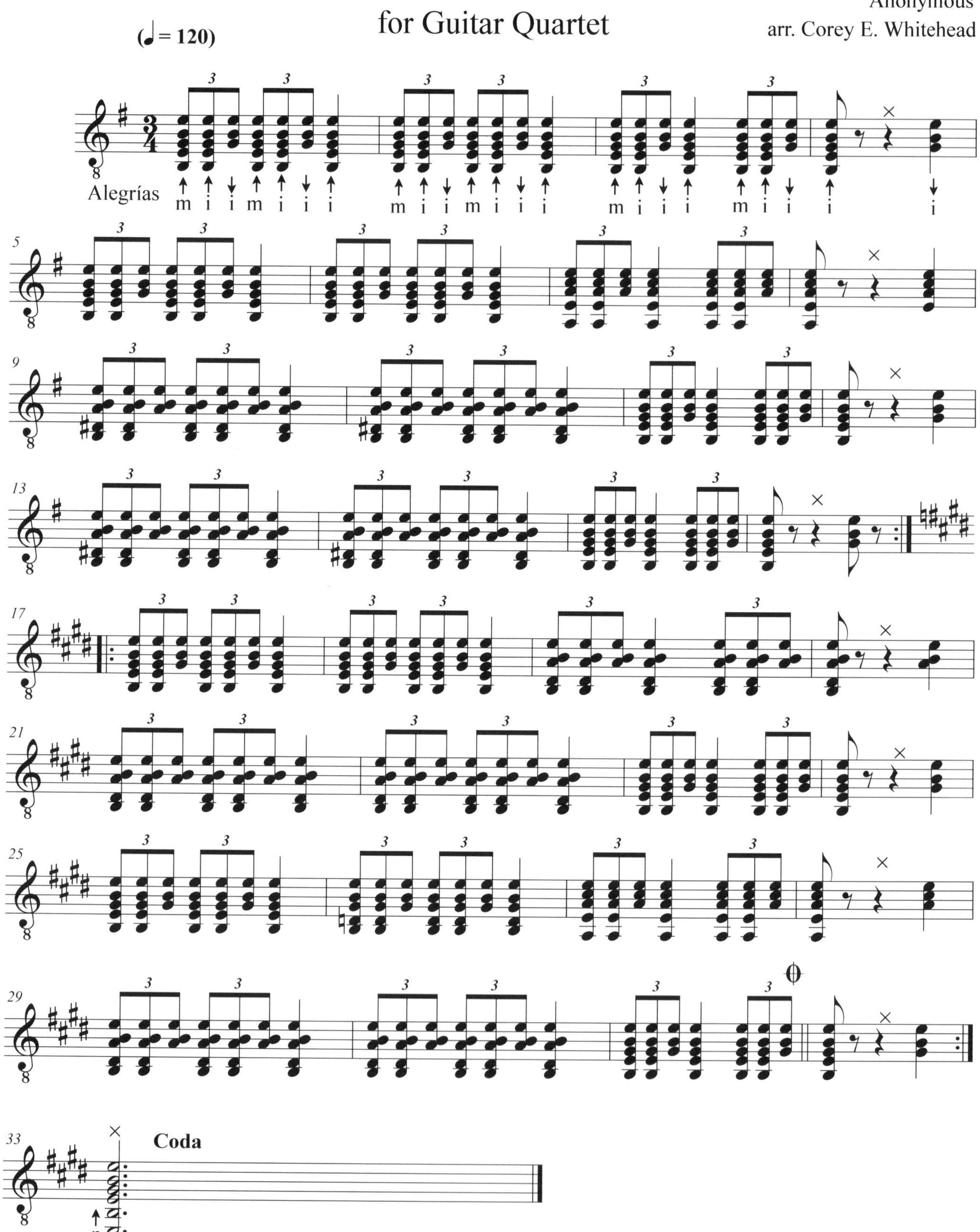